诸子百家智慧故事
Wisdom of Ancient Chinese Sages

WISDOM of ZHUANGZI

庄子
智慧故事

主编　陶黎铭　张　英
中文作者　陶黎铭
英文作者　顾　薇
英文审订　汪榕培

Editors-in-Chief　*Tao Liming　Zhang Ying*
Chinese by　*Tao Liming*
English by　*Gu Wei*
Revised by　*Wang Rongpei*

上海外语教育出版社
SHANGHAI FOREIGN LANGUAGE EDUCATION PRESS

图书在版编目(CIP)数据

庄子智慧故事：汉英对照 / 陶黎铭著；顾薇译.
—上海：上海外语教育出版社，2011
(诸子百家智慧故事丛书)
ISBN 978-7-5446-2004-8

I. ①庄⋯ II. ①陶⋯ ②顾⋯ III. ①庄周(前369～前286)
—哲学思想—通俗读物—汉、英 IV. ①B223.5-49

中国版本图书馆CIP数据核字(2010)第168637号

出版发行：**上海外语教育出版社**
（上海外国语大学内）　邮编：200083
电　　话：021-65425300（总机）
电子邮箱：bookinfo@sflep.com.cn
网　　址：http://www.sflep.com.cn　http://www.sflep.com
责任编辑：梁瀚杰　唐小春

印　　刷：上海申松立信印刷有限责任公司
开　　本：890×1194　1/32　印张8.125　字数226千字
版　　次：2011年1月第1版　2011年1月第1次印刷
印　　数：3 100册

书　　号：ISBN 978-7-5446-2004-8 / B・0014
定　　价：34.00元

本版图书如有印装质量问题，可向本社调换

前 言

2000多年前的春秋战国时代，是中国各种思想流派百花齐放的时期，涌现了孔子、孟子、老子、庄子、墨子、荀子、孙子、韩非子等思想家、哲学家，他们开创了儒、道、墨、法等各具特色、影响深远的思想派别，后世称为"诸子百家"。"诸子百家智慧故事"是一套介绍先秦诸子经典的汉英对照系列丛书，将先秦诸子的生平事迹、哲学思想、格言警句、哲理寓言以及与他们有关的历史故事串联成启迪智慧的短小故事，既能满足中国读者的普及型阅读需求，又照顾到国外读者的文化特点，让大家在轻松愉快的阅读氛围中走近春秋战国时代"百家争鸣"的先哲们。

为了让世界更好地了解中国的经典文化，"诸子百家智慧故事"在编写上突出了以下三个特点：

轻松阅读——本系列每本书中文不过七八万字，每个故事就是一个相对独立的阅读单位，仅几百字的内容十分钟就能读完，在当今信息爆炸的快节奏时代，这种文本便于读者随时取出翻阅。

经济阅读——中国的文字特别是古文字常常是外国人阅读中国经典的障碍，本丛书采取汉英双语对照，中文是浅显易懂的白话体，配以通顺晓畅的英语译文，读者无须钻研艰深的典籍，就能了解先哲的智慧。

趣味阅读——本丛书通过一个个短小生动的故事以及古意盎然的插图，为读者深入浅出地解读诸子经典。

先秦诸子经典是中国的宝贵精神财富，至今在中国乃至全世界都有广泛的影响。希望本丛书能够引起广大中外读者对先秦诸子百家的兴趣，并能通过书中的故事体会到博大精深的中国智慧。

编者

Preface

Over two millennia ago, China experienced a boom of ideas and philosophies in the form of "100 Schools of Thought". Confucius, Mencius, Laozi, Zhuangzi, Mozi, Xunzi, Sun Tzu, Han Feizi ... These are the stellar names behind the philosophical schools like Confucianism, Taoism, Mohism, Legalism, etc. in the Spring and Autumn Period and the Warring States Period (from 770 BC to 221 BC). The classics of these ancient sages contain great wisdom and have exerted profound influence on Chinese history and thought. While the classics themselves may seem difficult to understand today, you can find lucid and accessible explanations of the ancient philosophies in the books of *Wisdom of Ancient Chinese Sages*. With the help of a collection of short and interesting stories, you can get to know the lives and thoughts of the ancient sages, the axioms and allegories they employed to illustrate their ideas, and some facts about the historical era they lived in.

With the aim of presenting the ancient Chinese classics to the world audience, *Wisdom of Ancient Chinese Sages* boasts three advantages:

Easiness — Each book in the series is comprised of only a few dozen stories, each of which has no more than 2,000 words and can be glanced through in a 10-minute coffee break. Even in your busy life, you can always snatch some time to enjoy a story of wisdom and gain some spiritual nourishment.

Efficiency — The classics may seem a little obscure today since they are written in the ancient Chinese. In this Chinese-English version of *Wisdom of Ancient Chinese Sages*, however, the classics are rendered in simple, everyday English. Without having to tax your brains, you can readily comprehend the profound wisdom of the ancient sages.

Attractiveness — With all the short but lively stories accompanied by beautiful illustrations, *Wisdom of Ancient Chinese Sages* explains to you the ancient philosophical ideas in a friendly and agreeable way.

The ancient philosophical classics in the "100 Schools of Thought" are an important spiritual heritage of China and impose great cultural reverberations beyond the Chinese borders. We hope that the series may let the readers develop an interest in the ancient Chinese sages and their philosophies, and appreciate the quintessential Chinese wisdom that may prove useful in present day.

Editors

目 录

Contents

庄子生平 — 11
The Life of Zhuangzi

庄子智慧故事 — 19
Wisdom of Zhuangzi

1. 逞能的猴子 — 21
   The Conceited Monkey
2. 朝三暮四与朝四暮三 — 24
   Morning Three Evening Four or Morning Four Evening Three
3. 混沌开窍 — 27
   Creating Features for Chaos
4. 鱼快乐吗 — 30
   Are These Fish Happy?
5. 鞭策落后 — 33
   Whipping Up the Laggards
6. 儒士与儒服 — 36
   Confucian Scholars and Confucian Robes
7. 任公子钓大鱼 — 39
   Prince of Ren Catches a Giant Fish
8. 庄子梦蝶还是蝶梦庄子 — 42
   Zhuang Zhou or the Butterfly
9. 不能自测的神龟 — 45
   The Divine Tortoise Can't Tell Its Own Fortune

10. 没有累赘的骷髅   48
   A Carefree Skull
11. 鼓盆而歌   51
   Singing and Striking the Earthen Pot at the Funeral
12. 渔夫不为太师   54
   The Fisherman Refuses to Be the Grand Preceptor
13. 伯夷和叔齐的节操   58
   The Moral Integrity of Bo Yi and Shu Qi
14. 急流驾船的本领   62
   Skills of Boating in Torrents
15. 呆若木鸡   66
   Dumb as a Wooden Rooster
16. 杀龙的本领   70
   Dragon-Slaying Skills
17. 桓公见鬼   74
   Duke Huan Sees a Ghost
18. 不接受封赏的屠夫   78
   The Butcher Declines the King's Rewards
19. 一问三不知   82
   No to Every Question
20. 夔虫蛇风   86
   The Monster Kui, the Centipede, the Serpent and the Wind
21. 庄子拒绝相位   90
   Zhuangzi Declines the Offer of Being the Prime Minister
22. 鼻尖上削泥   94
   Chopping Plaster off Nose Tip
23. 废井里的青蛙   98
   A Frog in a Disused Well
24. 孔子弹琴   102
   Confucius Plays Music in Distress

25. 人籁、地籁与天籁   *106*
    Music of Man, Earth and Heaven
26. 窃贼士成绮   *110*
    Shi Chengqi the Thief
27. 鲁王养海鸟   *114*
    The King of Lu Keeps a Seabird
28. 大葫芦的用处   *118*
    The Uses of a Big Calabash
29. 长寿的诀窍   *122*
    The Knack for Longevity
30. 伯乐的罪恶   *126*
    Bo Le's Fault
31. 材与不材   *130*
    Use and No Use
32. 螳螂捕蝉，黄雀在后   *134*
    A Mantis Stalks a Cicada and Is Stalked by an Oriole
33. 望洋兴叹   *138*
    A Lament of Smallness Before the Vast Sea
34. 仁义乱人心   *142*
    Benevolence and Righteousness Disturb People's Minds
35. 言者不知、知者不言   *146*
    Those Who Talk Don't Know and Those Who Know Don't Talk
36. 机器与机巧   *151*
    Machine and Adroitness
37. 做老师的学问   *155*
    The Art of Tutoring
38. 列御寇与拍马   *159*
    Flatteries Are Poisonous
39. 子贡求教老子   *163*
    Zi Gong Seeks Advice from Laozi

40. 庄子卖鞋 … 168
    Zhuangzi Sells Sandals

41. 徐无鬼相面 … 173
    Xu Wugui Reads Appearances

42. 孔子求道 … 178
    Confucius Seeks Tao

43. 鲁太师谈孔子西游 … 183
    A Comment on Confucius's Travel to the West

44. 被砍去一只脚的人 … 188
    The Man with One Foot Cut off

45. 四大奇人 … 193
    Four Extraordinary Men

46. 黄帝求道 … 198
    The Yellow Emperor Seeks Tao

47. 庄子论剑 … 203
    Zhuangzi Talks About Swords

48. 宜僚替鲁侯解忧 … 209
    Removal of Mundane Worries

49. 宰牛的功夫 … 214
    Skills of Cattle Butchering

50. 心斋 … 219
    The Fast of the Heart

51. 季咸看相 … 225
    Ji Xian Tells Fortune

52. 小鸟与大鹏 … 230
    The Small Sparrow and the Giant Eagle

53. 也说白马非马 … 235
    A White Horse Is Not a Horse?

54. 虎狼也有仁爱 … 241
    Tigers and Wolves Are Benevolent Too

55. 长梧子的教诲 245
Teachings from Changwuzi

56. 盗跖怒斥孔丘 250
Zhi the Robber Rebukes Confucius in Anger

庄子生平
The Life of Zhuangzi

庄子

是中国文化史上的一位伟大人物。他既是一位哲学家,又是一位文学家,他以其巧妙讽喻的寓言故事、汪洋恣睢的丰富想像,给中国文化发展留下了浓墨重彩的一笔。有关庄子的历史记载现存不多,除了战国时期某些著作的零星记载和《庄子》中提供的一些相当分散的材料外,主要依据还是司马迁的《史记》。但即使在《史记》中,对庄子的叙述也没有单独成篇,而是作为"老庄申韩列传"中与老子、申不害、韩非并列的人物而出现的,全篇对庄子的介绍只用了280多个字。要想完整详细地了解庄子在目前看来是不可能的,就是以往对庄子的一些说法现在也受到人们的质疑。例如《史记》说庄子是宋国蒙人,但没有说蒙在什么地方。最新的说法有多种,有的说是山东的东明,有的说是山东的曹县,有的说是河南的商丘,有的说是山东的民权,也有的说是安徽的蒙城。尽管如此,我们还是可以介绍一些有关庄子生平的若干片段。

庄子姓庄,名周,具体生卒时间不详,大概属于战国的中后期,根据已有的研究成果可以认定公元前328年～前295年他在世。他曾做过"漆园吏",是管理漆园的小官,不过没有做多久就辞官隐居了。在先秦哲学家中,可能他算是最穷困了。根据他弟子的说法,生活窘迫的时候,他就靠打草鞋过日子,甚至出现吃了上顿没下顿、向别人借粮过日子的状况。有一次他去见魏王,穿的是补了又补的粗布衣服,草鞋上的带子也是断了再接的,但他并不为贫困所苦。所以当魏王问他为什么如此潦倒时,庄子马上说,"我是穷,不是潦倒,是生不逢时;如同落在荆棘丛里的猿猴,处势不利,被捆住了手脚,不能充分施展自己的才能。"《史记》中还说了这样一件事,楚威王听说庄子很有才干,就派两名使臣带重金聘他为相。庄子笑着对使者说:"千金固然是重利,宰相也当然是高位,但你们不妨看看那祭祀的牛,虽然平时吃的是美味,披的是锦绣,但一旦成为大庙的祭品时,想做自由的小猪也不可能了。你们快走开,不要玷污我,我宁愿像条小鱼,在污浊泥水中自得其乐,也不愿受国君们的束缚。"在另一个故事中,庄子把自己喻为高洁的凤凰,而惠施所任的梁国宰相这一高位就像腐烂的老鼠不值一提。

和先秦其他有名的思想家不同,庄子终生不出仕,过着隐士生活。他也有学生,但为数不多,不像孔子有72个弟子;也不像孟子,虽然学生没有孔子那么多,但《孟子》中确切记载的就有几十人,史书说孟子去齐国的时候,随者数十乘,从者数百人。庄子的朋友也不多,在当时的学者名人中,与庄子经常往来的是惠施。《庄子》书中有不少他和惠施进行讨论、争辩的故事,所以惠施的死对他来说是少了一个可以互相启发、相互切磋的朋友。在先秦诸子的书中,只有荀子一人提到了庄子,看来庄子与当时思想家的联系不多。这或许可以说明这样一个现象:尽管孟子名气很大,喜欢辩说,尽管孟子与庄子生活年代相当接近,但在孟子的书中看不到庄子的影子,庄子在把儒家的仁义作为鞭挞对象时也未将孟子列在其中。

Zhuangzi is a great figure in Chinese cultural history. As a philosopher and a litterateur, Zhuangzi made great contributions to the development of Chinese culture with his well-worded fables and brilliant imagination. However, not much information about Zhuangzi is available now. The most important records about Zhuangzi are found in *Records of the Grand Historian* written by Sima Qian (145–87 BC) besides some fragmentary materials provided by some writings in the Warring States Period and the book *Zhuangzi*. But even *Records of the Grand Historian* fails to provide a full chapter on Zhuangzi and only lists him in "Biographies of Laozi, Zhuangzi, Shen Buhai and Han Feizi", with only a few hundred words dedicated to Zhuangzi. As of today it is still impossible to make a detailed and complete introduction to Zhuangzi. Furthermore, even some of the widely accepted knowledge about Zhuangzi is now held under question. For example, *Records of the Grand Historian* says that he was a native of Meng in the State of Song, without mentioning the exact location of Meng. Today many people attempt to make out where Meng is located. Dongming in Shandong Province, Caoxian in Shandong Province, Shangqiu in Henan Province, Minquan in Shandong Province, or Mengcheng in Anhui Province? The latest claims have been quite a few. Nevertheless, we are able to gather a few facts about the life of Zhuangzi.

Zhuangzi's family name is Zhuang and his given name Zhou. The exact dates of his birth and death have remained unknown, possibly around the middle and late Warring States Period, and the research findings available have it that he was alive between 328–294 BC. He once held a position as superintendent (a watchman as a matter of fact) in a lacquer yard, and soon quit the job for a life as a recluse. He was probably the poorest among the philosophers of the 100 Schools of Thought before the Qin Dynasty. During the difficult times, according to his disciples, he had to earn his living by making straw sandals and even borrowed food from others when he did not know where his next meal would come from. Once he went to see the King of Wei in a patched dress of coarse cloth and a pair of straw sandals with broken strings, but he was not at all bothered about it. When the King of Wei asked him why he was so distressed, he immediately replied that he was not distressed, but just poor and born at the wrong time, just like a monkey finding itself among prickly thorns, trapped in an unfavorable situation, with its hands and feet tied, not being able to bring its abilities to full play. Here is another story in *Records of the Grand Historian*. Hearing that Zhuangzi was very talented, King Wei of Chu sent two envoys with a big reward to invite him to be the prime minister. Zhuangzi said to the envoys with a smile, "A thousand pieces of gold is indeed a large sum and the prime minister is of course a high position, but you might as well take a look at the ox serving as the sacrificial offering. It can usually enjoy good food and beautiful clothes. But once it becomes the sacrificial offering, it's no longer possible to live as carefree as a piglet. Please leave and do not try to corrupt me. I would rather be like a small fish having fun in the mud than being constrained by the lords." In another story, Zhuangzi compared himself to the noble phoenix, dismissing the high position of the prime minister held by his friend Hui Shi as a rotten rat.

Unlike other famous thinkers, Zhuangzi spent his entire life as a recluse, not willing to intervene in the outside world. He had disciples, but not many, unlike Confucius who had 72 or Mencius who had a few dozens. History books say that Mencius had dozens of horseback riders accompanying him and hundreds of followers when he went to the State of Qi. Zhuangzi had just a few friends. Among the renowned scholars and literati then, Zhuangzi was most close to Hui Shi, with whom he discussed and argued about important issues. Many such accounts can be found in the book *Zhuangzi*. So the death of Hui Shi meant to Zhuangzi the loss of a bosom friend with whom he exchanged ideas and shared a mutually enlightening relationship. Xunzi was the only one among the Pre-Qin philosophers to mention Zhuangzi in his book, which shows that Zhuangzi probably did not have much contact with the other thinkers of his time. This may well explain why not one word about Zhuangzi has been found in the writings of Mencius, a more famous and equally contentious contemporary of Zhuangzi. On the other hand, when Zhuangzi condemned Confucian benevolence and righteousness, Mencius was not among the targets to be attacked.

庄子智慧故事
Wisdom of Zhuangzi

1. 逞能的猴子

  吴王渡过长江,登上猕猴聚居的山岭。猴群看见吴王打猎的队伍,惊惶地四散奔逃,躲进了荆棘丛林的深处。有一个猴子却与众不同,它从容不迫地腾身而起,抓住树枝跳来跳去,一会儿晃晃脑袋,一会儿抓抓耳朵,在吴王面前显示它的灵巧。吴王用箭射它,它却一点都不害怕,当利箭飞速射来时,它敏捷地伸出前爪,相当麻利地接过箭杆。吴王不由得怒从心起,下命令让左右随从一起上前射箭,结果猴子躲避不及,抱树而死。

  看到猴子的尸体,吴王回身对他的朋友颜不疑说:"这只猴子夸耀它的灵巧,仗恃它的轻捷而蔑视我,以至受到这样的惩罚而失去了生命!而其他的猴子却能远离危险,得以活命。要以此为戒啊!不要因凭借技巧而傲气待人啊!"此事对颜不疑影响很大,回来后便拜贤士董梧为师,以铲除自己的傲气。他弃绝淫乐,辞别尊显,静心修炼。三年过后,全国的人个个都称赞他。

有本事的死了，没有本事的却活着，这样看起来技巧、智慧在一定的条件下不是什么好东西，这个条件至少包括骄傲，包括对人的藐视——当你看不起别人的时候，那你被别人抛弃的时间就快来临了。

THE CONCEITED MONKEY

Having crossed the Yangtze River, the King of Wu climbed up the mountain inhabited by the macaque monkeys. On seeing the hunting party of the King of Wu, the macaque monkeys ran for their lives in all directions in terror, hiding themselves in the depth of the thorn bushes and forests. But one monkey acted differently. It leapt up and jumped from one branch to another in a deliberately unhurried manner, shaking its head, scratching its ears, and displaying its agility in front of the king. It was not afraid when the king shot an arrow at it. Seeing the sharp arrow flying over, it held out its front paw deftly and took the arrow with ease. The king flew into a temper and ordered his immediate attendants to step up and shoot at the monkey together. Not being quick enough to avoid all the arrows, the monkey was killed while still hugging the tree.

Seeing the dead body of the monkey, the king turned to say to his friend Yan Buyi, "The monkey flaunted its agility and defied me because of its confidence in its smartness, due to which, however, it suffered due punishment and lost its life. But the other monkeys managed to escape from danger and survived. We must learn from this and never treat people arrogantly because of the abilities we have." This incident has had a great impact on Yan Buyi. After returning from the hunting, Yan Buyi immediately sought the tutelage of the virtuous sage Dong Wu, so that under Dong's guidance, he could get rid of his arrogance, give up indulgence in sexual and other worldly pleasures, distance himself away from aristocrats and nobilities and practice spiritual discipline in peace. Three years later, he won high acclaim from all over the country.

The fact that the talented dies while the less talented survives shows that skills and smarts are not that advantageous in certain cases, such as holding arrogance and contempt for others, to say the least. When you look down upon the others, you are not far away from being rejected by them.

2. 朝三暮四与朝四暮三

　　春秋时期的宋国有一个专门饲养猴子的老翁,他非常喜爱猴子,家里养了一大群活蹦乱跳的猴子。长期下来,老翁渐渐摸透了猴子的脾气,猴子好像也通人性,很称主人的心。

　　然而老翁的家境比较拮据,为了让猴子们吃饱,他只得常常省下家里人吃的东西。开始还能对付,时间一长,就有点捉襟见肘。连人都过着半饥半饱的日子,更难以保证每天为猴子提供足够的食物。无奈之下,老翁想出了一个对付的办法。

　　有一天,他开始对猴子的食物作了限制,采取定量供应的办法。他怕这些猴子平日里吃饱喝足、娇生惯养的,如今一下子限起食物来会不高兴,就把它们召集在一起,认认真真地说出了自己的打算:"从今天起我们按这样的标准吃饭,每一只猴子早上可分到三升橡子,晚上分到四升橡子。"猴子们听了非常愤怒,觉得那么少根本不够吃,于是就闹起来。

老翁一看情形不对,马上改口说:"那么就早上四升晚上三升吧。"这下猴子们都非常高兴,觉得老翁真好,开始抓耳挠腮,在地上打起滚来。

这个故事就是我们现在说的"朝三暮四"这个成语的由来,猴子们尽管得到的实际利益没有变化,却因为方式的不同表现为大喜与大怒,真是傻得可爱。人的智慧要高于猴子,就要居高临下,抓大放小,不执著于事物之间的细微差别,并认可对象世界的各种立场。需要指出的是,对朝三暮四的批评要注意条件,在一定的条件下,朝三暮四尽管是没有质变的量变,但是如果条件发生变化,就有可能真的造成朝四暮三优于朝三暮四。在总量不变的情况下,不同的组合带来的结果有很大不同,社会生活各领域中这种实例并不罕见。

MORNING THREE EVENING FOUR OR MORNING FOUR EVENING THREE

There was an old man who kept and trained monkeys in the State of Song during the Spring and Autumn Period. He was very fond of monkeys and kept a large number of them which were quite healthy and vigorous. Over the time, the old man gradually became familiar with the temperament of the monkeys, and the monkeys seemed to understand him.

However, the old man was poor. Quite often he had to reduce the amount of food for his family in order to feed the monkeys. At the beginning, he was able to cope, but after some time, it became more and more difficult for him to make ends meet and his family had to live a half-starved life. What was more, he was no longer able to guarantee enough food for the monkeys. Under the pressure, the old man came up with a solution.

The next day he began to limit the food for the monkeys and used a ration arrangement. Worried that the monkeys which had been used to a life of comfort and ample food might become angry at having their food limited all of a sudden, the old man gathered them together and told them his plan in earnest, "From now on, you'll have meals according to an arrangement. Each of you is to have three measures of acorns in the morning and four in the evening." On hearing this, the monkeys got very angry and noisy, believing that the food was not enough to meet their needs. The old man, seeing this, immediately corrected himself and said, "Well then, I'll give you four measures in the morning and three in the evening." At this all the monkeys were delighted and began to roll on the ground, touching their heads and feeling very pleased.

    The above story is the source of what we now use as an idiom "three in the morning and four in the evening". The actual amount of benefits remained the same, but the monkeys, owing to the change in the way of allotment, displayed either anger or pleasure, which in fact was absolutely not necessary. Humans are much superior to monkeys. Standing high and seeing far, humans should focus on the major issues instead of the minor ones and acknowledge the varied standpoints existing in the real world without being overly concerned about insignificant difference among things. It is also worth noting that the evaluation of "three in the morning and four in the evening" depends on the conditions available. Under certain conditions, it means quantitative adjustment with no qualitative change. But if the conditions are different, "four in the morning and three in the evening" might be more desirable than "three in the morning and four in the evening", as different combinations may bring about quite different results, even though the total amount remains the same. Examples are not at all rare in the various aspects of social life.

3. 浑沌开窍

古代的时候,有三个帝王成了好朋友。一个居住在南海,名叫儵,一个居住在北海,名叫忽,居住在大地中央的叫浑沌。儵与忽做事比较机灵,行走也很神速,他们两人经常走动,互相串门,后来为了图方便,就常常在大地中央相会。作为主人的浑沌十分好客,招待也很周到,为他们聚会提供了很好的条件。儵和忽很是感激,时间长了,他们就在一起商量如何报答浑沌的深厚情谊。两人认为,人人都有眼耳口鼻七窍,眼睛可以享受美色,耳朵可以听见美妙的音乐,嘴巴可以尝遍美味,鼻子可以闻到各种香味,偏偏浑沌没有办法享受生命的乐趣,因为他上下无别,内外不分,没有七窍,囫囵一个,于是他们决定要用凿为他开窍。在征得浑沌的同意后,他们捧住浑沌的脑袋凿起来。他们每天凿出一个孔窍,眼睛、耳朵、鼻子相继成型。凿到第七天,最后一窍——嘴巴也完成了。看到浑沌有了凡人的形态,他们十分高兴,觉得大功告成了,然而这时浑沌却死了。

好心结果办成坏事，这是因为儵和忽两位帝王不知道"浑沌"也是认识世界的一种方式。他们错误地认为，对世界的把握是越精细、越准确越好，其实并不尽然。世界上的事物是处于复杂的联系中，在一定的条件下，模糊、混沌更能把握世界。现代科学中模糊数学、模糊语言学、模糊逻辑的出现，多少证明了这个道理。中国人常吃的馄饨，其文化意义与浑沌相近。如果馄饨也被凿开，恐怕就食之无味了！

CREATING FEATURES FOR CHAOS

In ancient times, there were three emperors who became good friends. One of them whose name was Helter lived on the South Sea, another whose name was Skelter lived on the North Sea, and the third whose name was Chaos lived in the Central Region. Helter and Skelter were very clever in managing things and both of them walked fast, so they paid constant visits to each other. Later, to save trouble, they often met in the Central Region, where they were entertained with generous hospitality by Chaos, who played the kind host and provided good conditions for their get-together. Helter and Skelter were very grateful and after some time, they began to talk about how to repay Chaos' hospitality. They believed that everybody had seven facial apertures: eyes, ears, mouth and nostrils. With the eyes, people could see beautiful sceneries; with the ears, people could appreciate wonderful music; with the mouth, people could taste all the delicious food; with the nostrils, people could smell various fragrances. Unfortunately, Chaos was denied of all these funs of life, for he was a big blurry whole with no up or down, no inside or outside, and no facial apertures. So they decided to chisel out the apertures for him. With Chaos' permission, they began the chiseling.

Every day, they dug one aperture in Chaos and one after another, the eyes, the ears and the nostrils took shape. On the seventh day, the last aperture, the mouth, was completed. On seeing Chaos taking the shape of an ordinary man, they were very delighted that a big project had been successfully completed. However, Chaos died as a result.

The two emperors Helter and Skelter had good intentions but met bad results because they did not realize that a blurry whole (Chaos) was also a way of existence in the world. They mistakenly believed that the more precisely they knew the world, the more accurate their knowledge would be, which was not always the case. As everything in the world exists in the midst of complicated connections, a blurry and fuzzy whole (Chaos) actually allows people to better grasp the world under certain conditions. The emergence of fuzzy mathematics, fuzzy linguistic and fuzzy logic in the modern science somehow serves as testimony to the above theory. The dumplings, a kind of food the Chinese people often eat, are close to Chaos in terms of cultural significance. If the dumplings had holes in them, they would lose all the flavor and taste and be hardly worth eating, instead of being favored by the Chinese people of one generation after another until today.

4. 鱼快乐吗

有一天,庄子和他的好朋友惠施一起出游。他们走到了濠水的一座桥上,两人倚栏观赏。微风中碧波荡漾,一条条银灰色的鱼在水中摇头摆尾,鼓鳃吐泡,时而窜入水底,时而跃出水面。看到这一景象,庄子若有所思,他对惠施说:"你看,这些鱼成群结队,互相嬉戏,游得多么悠闲自在,天地之间任它们快活,真是太快乐了,哪像咱们做人的那样整天忙忙碌碌。"惠施觉得很奇怪,说:"你又不是鱼,怎么知道鱼的快乐?"庄子针锋相对,说:"你不是我,怎么知道我不知道鱼儿的快乐?"惠施马上接口说:"对啊,我不是你,固然不知道你是否知道;同样,你不是鱼,你不知道鱼的快乐,也是完全可以肯定的。"庄子听后,哈哈大笑说:"看来我们还是有必要梳理一下我们讨论的问题。先回到最初讲的话,你刚才说'你又不是鱼,你怎么知道鱼的快乐',其实这句话就表明你已经知道了我虽然不是鱼,但却知道鱼儿的快乐,否则你不会问我这样的问题。世界上甲要了解乙,并不一定要甲本身是乙才能了解乙。要说我是怎么知道鱼的快乐,那是因为我来到了濠水的桥,看见鱼在水中游得自由自在,就知道鱼儿快乐的。就像你不是我,但却了解我一样。"

庄子与惠施的这场辩论,在中国哲学史上相当有名。它触及到有关人的认识的一个重要问题:人到底能不能认识世界?如果不是鱼就不能知道鱼的快乐,不是马就不能知道马的性情,那么,人对世界将是一无所知,这和不可知论就相差无几了。

ARE THESE FISH HAPPY?

One day, Zhuangzi and his good friend Hui Shi went for an outing. They strolled onto a bridge over the Haoshui River, where they stopped and leaned over the railings to gaze into the water. A breeze was rippling the limpid surface and silvery fish were waving their heads and tails and blowing bubbles with puffing gills. Sometimes they would delve to the bottom of the river and sometimes they would jump out of the water. Zhuangzi looked at this thoughtfully and said to Hui Shi, "Look, these fish swim in shoals in a leisurely way, sporting about in fun. They can enjoy themselves between Heaven and Earth, so free and so easy. How happy they are swimming around, never as busy as the human beings who bustle about all the time!" Hui Shi looked puzzled at this remark and said, "As you are not the fish, how can you know the happiness of the fish?" "As you are not me," retorted Zhuangzi, "how can you know that I don't know the happiness of the fish?" "That's right." Hui Shi replied immediately, "As I am not you, I cannot know what you know. Therefore, as you are not the fish, you won't know about the happiness of the fish." On hearing this, Zhuangzi laughed and said, "It seems necessary that we'll first sort out our discussion. Let's start from the very beginning.

You said, 'As you are not the fish, how can you know the happiness of the fish?' It showed that you were aware that I knew the happiness of the fish although I was not the fish. Otherwise, you wouldn't have asked me such a question. In this world, if A wants to know about B, it's not necessary for A to become B. As to how I know about the happiness of the fish, that's just because I come to the bridge over the Haoshui River and see these fish swim about freely and at ease — there I know that they are happy. It's the same as you know me though you are not me."

The argument over the happiness of the fish between Zhuangzi and Hui Shi is famous in the history of Chinese philosophy. It touches upon a very important issue on human cognition: Can human beings actually understand the world? If a man who is not a fish cannot know the happiness of the fish, and if a man who is not a horse cannot know the temperament of the horse, the human beings will know nothing about the world — that is on the verge of agnosticism.

5. 鞭策落后

　　周威公继承王位后,四处召集天下义士。有一个人叫田开之,是当时被称为"胸怀大道者"的祝肾的学生。他去拜见周威公,周威公和他交谈一番后说:"我听说祝肾在学习养生,你跟祝肾交游,从他那儿听到过什么有关养生的信息吗?"田开之回答说:"我只不过是拿着扫帚打扫门庭的杂役而已,怎么能从先生那里听到这种信息呢!"周威公说:"先生不必谦虚,我真心希望能听到你关于这方面的见解。"推脱不下之后,田开之说:"我曾听先生说,善于养生的人,就像是放牧羊群似的,看到哪只羊落后了,便用鞭子赶一赶。"周威公听后迷惑不解,连忙问:"这话说的是什么意思呢?我怎么不明白?"田开之说:"先生这句话的意思是,人的身体哪一方面有缺陷,就应该有针对性地作补充。大王一定听说过鲁国发生的事吧。有两个人,一个叫单豹,一个叫张毅。单豹隐居在岩穴里,在山泉边饮水,不跟任何人争利,活得很轻松,到了七十岁还有婴儿一样的面容，不幸的是后来遇上了饿虎，被饿虎吃掉了。那张毅，每次经过高门大户或挂着帘子的富贵人家，便快步前去参谒，结果活到四十岁便患内热病而死去。单豹注重内在的修养，可是老虎却吞食了他的身体；张毅注重身体的调养，可是疾病却侵蚀了他的内在——这两个人，都不是能够鞭策自己落后之处的人啊。"

　　鞭策落后，虽然讲的是养生之道，强调养生要内外并养，但更有价值的是人要注意自己的弱项。后就是缺点，就是不足。如果只看到自己的长处，并满足于自己的长处，而看不到自己的短处，或置短处而不顾，一味向前冲，就容易身受其害。

WHIPPING UP THE LAGGARDS

Having ascended to the throne, Duke Wei of Zhou began to recruit talents from all parts of the world. Tian Kaizhi, a disciple of Zhu Shen, a master who was regarded at that time as "having known the Great Tao", went to see Duke Wei of Zhou. Having talked with him for a while, Duke Wei of Zhou said, "I have heard that Zhu Shen has been studying the cultivation of life. As you have learned from and traveled with him, what have you heard from him about it?" Tian Kaizhi replied, "I'm just a handyman who sweeps his front courtyard. What could I possibly have heard from the master about it?" "Don't be so modest, sir," said the duke, "I sincerely wish to hear your view on it." Knowing that it was not possible to avoid the question, Tian Kaizhi said, "I have heard from the master that those who are good at cultivating their lives are like shepherds who whip up the sheep that they see lagging behind." The duke was perplexed over what he had heard and asked, "What does it mean? I don't understand." "My master meant to say," replied Tian Kaizhi, "that one should make concentrated efforts to improve the part of his body which is less than perfect. Your Highness must have heard the story in the State of Lu. There were two men living in the State of Lu, one called Shan Bao and the other Zhang Yi. Shan Bao lived among the rocks as a recluse and drank springwater only. He never fought for worldly interests with others and lived a carefree life. By the age of seventy, he still had the complexion of a baby. Unfortunately he encountered a hungry tiger, which killed and ate him. The other man, Zhang Yi, would hurry to pay visits to all the rich families with grand and lofty doors or with hanging screens over them. He died of a fever at the age of forty. Shan Bao took care of the refinement of his inner world but a tiger ate his external body; Zhang Yi took care of the nourishment of his external body but disease attacked his inner world. Neither of them could whip up the part that lagged behind."

The story of "whipping up the laggards" is about life-cultivation methods, which focus on the nourishment of both the internal and the external parts of the body. But what is more meaningful is that one should watch one's weaknesses. "Lagging behind" means one has weaknesses and limitations. If one notices and revels in his strong points only and pushes forward blindly without realizing his weak points or simply ignoring them, one is likely to suffer harms.

6. 儒士与儒服

　　鲁国是孔子的家乡，受儒家思想影响很大。有一次，庄子来到鲁国拜见鲁哀公。鲁哀公对道家不太以为然，他对庄子说："鲁国多儒士，很少有信仰先生学说的人。"庄子说："我看鲁国很少儒士，懂得儒家学说的人也很少。"鲁哀公说："怎么能这么说呢？你看全鲁国到处都是穿着儒士服装的人，可以说是儒士遍地。"庄子摇摇头说："我听说，儒士都戴圆帽，表明他们知晓天时，说明天是圆的；儒士都穿方鞋，表明他们熟悉地形，说明地是方的；儒士都身佩用五色丝绳系着的玉玦，表明他们遵守儒家的礼俗，遇事能决断。其实，身怀那种学问和本事的人，不一定要穿儒士的服装；穿上儒士服装的人，不一定会具有那种学问和本事。你如果不相信我说的话，何不在国中下一道命令：'凡是没有儒士的学问和本事而又穿着儒士服装的人，一律处以死罪！'"

　　听了庄子这番话，鲁哀公半信半疑，于是就按庄子的说法做了试验。

结果五天之后，鲁国国中差不多没有人敢再穿儒士服装，只有一个男子身着儒士服装站立于朝门之外。鲁哀公立即召他进来，以国事征询他的意见，天文地理、社会人文、儒术道术，无论多么复杂的问题他都能滔滔不绝地做出令人满意的解答——这是一个真正懂得儒学的人。于是庄子就对鲁哀公说："这么大的鲁国，儒士只有一人呀，怎么能说是很多呢？"

鲁国是不是就只有一个儒士，其实也难以做出定论，因为穿儒服的不一定是儒士，是儒士也不一定穿儒服，内容与形式常常是不一致的。这则故事说明如下道理：当一种学说与思潮比较流行的时候，总有人出来赶时髦，哗众取宠。特别是当社会舆论形成一种压力时，人们说的不一定是心里想的，所做的也不一定是真心愿意做的。所以千万不要仅仅从外表来判断事情的对错。

CONFUCIAN SCHOLARS AND CONFUCIAN ROBES

The hometown of Confucius was located in the State of Lu, where the influence of Confucianism was strong. Once Zhuangzi went to the State of Lu and paid a visit to Duke Ai of Lu who expressed his disapproval against Taoism. The duke said, "There are many Confucian scholars in the State of Lu, but few of your school." Zhuangzi said, "In the State of Lu, I see few Confucian scholars and few people who are well-versed in Confucianism." "How can you say so?" Duke Ai of Lu said, "You can see men wearing Confucian robes everywhere in Lu. We may say that the State of Lu is thronged with Confucian scholars." Shaking his head, Zhuangzi replied, "I have heard that Confucian scholars wear round hats to show that they know the round shape of the heaven, wear square shoes to show that they know the square contour of the earth, and wear rectangular jade with five-colored silk threads to show their adherence to Confucianism and their determination in handling problems. However, a gentleman of ample knowledge and talents does not have to wear a Confucian robe while a man in a Confucian robe may not possess such knowledge and talents. If Your Highness doesn't believe me, why not issue an order throughout the state that there should be a death penalty for those who wear the Confucian robes without the knowledge and talents befitting a Confucian scholar?"

Feeling dubious about this, Duke Ai of Lu issued the order as an experiment based on Zhuangzi's suggestion. Five days later, there was almost no one in Lu who dared to wear the Confucian robes. There was only one exception: a man dressed himself in a Confucian robe and stood in front of the palace gate. Immediately summoning him inside, Duke Ai of Lu consulted him on affairs of the state. The man talked at great length and offered excellent explanations on diverse topics, no matter how sophisticated they were, such as geography, astronomy, society, humanities, Confucianism and Taoism. So Zhuangzi said to Duke Ai of Lu, "There is only one Confucian scholar in such a big state as Lu. How can we say there are many?"

Of course it is hard to say whether there was only one Confucian scholar in the State of Lu, as those in the Confucian robes might not necessarily be Confucian scholars, and the Confucian scholars might not necessarily wear the Confucian robes. The appearance and the content are often not in accordance with each other. What is to be noted is that when one particular doctrine or school of thought prevails, there are always people who are eager to follow the trend and curry favors from the public. Especially when the social pressure becomes strong, people may say things which are far from what they really think and do things that they do not really wish to do. So never take the appearance as the inherent truth.

7. 任公子钓大鱼

　　任国公子做了个巨大的鱼钩，鱼钩上系上了又粗又长的黑绳，用了五十头牛做钓饵，整天蹲在会稽山上，把钓竿投向东海，每天早出晚归。就这样一天天过去了，整整一年的时间一条鱼也没钓到。后来终于有一天，有一条大鱼游过来，看到鱼饵张嘴就吞，鱼钩深深地卡在鱼的喉咙里。只见它牵着巨大的钓钩，急速沉向海底深处，把海水搅成一个猛烈旋转的巨大漩涡；忽一会它又迅速地扬起脊背，腾身而起，掀起如山的白浪，海水剧烈震荡，发出的响声犹如鬼叫神嚎，千里之外都可以感受到震动。任公子丝毫不敢放松，最后终于把这条大鱼捉住了。随后，他将大鱼剖开，制成鱼干，从浙江以东到岭南的苍梧山以北，没有谁不饱饱地吃上这条鱼的。后来那些学识浅薄、以道听途说为真知，并以此作为品评议论标准的人，都非常吃惊地到处奔走相告。

　　由此看来，那些平时拿着小渔竿、细丝绳，奔走在山沟小渠旁，等候小鱼上钩的人，虽然会时不时地钓上几条小鱼，但要想抓上大鱼那就很困难。把浅薄的说法作一些修饰，向县令献计献策以求得赞誉的人，距离达到通晓大道的境界很远很远。因此不了解任公子远大志向的人，恐怕也不可以说是善于治理天下，而且两者之间的差距也是很大的了。

　　任公子钓鱼讲究的是大。大首先说的是人的志向要大、目标要高、要远，不要在乎一时一地的得失，不要被一些蝇头小利捆住手脚。一个人如果能经受长时期一无所获的寂寞，默默地承受各种风险的煎熬，一旦成功，就会惊天动地，惠及天下。大还要求人去学会抓大放小，懂得放弃，要知道有所失才能有所得，有所得总会有所失。一个人如果眉毛胡子一把抓，最终是什么东西也得不到的。

PRINCE OF REN CATCHES A GIANT FISH

　　Having made a huge fishhook fixed with a long and strong black rope, Prince of the State of Ren baited with 50 bulls, squatted on Mount Kuaiji all day long, and cast his fishing rod into the East Sea. Morning after morning, day after day, a whole year passed but he caught nothing. Then one day, a giant fish swam over and took the bait with its mouth. With the hook cutting deep into its throat, the giant fish sank quickly into the depth of the sea, dragging the huge hook behind it and turning the sea into a big boisterous maelstrom. After a while, it suddenly bucked and jumped out of the water, stirring huge white wave, while the seawater shook wildly. The noise was like the howling of ghosts and spirits which could be heard a thousand *li* away. Prince of Ren held the rod tightly and finally managed to catch the giant fish with great efforts. Then he cut the fish open into slices and dried them. From the east of Zhejiang to the north of Mount Cangwu of Lingnan, there was no one who did not eat the fish to his full. Later, those who were not knowledgeable enough and based their judgment on hearsay told and retold the story everywhere in astonishment.

From the story we can see that it would be very difficult for someone to catch a big fish if he just takes a thin fishing rod with a fine line and goes to the hillside ditches to bait the small fish, even though he may catch a few minnows from time to time. Those who dress up their shallow ideas and try to offer proposals in order to curry favor with the county magistrates are indeed far away from being able to understand the all-pervasive Tao. Therefore, those who have never understood the ambitious Prince of Ren are far away from being good at managing the state affairs. There is a great difference between them and Prince of Ren.

Prince of Ren aimed at the giant fish. On the one hand, one must have a big ambition, a lofty aim and a far-reaching foresight, instead of minding the temporary gains and losses and being handicapped by the pursuit of petty interests. If one can bear the loneliness of not being able to make any progress for a long time and withstand the ordeal brought about by the numerous risks without complaints, then once he succeeds, his success will be great and benefit the rest of the world. To aim high also demands that people learn the knack of making choices by grasping the important issues and letting go the trivial ones. One must know that one cannot make an omelet without breaking eggs and the gains usually accompany the losses. If one tries to attend to significant and insignificant matters at the same time without priorities, one is doomed to achieving nothing.

8. 庄子梦蝶还是蝶梦庄子

一个炎热的夏天,庄子与几个学生一起去游泳。他在河里畅游了好一会儿,便独自爬上岸来,随意倒在棉毯一样柔软的草地上。他脸朝着天空,只见一朵朵白云像羔羊在蓝天中随风散步,不少美丽的蝴蝶在原野中上下飞舞,周围一片宁静。这时他全身舒展,情不自禁地闭上眼睛,陶醉在这美好的自然中。慢慢地他忘掉了时间的流逝,忘掉了小鸟的眼睛,忘掉了孔子的教诲,忘掉了自身的存在,变成了一只五彩缤纷的大蝴蝶。他摆动着轻盈的翅膀,冲破了层层罗网,在宇宙中浮游。他一会儿来到野花盛开的原野上,一会儿来到树木茂盛的山谷中,忽然是白云蓝天,忽然是大海波浪。他与蜜蜂说话,与水鸟赛跑;他蹲在猴子的头顶上嬉戏,他在杨树叶上睡觉。他好像在拥抱整个自然,充满愉快和惬意,感受着从未有过的潇洒、超脱与自由。忽然,一阵黑风铺天盖地而来,将他吹得摇摇晃晃。风越来越猛,吹折了他的翅膀,把他从九万里高空吹落到一片荆棘之中，他被刺得遍体鳞伤。这时庄子醒了，惊惶不定之间发现自己仍然躺在草地上，边上还有一起来的两个学生，原来自己是庄周。他懵懵懂懂地看着四周，又摸摸自己后脑勺，自言自语地说："哎呀，这是怎么搞的，蝴蝶本来自是它蝴蝶，庄周本来自是我庄周，两者肯定是有区别的。但在梦中，蝴蝶与庄周已经融化为一体了，蝴蝶变成了庄周，庄周又变成了蝴蝶，他们之间没有确定的界线，不知是庄周梦中变成蝴蝶呢，还是蝴蝶梦见自己变成庄周呢？"庄子的看法是，这可叫做物我的交融与变化。

庄子梦蝶是一个相当有名的故事。在常人看来，到底是庄子梦蝶，还是蝶梦庄子，其真伪是不言而喻的。但恰恰是这个问题，给人们以深刻的思考：除了在艺术审美的过程中要物我交融，更重要的是，如果一个人把自己都可以忘掉，那么还有必要固守个人的名利是非吗？

ZHUANG ZHOU OR THE BUTTERFLY

On a hot summer day, Zhuangzi went swimming with several disciples. Having swum with pleasure for quite a while, he climbed onto the shore by himself. He lay on his back on the soft green grass thick as a cotton blanket and gazed at the blue sky. Soft clouds were floating in the breeze like little lambs taking strolls and beautiful butterflies were dancing above the green fields. Everything around him was so quiet and peaceful that he could not help but close his eyes and get lost in the beauty of nature. He gradually forgot about the passage of time, the eyes of the birds, the teachings of Confucius, or even his own existence. He seemed to have turned into a big colorful butterfly with delicate wings, breaking through one trap after another and roaming freely in the vast universe. For a while he rested himself in the green fields with flowers in full bloom; for another while, he found himself in the mountain valleys with thriving lush trees. For one minute he saw white clouds in the blue sky; for the next minute, he saw roaring waves in the vast ocean. Talking with the bees and racing with the water birds, playing on the monkey heads and sleeping on the poplar leaves, he felt as if he were embracing the entire nature in a sense of happiness and coziness, enjoying a free and unrestrained life that he had never lived. Then all of a sudden, a gust of dark wind engulfed him and sent him staggering about. The wind became stronger and broke his wings, throwing him from the height of ninety thousand *li* into a thorny bush and turning him into a mess of cuts and bruises. Zhuangzi woke up from his dream and found in bewilderment himself lying on the green grass with two disciples on his side. So he was Zhuang Zhou again, not a butterfly. Still puzzled, he looked around and felt the back of his head with his hands, murmuring to himself, "Oh, what has happened? A butterfly is a butterfly and I am Zhuang Zhou. There is definitely a distinction between a butterfly and a man. But in my dream, a butterfly and Zhuang Zhou became one and the same. A butterfly was turned into Zhuang Zhou while Zhuang Zhou was turned into a butterfly. There seemed no clear distinction between the two. Was it Zhuang Zhou who dreamt that he became a butterfly, or was it a butterfly who dreamt that it became Zhuang Zhou?" His conclusion was that it was the mergence and transformation between material objects and human beings.

"Zhuang Zhou dreaming of a butterfly" is a well-known story. To the ordinary people, it goes without saying as to whether Zhuang Zhou turned into a butterfly in his dream or the other way round. Yet, this puzzle, although seemingly solvable with mere common sense, does give people deep thought. While the mergence and transformation is definitely useful in the appreciation of artworks, the more important moral of this story is: If one can easily forget oneself, is it necessary for him to be entangled in the strife for fame and wealth, or the argument for right and wrong?

9. 不能自测的神龟

　　宋元君半夜里做了一个梦，梦中见到有人披散着头发在侧门旁窥视，就把他叫进来问话，那人回答说："我来自名叫宰路的深渊，作为清江的使者出使河伯的居所，渔夫余且捉住了我。"宋元君醒来，觉得有点奇怪，就派人去占卜。占卜的结果说这是一只神龟，是神龟托梦给君王，求君王把他解救出来。宋元君马上问："有没有一个名叫余且的渔夫？"左右侍臣回答说："有。"宋元君说："那叫余且来朝见我。"第二天，余且来朝。宋元君问："你捕捞到了什么？"余且回答："我捕捉到一只白龟，有五尺长。"宋元君说："把你捕获的白龟献出来。"听了宋元君的吩咐，余且马上把白龟送到朝廷。看到这个神龟，宋元君一会儿想把它杀了，一会儿又想把它养起来，心中犹豫不定，最后还是通过占卜问吉凶。占卜的人说："杀掉白龟用来占卜，一定大吉。"于是宋元君让人把白龟剖开挖空，用龟板占卜数十次，没有一点失误，每卜每中。后来孔子知道了这件事，很为感慨，说："神龟能显梦给宋元君，却不能避开余且的渔网；运用才智占卜数十次没有一点失误，却不能逃脱被剖腹挖肠的灾祸。如此说来，才智也有困窘的时候，神灵也有考虑不到的地方。即使最高超的智慧，也敌不过万人的谋算。鱼儿即使不畏惧渔网，也会害怕水鸟。摒弃小聪明方才显示大智慧，除去矫饰的善行方才能使自己真正回到自然的善性。"

龟是中国传统"四灵"之一，具有很高的灵性。过去用于算命的象数之学，是先有象，后有数，后来象与数才慢慢合起来。这个象，就与龟有关。古人占卜时用火把锐利的金属烧得通红，然后穿透龟板，由此形成的裂纹成了判断事情吉凶的依据。白龟虽然很神，对自然、人事的预测十分灵验，但对自身未来的把握却无能为力。看来，无论是谁都有认识的盲点，无论什么样的智慧都有难以克服的局限。

THE DIVINE TORTOISE CAN'T TELL ITS OWN FORTUNE

Lord Yuan of the State of Song had a dream: He saw a man with disheveled hair peeping in at him by a side door, so the lord summoned the man in for questions. The man replied, "I come from the abyss of Zailu as an envoy of Qingjiang to visit the residence of Hebo (the God of the Yellow River), but was caught by Yu Qie the fisherman." Feeling puzzled when waking from the dream, Lord Yuan sent for a diviner to tell him the meaning of the dream and was told that it was a divine tortoise who visited him in the dream for the purpose of asking him to rescue it. Lord Yuan immediately asked around, "Is there a fisherman named Yu Qie?" "Yes, there is," his attendants answered. "Summon him to my court," Lord Yuan ordered. When Yu Qie appeared in the court the next day, Lord Yuan asked him, "What have you caught?" Yu Qie answered, "I have caught a five-*chi* white tortoise with my fishing net." "Present the white tortoise you've caught to the court," said the lord. Yu Qie complied and sent the tortoise. On seeing the tortoise, Lord Yuan hesitated as to whether he would kill it or keep it alive. At last, he went to the diviner again for signs of good or ill luck. The diviner said, "It would bring good omen to kill it and use it for divination." So Lord Yuan had the tortoise cut open and disemboweled. Later, the tortoiseshell was used for divination for dozens of times, and the results were correct each time. Confucius sighed with emotion at the story, saying, "The divine tortoise was able to appear in Lord Yuan's dream, but was unable to escape from Yu Qie's fishing net. It was able to provide dozens of accurate divinations without a single mistake, but was unable to escape disembowelment. From this we can see that a man of wisdom may be perplexed and a divine being may also have a miss. The greatest wit may fail in the hands of ten thousand people. Fish may not be afraid of the fishing nets, but may fear the water birds. Put aside petty tricks and great wisdom will rise; do away with pretentious deeds and natural kindness will take over."

The tortoise, one of the "Four Divine Creatures" in the Chinese tradition, is endowed with divine power. The divinatory theories in traditional Chinese fortune-telling developed from the images on oracle bones and tortoiseshells. The ancient people chiseled the tortoiseshell with a blazing rod for divination and based their judgment of good or ill luck on the cracks on the shell. In spite of its accurate prediction of the natural phenomena and the worldly affairs, the white tortoise was unable to control its own future. Therefore, everybody has a blind spot in his mind's eye while every wit has its unavoidable limitations.

10. 没有累赘的骷髅

在去楚国的路上,庄子经过了一块墓地,那里野草丛生,一片荒凉景象。突然,庄子见到一个骷髅,枯骨突露,但还保持着活人头颅的形状。庄子用马鞭在骷髅的脑门上敲了敲,问道:"先生所以成为这个样子是因为你贪求生命、失却真理,还是你遇上了亡国的大事,遭受到刀斧的砍杀?是你有了不好的行为,担心给父母、妻儿留下耻辱,羞愧而死,还是你遭受寒冷与饥饿而活不下去?抑或你什么都不是,只是年龄的关系寿终正寝?"说完了这些话,庄子就拉过骷髅,将头枕在上面躺下了。到了半夜,庄子做了一个梦,梦中见到骷髅对他说:"你先前谈话的情形真像是一个善于辩论的人。不过你所说的那些话、所举的那些例子,全属于活人的牵累,就像是长途跋涉时压在背上的沉重包袱,压得人喘不过气来。而人死了就没有这种负担了。你愿意听听人死后的事吗?"庄子说:"好啊。"于是骷髅就娓娓道来:"人一旦死了,就可以从苦恼中解脱出来，没有忧愁，没有羁绊，整天逍遥自在，悠然自得。上没有国君的统治，下没有官吏的管辖；没有一年四季的冷冻热晒，也无需耕种收割的辛劳，从容安逸地把天地的长久看作时令的流逝。人即使南面为王，也常常要绞尽脑汁，四处算计，绝对不可能享受到死后的快乐与自由。"对于这番话，庄子不相信，摇着头说："我让主管生命的神来恢复你的形体，为你重新长出骨肉肌肤，返回到你的父母、妻子儿女、左右邻里和朋友故交中去，你希望这样做吗？"骷髅皱眉蹙额，深感忧虑地说："我怎么能抛弃现在的快乐而再次经历人世的劳苦呢？"

现实生活中，人们多是趋生避死，厌死不厌生，所以听到的多半是生的愉悦，而不是死的快乐。而庄子则在至乐的背景下谈论死亡，把生与死看作自然的两端，把自由作为快乐的根本。他提出的一个问题是，人如果没有自由，活着还有意义吗？

A CAREFREE SKULL

Once on his way to the State of Chu, Zhuangzi was passing a desolate graveyard overgrown with wild weeds when he saw an arid skull in the shape of a human head. Tapping it with his riding crop, Zhuangzi asked, "Was it because of your lust for life or your abandonment of truth that you end up like this? Was it because of the fall of a kingdom and the beheading by an axe? Was it because of your misdemeanor or cold and hunger? Or did you simply die a natural death when you had completed your lifespan?" Having finished these questions, Zhuangzi pulled over the skull, placed it under his head like a pillow and went to sleep. Zhuangzi dreamt that the skull said to him, "Judging from your manner of speaking, you sound like an eloquent orator. But the words you said and the examples you cited are all entanglements of the living, like the heavy burdens on the backs of the exhausted wayfarers. However, the dead is free of such burdens. Would you like to hear about the afterlife?" "Yes," Zhuangzi replied. So the skull went on in a leisurely manner, "A man after death is set free from all the slings and arrows of life, with no worry or restraint, but with ease and leisure all day long, neither ruled by the lord nor governed by the officials. He is free from the torment of the cold and heat of the year and from the drudgery of plowing and reaping, forever at ease and in tranquility to enjoy the longevity of Heaven and Earth with the passage of seasons. A king will not surpass him in joy or freedom, because the mighty king has to rack his brains to plot and scheme all the time." In doubt with these words, Zhuangzi shook his head and said, "Would you be happy if I had the god in charge of the human destiny to restore your body in flesh and bones so that you could return to your parents, wife and children, together with your neighbors and friends?" Lost in consternation with a deep frown on its brow, the skull asked, "Why should I discard the present happiness for a second encounter with the human hardships?"

People in the real world love life and hate death. They talk about the pleasure of life instead of the bliss of death. However, Zhuangzi talked about death in terms of ultimate joy, seeing life and death as the two extremes of nature and freedom as the root of happiness. Here is the question he raised, "Would there be any value in life if one loses his freedom?"

11. 鼓盆而歌

庄子的妻子死了，惠施听到这个消息后，立刻急匆匆地前往吊唁。一路上惠施琢磨着如何劝慰庄子，让他忍痛节哀，不要过分悲伤，免得伤了身体。快要到庄子家门的时候，只听到里边传出一阵婉转悠扬、动人心弦的歌声，同时还有乐器的伴奏声。惠施很纳闷，连忙三步并作两步走进大门，只见庄子正盘腿坐在蒲草编织的垫子上，一边用筷子敲打着瓦盆，一边唱着歌，看不出有多少悲伤的样子。惠施带着半是不解、半是不快的口气说："你跟妻子生活了一辈子，她生儿育女直至衰老而死。人死了你不伤心哭泣也就算了，还敲着瓦盆唱起歌来，有点过分了吧！"

庄子站起来慢吞吞地说："你这话就不对了。'人非草木，孰能无情？'你知道吗，我妻子刚死的时候，我伤心极了，饭吃不下，觉睡不好。后来仔细想想，我算是想明白了，也就不伤心了。想想人类的前身，宇宙本来是没有生命的，盘古开天辟地之前，整个宇宙混混沌沌，哪里有什么人。后来，随着自然界的潜移默化，渐渐形成了适宜生命的环境，诞生了生命，诞生了人类。其实，我妻子她开始是没有生命的，不但没有生命，而且也不具有形体；不但不具有形体，而且连元气也没有。后来她夹杂在恍恍惚惚的境域之中，慢慢变化而有了元气，元气变化而有了形体，形体变化而有了生命。如今她死了，又从有生命的东西变回到无生命的东西，之后形体消失，元气泯灭，这就跟春夏秋冬四季运行一样，循环往复以至无穷。当你看到我那死去的妻子安安稳稳地寝卧在天地之间，而我却呜呜地围着她啼哭，这实在是不懂得大自然运行的道理。正因为如此，我擦掉了眼泪，停止了哭泣，再也不感到悲伤了。"

　　面对庄子的这番言论，惠施无言以对。

　　庄子为妻子去世鼓盆而歌看似不近情理，却是超越世俗观念、把生死看作大自然循环运行的真实展现。一个人如果不畏死，不趋生，就向自由跨了一大步。后来的道教讲得道成仙，追求长生不老之术，那就与庄子的想法差得有点远了。

SINGING AND STRIKING THE EARTHEN POT AT THE FUNERAL

Hearing the news that Zhuangzi's wife died, Hui Shi hurried to Zhuangzi's home to convey condolences. On his way there, he thought about how to comfort Zhuangzi and how to persuade him not to be overwhelmed with grief. When he was about to reach Zhuangzi's house, he heard beautiful and attractive songs accompanied by the tunes of musical instruments. Bewildered at the music, he hurried inside the house and found Zhuangzi sitting cross-legged, striking an earthen pot with chopsticks and singing without much grief. "You lived with you late wife all your life. She gave birth to and raised your children, and passed away in her old age. Not weeping for her at her death is bad enough. Aren't you going too far by striking the earthen pot and singing songs?" said Hui Shi, half in bewilderment and half in dissent.

Zhuangzi stood up and said slowly, "You are wrong. Humans are not as heartless as trees or grass. You know, when my wife died, I was so overwhelmed with grief that I could not eat or sleep. When I thought it over, I began to understand and became less grieved. Before Pan Gu created the world and the human beings, there had been no life in the chaos of the universe. However, with the passage of time, environments suitable for life began to grow in the universe, where living species and human beings were born. In the beginning, my wife had neither life nor shape. Then in the midst of the chaos, a slow change took place and she began to assume spirit and form and obtained life. Now that she is dead, she evolves from life to death, losing her spirit and form like the shift of the seasons, which recurs until infinity. My dead wife is now lying at peace between Heaven and Earth. If you find me weeping by her side, it means that I know nothing about the functioning of nature. Thus, I've dried my tears and stopped crying. I don't feel the grief now."

Hui Shi kept silent when he heard Zhuangzi's words.

Striking on an earthen pot and singing songs at one's wife's death may seem odd and unreasonable, but life and death is indeed the true course of nature. If one neither dreads death nor clings to life, he is a big step closer to freedom. The Taoism of the later ages that sought immortality and longevity, however, was worlds apart from Zhuangzi's ideas.

12. 渔夫不为太师

  周文王在臧地巡游,看见一位老人在水边钓鱼。周文王觉得他很特别,说他在钓鱼却又不像是在钓鱼,手拿着钓竿却又漫不经心,不像是真正钓鱼的样子。

  文王一心要起用他,并把朝政委托给他,可是又担心大臣和宗族的反对;打算就此放弃这个念头,却又不忍心天下的百姓得不到天子的庇护。反复考虑后文王总算想出了一个办法。他在清早议事时向诸大夫说:"昨晚我梦见了一位非常贤良的人,他黑黑的面孔,长长的胡须,骑着一匹杂色马,而且有只马蹄是红的。他对我大声说,'把你的朝政托付给那位臧地的老人,恐怕你的百姓也就差不多有救啦!'"诸位大夫惊恐不安地说:"这个显梦的人就是陛下的父亲!"文王说:"那么我们还是占卜问问这件事吧。"诸位大夫说:"既是先君的命令,陛下不必多虑,哪里还需要问呢?"

于是文王就命人把这位臧地老人请来，让他主持朝政。谁知他既不更改典章法规，也不发布新的政令。三年时间过去了，文王在国内遍访考察，发现儒士们解散了各自的地方势力集团，各级长官不再夸耀自己的功德，他国的粮食量器不再能进入国内使用。地方势力集团纷纷解散，意味着人民同心同德；各级长官不再夸耀个人的功德，意味着大家都变得务实了；他国的粮食量器不再能进入国内使用，诸侯就不会生出异心。看到这一切，文王十分高兴，于是就拜臧地老人为太师，以臣下的礼节恭敬地向他问道："这样的政事可以推行于天下吗？"臧地老人含含糊糊不作回应，抑或漫不经心地予以推辞。早晨还在发布命令，到了夜晚他就偷偷跑掉了，从那以后人们就再也听不到他的消息了。

文王认为渔夫的成功是因为他有高超的治国才能，所以请他做太师。太师是多少人梦寐以求的高位，可是渔夫却不当回事，因为渔夫的成功在于不治，运用的是"不是才能"的才能。现在人们多认为法令越多、规定越详、政策越细、方法越具体，治理国家就越有效，不知道这位渔夫的无为治国之术对他们会有什么启发。

THE FISHERMAN REFUSES TO BE THE GRAND PRECEPTOR

During his inspection tour to the Zang area, King Wen of Zhou saw an old man angling by the riverside. Yet his angling was not real angling. He was not angling for fish, but for something else. He was always there, angling for angling's sake.

King Wen was determined to call the fisherman to office and entrust the state affairs to him, but the king was also aware that the ministers and the royal family would worry about this. He even considered dropping the idea, but thought better of it because he did not want to see his people falling out of his protection. After long deliberation, he came up with an idea. When holding court in the morning, he said to his ministers, "Last night I dreamt of a very virtuous person with a dark complexion and a heavy beard, riding on a dappled horse with red hoofs. He said to me loudly, 'Entrust the old man from Zang with the state affairs and your people will most probably be relieved.'" The ministers were awe-stricken and said, "The man in the dream was your late father." King Wen said, "We'd better ask a diviner about it." But the ministers said, "Since it is the order of the late king, you should not hesitate. Surely there's no need for divination."

So King Wen sent for the old man from Zang and asked him to run the state. However, not a law or regulation was modified and not a statute was issued by the old man when he was in office. When King Wen made another inspection tour around the country three years later, he found that the scholars had disbanded their local cliques, the officials at different levels no longer lauded their personal achievements and merits, and the scales and bushels from other states were no longer used in the country. King Wen was very pleased to have discovered all these, since the disbandment of the local cliques meant that the people of the country were now of one heart and one mind; no more lauding of one's personal achievements and merits on the part of the officials meant that they were shouldering their official duties; and the vassals would not brood ulterior motives when scales and bushels from other states were not allowed to be used. King Wen was so happy that he asked the old man from Zang to be the grand preceptor. The king asked him respectfully in the manner of a liege subject, "Can this way of managing the state affairs be extended to the other parts of the world?" Hearing the question, the old man either evaded a definite answer or kept silent with indifference. He was issuing orders in the morning, but sneaked away in the evening, never to be heard of again.

King Wen believed that the success of the fisherman from Zang was due to his superior ability in managing the state affairs, thus asking him to be the grand preceptor, a much sought-after high position. But the fisherman thought differently, as his success was attributed to inaction, relying on abilities which could hardly be called abilities. It seems that more decrees, more detailed regulations, more minute policies and better-defined approaches do not necessarily guarantee that the country will be more effectively governed.

13. 伯夷和叔齐的节操

当年周朝兴起的时候,孤竹国有两位贤人,名叫伯夷和叔齐。两人相互商量道:"听说西方有个人,好像是有道的人,我们何不前去看看。"于是他们来到岐山的南面。周武王听说他们来了,就派他的弟弟旦前去拜见,和他们谈论讨伐纣王的事,并且跟他们立下誓盟,对他们作出"增加俸禄二等,授予一等官职"的许诺,为郑重起见,还将牲血涂抹在盟书上埋入祭坛之下。

看到这一情景,伯夷、叔齐二人相视而笑说:"咦,真是奇怪啊!这不是我们所谈论的道。从前神农氏治理天下,按时祭祀,竭尽虔诚而不祈求赐福;他对于百姓,忠实诚信,尽心治理而不向他们索取什么。人们乐于参与政事,就让他们参与政事,乐于从事治理,就让他们从事治理;不趁别人的危难来成全自己,也不因别人地位的卑下来抬高自己,不抓住各种机遇来图谋私利。如今周人看见殷商政局动荡,就想急速夺取统治天下的权力,崇尚谋略收买臣属,依靠武力威慑他国,宰牲结盟表示诚信,宣扬德行取悦众人,凭借征战求取私利。这样用推动祸乱的办法替代已有的暴政是以暴代暴,乱上加乱。我听说上古的贤士,遭逢治世不回避责任,遇上乱世不苟且偷生。如今天下昏暗,周人如此做法说明德行已经衰败,与其跟周人在一起而玷污我们的身体,还不如逃离他们保持品行的高洁。"于是两人向北逃到了首阳山,后来周克商,两人不食周粟,不饮周水,最终饿死在那里。

像伯夷、叔齐这样的人,他们对于富贵的态度就是,即使真有机会得到也决不会去获取。高尚的气节和迥异于流俗的行为,自适自乐而不追逐于世事,这就是两位贤士的节操。

司马迁讲过这样的话:天下人熙熙攘攘、忙忙碌碌,都是为利而来,为利而去。伯夷和叔齐的节操给人展示的则是另一种境界,利禄不可取,王位可以让,因为他们认为外物有碍生命、有碍自由。《庄子·让王篇》中讲的几乎都是这个话题。庄子要说的是,人宁可贫穷也不能窝囊。如果一只鸟找到了鸟笼为安身之处而沾沾自喜,那么,它还有自由吗?

THE MORAL INTEGRITY OF BO YI AND SHU QI

During the rise of the Zhou Dynasty, there were two virtuous sages living in the State of Guzhu named Bo Yi and Shu Qi. Once they had a conversation and one said to the other, "I've heard that there is one man living in the west who is said to have known Tao. Why don't we go and pay him a visit?" So they went to the south of Mount Qi. By the time they reached there, King Wu of Zhou had heard of the news and sent his younger brother, Dan, to visit them. On behalf of King Wu, the younger brother Dan talked about the crusade against King Zhou of Shang and offered a solemn contract to them, promising that their salary would be increased to the grade of second-rank officials, and they would immediately be promoted to the first rank. Finally Dan sealed the deal in earnest by dripping the blood of an ox on the document and burying it under the sacrificial alter.

At this, the two sages looked at each other and laughed, saying, "Oh, how strange! This is not what we referred to as Tao. When the legendary emperor Shennong put the world in order, sacrifices were regularly offered with the utmost reverence, but not for the sake of god's blessings. He was faithful and trustworthy in his running of the world, never asking for anything in return from his people. He allowed those who had an interest in state affairs to participate in the running of the government and those who loved farming and husbandry to engage in such agricultural activities. He did not take advantage of those in difficulties to achieve success; he did not make himself appear higher by looking down on those who were less fortunate in terms of social status; neither did he take various opportunities to advance his own interests. But now the people of Zhou see that the Kingdom of Shang is in political unrest and they wish to rush over and take control of Shang so that they can control the whole world. They maneuver to buy off officials and subjects, intimidate others with a display of force, seal alliances by killing animals to show their trustworthiness, advocate virtuous behavior to please the mass, and send troops to conquer other states for their own benefits. To overthrow the existing oppression in a way which actually spreads disorder is to replace tyranny with tyranny, which would result in more troubles. I have heard of virtuous people in ancient times who never ran away from their official responsibilities when they were in peaceful times and who did not care to drag on with their lives in shame when troubled times came. Now that the world is in such darkness and what the people of Zhou are doing shows clearly that virtue has been ruined, we'd rather run away from them to keep our morals pure than messing around with them to get ourselves soiled." Therefore the two of them fled north to Mount Shouyang. After Zhou conquered Shang, they stopped eating and drinking because they believed that food and water all belonged to the Kingdom of Zhou. In the end, they died of starvation.

People like Bo Yi and Shu Qi will never seek fortune and high position even when they are presented with the right opportunities. With their high principles, they remain uncorrupted and very much contented with what they have, instead of having too many worldly concerns — such is the moral integrity of these two virtuous sages.

Sima Qian made comments similar to the following. Bustling around every day, people in the world live for benefits and die for benefits, but the moral integrity of Bo Yi and Shu Qi leads us to another realm where benefits are not to be scrambled for, and where even the throne can be given away, as external things will interfere with life and freedom. The chapter "Kings resign the throne" in *Zhuangzi* discusses nothing else but the same topic. What Zhuangzi wanted to say was that one can be poor but should not be stupid and cowardly. If a bird gloats over a bird cage for it has found its safe haven, will it still enjoy freedom?

14. 急流驾船的本领

  颜渊问孔子说:"有一次我在觞深这个渡口过河,那是一条又大又深的河,有不少漩涡,水流也很急。那摆渡人操纵着船,如同神仙那样,驾船的技巧高超极了,很快就把船摇到了对岸。我问他,'驾船好学吗?'摆渡人说:'当然。会游泳的人很快就能学会驾船。假如是善于潜水的人,因为熟悉水性,即使他不曾见过船,也会熟练地驾驶。'我又问他这是什么道理,他却不再回答我。我实在不明白他为什么这样?老师,他的话究竟是什么意思呢?"

  孔子回答说:"所谓会游泳的人很快就能学会驾船,这是因为他们习以成性,适应于水而处之自然,忘掉了那是水。至于那善于潜水的人不曾见过船就能熟练地驾驶,是因为他们眼里的深渊就像是陆地上的小丘,看待船翻倒就犹如车子向后倒退一样。船翻也好,车子倒退也好,各种挫折、危险展现在他们眼前,都不能扰乱他们的内心,他们依然毫不在乎，旁若无事！就拿下赌来说，同一个人，用瓦片作为赌注时心里坦然，因为即使输了也不过是块瓦片，所以显得很放松，没有心理负担；用银质带钩作为赌注时则心存疑虑，计算着输赢的成本；用黄金作为赌注，则唯恐输得倾家荡产，常常头脑发昏内心迷乱。一个人的赌博技巧原本是一样的，各种赌注体现的赌博原理也没有什么差别，但是因为怕输掉了贵重的东西而有所顾惜，那就是以身外之物为重了。大凡注重外物的人，其内心世界一定笨拙。"

外物看得过重的人，其内心世界一定笨拙，这是道家养生、养神、通达生命的理念，其基本要求是心神宁寂，摒除各种外欲。老子告诫说，人要知足，人知道满足就不会受到侮辱，知道休止就不会遇到危险，人最大的祸害就是不知足；要寡欲，人有欲望很危险，因为五色使人眼睛瞎，五音使人耳朵聋，五味使人口味败，纵马追逐、打猎行乐使人心发狂，难得的财物使人干坏事。不为外物所累，成了中国许多志士仁人推崇的理想，现在我们常说的无欲则刚，说的也是这个道理。

SKILLS OF BOATING IN TORRENTS

Yan Yuan asked Confucius, "Once I was crossing a river at a ferry called Shangshen. The river was wide and deep with strong currents and a lot of eddies. But the ferryman handled the boat with superior boating skills, almost like a super-natural being, and soon took the boat across to the other side. I asked him, 'Can anyone learn the skills to pilot a boat like that?' 'Of course,' said the ferryman, 'Good swimmers can pick it up quickly. As for the divers, even if they haven't seen a boat before, they can pull it over and manage it well since they know the water well.' I went on to ask him why it was like that, but he no longer offered any explanations. I was puzzled, wondering why he said that. Master, can you tell me what he meant?"

Confucius answered, "Good swimmers can learn it quickly because they are so used to water and feel so comfortable in it that they forget it is water. As for the divers, they are able to manage a boat well even if they've never seen it before. That is because they see a deep abyss as though it were a small hill on the land and a capsized boat as though it were a cart going backwards. Be it a capsized boat or a cart going backwards, all the setbacks and dangers have occurred right in front of them but will not disrupt their innermost world. They carry on at ease as if nothing has happened. Let's take gambling for an example. One who stakes on a piece of earthen tile feels clear of burden, since even if he loses, it's nothing but a piece of tile. If he stakes on a silver hook, he gets more apprehensive with the calculation of the cost. But if he gambles with an article of gold as his stake, he gets giddy and confused, afraid of losing everything to his name. Actually the skill of the gambler is the same in each case, and the basic principles of gambling as reflected by different stakes do not vary. Being afraid of losing something of value and becoming over-worried means the gambler looks on the external things as most important. Anyone who attaches importance to what is external must be clumsy and awkward in their inner world."

Too much importance attached to what is external results in a clumsy and awkward inner world — that is the concept advocated by Taoism in terms of the nourishment of body, the cultivation of spirit and the understanding of life. The basic requirement is to suppress all kinds of external desires in favor of inner tranquility. Laozi advised that one should be contented with one's lot, and then one would not get humiliated. Knowing when to stop takes one away from danger. The biggest enemy of human beings is discontentment. One should have few needs and wants since it's very dangerous if one has too many. The five colors make people blind; the five sounds make people deaf; the five tastes ruin the tasting buds; riding horse and hunting animals make people go wild at heart; and hard-to-get wealth tricks people into doing something bad. So for many Chinese people who have ideals and principles, the dreams and the moral integrity which they praise highly are to be free of concerns over what is external. Now we often say that one is the strongest when one has few desires, which is of the same idea.

15. 呆若木鸡

　　西周时期,有一个奇人名叫纪渻子,他善于训鸡,名气很大。那时的周宣王酷爱斗鸡,便把纪渻子召进宫来,专门替他精心养鸡。时间过得很快,转眼之间已过去了十天,周宣王有点心急,问道:"鸡养得怎样,可以斗了吗?"纪渻子说:"不行,您看那只大公鸡昂首挺胸,目空一切,全凭一股傲气,没有真本事,这种样子打起来是不能持久的。"再过了十天,周宣王忍不住又问了。纪渻子说:"还没有呢,那鸡虽然没有了傲气,但还好斗。你看它,只要看到鸡的影子,听到鸡的走动,便竖起头颈,咯咯地叫,挑衅滋事,还是不行。"又过了十天,周宣王想这下总差不多了,于是又问了。纪渻子解释说:"还没有呢,圣上别急,还要等一下。虽然它不想滋事了,可有时还会抖抖冠子,眼睛睁得大大的,神气十足,志在必胜,训练还没有到家。"周宣王听得晕头晕脑,心里很不高兴。他心想这纪渻子年龄不大,说起来头头是道,莫不是一个骗子?不知训出来的大公鸡究竟会怎么样，如果再过十天还是这样，非要他的命不可。

好不容易又过了十天，周宣王忍不住又问训鸡的进展状况。这时纪渻子满脸喜气，高兴地把鸡抱到周宣王跟前。周宣王一看十分茫然，昔日那雄赳赳气昂昂的大公鸡如今双目发呆，无精打采，呼之不应，驱之不动，不要说上战场了，就是叫它自己求食好像都有问题，这样的木鸡还能斗吗？怀疑之下，周宣王就让人另取凶鸡来斗。铁笼里的凶鸡原本气势汹汹，但看到周宣王的木鸡却愣住了。这只木鸡似有鸡身鸡型，听起来似有鸡声鸡鸣，但双眼没有生气，神态没有活力，呆若木桩，没有生死的界限。然而，不分生死就不知死亡，不知死亡就不会停战，不知疼痛就不会退逃。面对这样的对手，凶鸡的斗志顿时丧失了，不敢往前走一步，最后掉头逃走了。

可以把"呆"看作一种境界，一种高层次的认识。当人们在实现自己的奋斗目标时，要有一种"呆"劲，要全身心地沉浸在"呆"境中，抵挡一切诱惑，排除一切干扰，不在意细小的差距，不在意一时一地的得失，从而顺利地到达自己的目的地。

DUMB AS A WOODEN ROOSTER

In the Western Zhou Dynasty, there was a wizard named Ji Shengzi who enjoyed a great reputation in training roosters. At that time, King Xuan of Zhou loved rooster-fighting and therefore hired Ji Shengzi to train fighting roosters for him. Time flew quickly and ten days passed before King Xuan seemed to be a bit anxious and asked, "How is the training going on? Is the rooster ready for fight?" Ji Shengzi replied, "No, not yet. You see the big rooster holds its head up high and looks proud and conceited. It relies on its vigor instead of real skills. In this state, it won't last long in a fight." Another ten days passed and King Xuan ran out of his patience and once again asked about the rooster. Ji Shengzi said, "Not yet. Though without conceit, the rooster is still haughty. It jumps and rushes to attack with threatening squawks and raises its head at the slightest movement and sound made by other roosters." Still another ten days passed and King Xuan thought that now it would be time. He asked Ji again. Ji Shengzi explained, "Still not yet. Would Your Majesty wait a bit longer? Though the rooster no longer heads for trouble, it still puts on airs with a determination to win, and so it raises its hackles and stares fiercely from time to time. The training is not done yet." At this, King Xuan found himself dizzy with confusion, and what was more, very unhappy about everything. He thought that as someone who looked not very old, Ji was for sure a good talker, rambling on with eloquence. He wondered what the rooster would be like after being trained by Ji and if Ji was a cheater. The King was suspicious and decided that if it was still like this after another ten days, he would have the rooster trainer beheaded.

At last another ten days went by. King Xuan was impatient with his doubt and inquired about the training again. With a big smile, Ji Shengzi held the rooster in his arms and took it to the king, who took one look at the rooster and found himself utterly confused. The once proud and dashing rooster now looked spiritless and lazy with dull eyes, not responding to calls and prompts. It seemed that the rooster even had trouble feeding itself, let alone going to the fight. Could such a wooden rooster fight? With suspicions as such, the king sent for some most terrible roosters. Yet, no matter how vicious they appeared in their cage, they froze at the sight of the king's "wooden rooster". It looked like a rooster and sounded like a rooster, yet its eyes were lifeless, its manners were listless, and it looked as dumb as a piece of wooden stick without distinction between life and death. Yet with life and death thus blended together, it knew no death; with no knowledge of death, it would not stop fighting; and with no taste of pain, it would not give up and run away. In face of such an opponent, all the vicious roosters lost their will to fight, and not daring to take one step forward, they turned around and fled.

Being dumb can be taken as a kind of state, an understanding on a superior level. In the process of realizing one's goals, one needs the kind of dumbness so that one can be immerged in the "wooden" state, resisting temptations of all kinds, avoiding interferences from all parties, and disregarding small differences and the present gains and losses. Thus one is able to smoothly reach one's destination.

16. 杀龙的本领

  从前有个人名叫朱评漫,他很有志向,总想学点独一无二的技能。可是世界上的知识门类很多,究竟学什么好,学什么才能高人一筹,朱评漫一直拿不定主意。

  有一天,朱评漫听说远方有个人叫支离益,他本领出众,有一手杀龙的绝活。朱评漫很高兴,觉得这是一个千载难逢的好机会,就告别家人,带上一千两黄金,兴致勃勃地去找支离益,向他学习屠龙的本领。一进支离益的家,只见墙上贴满了大大小小的龙画,威风凛凛,让人感到很是恐怖。支离益收了朱评漫为徒弟后,就把他领到墙边,指着龙画一一告诉他,何处用刀可以致龙于死地,怎样用刀可以顺利取下龙胆,割龙肝的最佳位置在那里等等。朱评漫听得很认真,不时地做些记号,唯恐漏掉些什么。由于朱评漫看到的龙只是一副副平面画,所以相当长的时间还是像瞎子摸象一样,对龙没有确切的感觉。

就这样整整学了三年，朱评漫把带来的千两黄金都用完了，总算完成学业。他告别了师傅，回到了自己的家乡。朱评漫想到自己掌握了杀龙的绝技，心中十分得意。周围的人看到他，都十分关切地问他究竟学了什么，这时朱评漫显得十分兴奋，滔滔不绝地把杀龙的技术——例如怎样按住龙头，怎样踩住龙的尾巴，怎样割龙的咽喉，怎样从龙身上提取宝物——边说边用手势比划给大家看。

这时，有个天真的孩子插话了，他问："哪儿有龙，什么是杀龙？"听到小孩子的问话，大家都笑了。而朱评漫却涨红着脸，不知怎么回答，但他终于明白了，世界上根本没有什么龙，三年的苦功算是白花了。

花了千金，苦学三年，却一无所获，庄子用屠龙之技这个故事来批评儒家、墨家，说它们的学说是无用之学，但这个故事的实质，谈的还是自然与人为的关系问题。庄子讲了个笑话：有人怕别人偷东西，就把东西整理好，然后用绳子把它捆扎起来，结果小偷轻而易举地把东西偷走了。学习本来是使人聪明的，但聪明是有区别的。世俗的聪明习惯于人为的摆布，常常在浅薄的事情上耗费精力，把心思用在鸡毛蒜皮的事情上，虽然付出很多，但结局却是事与愿违。顺应自然，安于宁静，才算得上是真正的聪明。

DRAGON-SLAYING SKILLS

Once there was a man named Zhu Pingman who was quite ambitious and wanted to learn some unique skills. However, knowing that there were many different skills and knowledge in the world, he was at a loss as to what to learn to make him superior to others.

One day Zhu Pingman heard that there was a man living far away named Zhi Liyi, who was endowed with exceptional abilities and was distinguished in dragon-slaying. Delighted at the news, Zhu Pingman believed that it was a chance of a lifetime. Therefore, in high spirits, he said goodbye to his family and went to see Zhi Liyi with one thousand taels of gold on him for the hopes of learning the dragon-slaying skills. Stepping into the house of Zhi Liyi, he saw the walls were covered with pictures of dragons of all sizes in their full majesty, making one feel a bit scared. Having agreed to take on Zhu Pingman as his apprentice, Zhi Liyi took Zhu in front of the walls and pointing at the dragon pictures one by one, he explained where to drive in the knife to make it a fatal strike, how to drive in the knife to take out the dragon gallbladder smoothly and what was the best place to cut apart dragon liver, etc. Zhu Pingman listened to everything carefully and took down notes from time to time, not willing to miss anything. Since all Zhu Pingman had seen of the dragons were only on pictures, he still lacked tangible experience on the dragons even after a long time, much like a blind man feeling an elephant.

Having studied in this manner for three whole years, Zhu Pingman used up the one thousand taels of gold he had brought with him and finally completed his study. He said goodbye to his master and returned to his hometown, feeling very satisfied now that he knew that he had learnt the dragon-slaying skills. The neighbors, seeing his return, all asked him in a caring way what exactly he had learned. Zhu Pingman appeared to be very excited and talked on and on about the dragon-slaying skills, such as how to hold the dragon's head down, how to step onto the dragon's tail, how to slice open the dragon's throat, and how to remove valuable parts from a dragon, all accompanied with gestures to make people understand.

Just then, an innocent child interrupted him by asking, "Where is the dragon? What is dragon-slaying?" Everyone laughed at this. But Zhu Pingman turned red in the face, not knowing how to answer. It dawned on him that there were no dragons in the world, and his three years of hard work were all for nothing.

Having spent one thousand taels of gold and studied hard for three years, Zhu Pingman only found that he had achieved nothing in the process. Zhuangzi used the story of the dragon-slaying skills to criticize the teachings of Confucius and Mancius as being useless. But in essence, what Zhuangzi talked about was still the problem about the human behaviors and nature. Zhuangzi told a funny story about someone who was worried about thefts. He tidied up everything into a bundle and tied it with a rope. Then a thief came and took everything easily. Learning is supposed to make people smart, but there are different kinds of smartness. Being smart in a worldly way makes one subject to the manipulations of others, wasting too much time and attention on trivialities. And in the end he is made utterly exhausted both in mind and body with the results being very much undesired. To tune in with nature and be content with quietness are what is indispensable in true smartness.

17. 桓公见鬼

有一次,齐桓公在草泽中打猎,管仲替他驾车。突然桓公见到了鬼,只见那鬼个子很高,披着长发,穿着紫袍,头戴红帽,迎面站着,一动不动。惊得桓公拉住管仲的手不放,连声问:"仲父,你见到了什么没有?"管仲回答说:"主公,我什么也没有见到。"受了这一惊吓,桓公再也没有心思打猎了。回来后,桓公便感疲惫困怠,失魂落魄,一病不起,连着好几天都不出门。

桓公见鬼的事很快就传开了。这时,齐国有个叫皇子告敖的士人前来求见。他来到桓公的病榻前,对桓公说:"君王这是自己伤害自己,鬼怎么能伤害到君王呢?人健康与否与气很有关系,存于身体内部的气,如果和谐,人就感到舒畅;如果不和谐,就会全身不适。人的郁结之气,容易散泄而不返归于身,对于来自外界的骚扰也就缺乏足够的精神力量加以抵御。郁结着的气如果只能上通而不能下达,就会使人易怒;只能下达而不能上通，就会使人健忘；不上通又不下达，阻滞在胸中，那就会生病。"桓公说："这样说，那么世上到底还有鬼吗？"告敖回答说："鬼是有的。水中污泥里有叫履的鬼，灶里有叫髻的鬼。门户内的各种烦攘，是那名叫雷霆的鬼在活动；东北的墙下，有阿鲑龙鬼在那里跳跃；西北方的墙下，名叫泆阳的鬼住在那里。水里有鬼罔象，丘陵里有山鬼峷，大山里有山鬼夔，郊野里有野鬼彷徨，草泽里还有一种名叫委蛇的鬼。"桓公接着问："请问，那委蛇的形状是怎么样的？"告敖回答："委蛇，身躯大如车轮，长如车辕，穿着紫衣，戴着红帽。这种东西长得很丑陋，它讨厌听到雷、车的声音，一听见就两手捧着头站着。谁见到了他，谁就会称霸于天下。"

桓公听了后开怀大笑，说："这就是我所见到的鬼。"于是连忙起身，穿好衣服，跟皇子告敖坐着谈话。不到半天的工夫，病就不知不觉地消失了。

世界上是没有鬼的，但历史上就有不少人相信鬼。中国古代思想家墨子就说鬼无处不在。其实，说人间有鬼的人是心中有鬼。看来，人的认识器官大脑——古人说的心——在人的认识过程中有着决定性的作用，所以后人就把心比作水中的珍珠，要不断地加以擦洗。如果心净了，鬼还有吗？

DUKE HUAN SEES A GHOST

Once when Duke Huan of Qi was hunting in the marshes with Guan Zhong driving the carriage for him, he suddenly saw a ghost that had a big build and long flowing hair and wore a purple robe and a red hat. It stood in front of him, motionless. In shock, Duke Huan grasped Guan Zhong's hand tightly and asked over and over, "Do you see anything, Uncle Zhong?" "Nothing, Your Grace," answered

Guan Zhong, "I don't see anything." Thus shocked, Duke Huan was no longer in the mood for hunting. After his return, he felt exhausted and mentally disturbed. He went sick and stayed home for several days.

Words soon got out that Duke Huan had seen a ghost and was ill. Among the scholars in the State of Qi, there was a Huangzi Gao'ao who asked to be granted an audience. He went up to the sickbed of Duke Huan and said, "Your Grace is hurting yourself. How would a ghost be able to harm you? One's health has a lot to do with *qi* (energy). If *qi*, which is contained within the human body, is in harmony with the body, one feels at ease; but if it disagrees with the human body, then one feels uncomfortable all over. It is easy for the bound-up *qi* to disperse. If it doesn't return to the body, the body will be left with insufficient spiritual energy to resist external disturbance. When the bound-up *qi* ascends and does not descend, it makes one lose temper easily; when it descends and does not ascend, it makes one forgetful; and when it neither ascends nor descends, but remains about the heart in the center of the body, it makes one ill." Duke Huan said, "Yes, but are there such things as ghosts in the world?" Gao'ao replied, "Yes, there are. Amid the mud deep in water, there is the shoe ghost Lü; in the kitchen stove, there is hair bun ghost Ji; inside the door, the various troubles are the works of the thunder ghost Lei Ting; under the northeast wall, the ghost Ah Gui Long is jumping about; under the northwest wall, there lives a ghost named Yi Yang. In the water, there is Wang Xiang. In the hills, there is the hill ghost Xin. In the mountains, there is the mountain ghost Kui. In the wildness, there is the wandering wild ghost Pang Huang. And in the marshes, there is the ghost named Wei She." Duke Huan went on with another question, "May I ask what Wei She looks like?" Gao'ao answered, "Wei She is as big as the hub of a wheel, long as a wagon shaft, and wears purple clothes and a red hat. It looks ugly and it hates the sounds made by thunders and carriages. Every time it hears such sounds, it will stand up with both hands holding its head. He who sees it is to become the leader of the world."

Duke Huan burst out laughing at what he had just heard and said, "That's the ghost I saw." Saying that, he got up from bed, put on his robes and sat down with Huangzi Gao'ao. In a couple of hours, his illness had gone without him noticing it.

There are no ghosts in the world, but still not a few in the history said that they believed there were. Mozi, another great thinker in ancient China, claimed that ghosts were everywhere. In fact, he who says there are ghosts harbors one in his heart. The brain, the cognitive organ of the human body, or according to the ancient people, the heart, seems to play a very important function in the understanding process of human beings. That is why the later generations have compared the human heart to the pearl in water, which needs constant polishing. If the heart stays clean, will one see ghosts?

18. 不接受封赏的屠夫

　　由于吴国的入侵,楚昭王被迫出逃,有一个以屠羊为生的名叫说的人跟随他一起逃亡。后来昭王收复了国土,返回楚国,那位屠夫也跟着回国,重操旧业。楚昭王没有忘记那些与他共患难的官吏、百姓,打算赏赐跟随他逃亡的人,其中也包括这位屠夫。当昭王的使者把奖赏送到屠夫家中时,屠夫谢绝了,他说:"当年大王丧失了国土,我也失去了屠羊的职业;大王返归楚国,我也恢复了原先的职业,我已经像过去一样得到了从业的报酬,又何必再另外赏赐什么!"昭王听到左右的汇报后,下令一定要他接受奖赏。于是使者再次来到屠夫家,传达了昭王的旨意,但屠夫仍不接受。他对使者说:"大王失去楚国,不是为臣的过失,所以我不愿坐以待毙、伏法受诛;大王返归楚国,也不是为臣的功劳,所以我也不该接受赏赐。"得知屠夫的态度后,楚昭王就对左右说:"这样,我来见见他!"屠夫被叫到宫里,昭王又谈到封赏的事情,屠夫说:"按照楚国的法令，只有立了大功、受过重赏的人才能够得到君王接见的礼遇。现在我的才智不足以使国家得到保全，勇力又不足以杀死敌寇。吴国的大军攻入国都，我怕遇到灾难，就逃走躲避敌寇，并不是有心追随大王。如今大王意欲弃置法令和制度来接见我，这不是我所希望传扬天下的办法。"

听了这番话，楚昭王就对大司马子綦说："屠夫虽然地位卑贱，但陈述的道理却很深刻，你还是替我用三卿之位把他请来。"于是子綦就去见屠夫，屠夫知道来由后说："三卿的高位，我知道比起屠羊的店铺实在是高贵得多；优厚的俸禄，我也知道比起屠羊的报酬实在是丰厚得多。然而，怎么可以贪图高官厚禄而使国君蒙受胡乱施舍的坏名声呢！我实在不敢接受公卿之位，还是让我回到那宰羊的店铺吧。"

到最后，屠夫还是没有接受楚昭王的封赏。

老子说反者道之动，就是说事物的发展如果过了头，就会向相反方面转化。屠夫之所以力拒封赏，安贫乐道，是因为他知道，外面的世界固然很精彩，很诱人，但人对世界的追求是有限的，人所拥有的只能是属于自身的东西。所以人必须为自己的欲望划定一个界线，超出这个界限，就有可能害得自己一无所有。

THE BUTCHER DECLINES THE KING'S REWARDS

Under the attack of the State of Wu, King Zhao of Chu was forced to leave his state and a sheep-butcher followed him in his flight. When King Zhao recovered his territory and returned to the throne later, the butcher returned with the king and took up his old job again. Not wanting to forget the officials and the common people who stood by him and followed him in times of trouble, King Zhao of Chu decided to reward them, including the butcher. But when King Zhao's envoy took the reward to the butcher's house, the butcher declined, saying, "When the king lost his state, I lost my job as a sheep-butcher; when the King returned to Chu, I regained my old job. Now I have got my income from my job like before, why is there the need for a reward?" King Zhao, on hearing this from his envoy, issued the order that the butcher should accept the reward. So the envoy once again came to the house of the butcher and told him the order of the King. Declining the reward for the second time, the butcher said to the envoy, "It was not due to any fault of mine that the king lost his state, so I don't deserve any punishment for that. It was not through any effort of mine that the king was able to return to Chu, and so I should not accept any rewards, either." Learning the butcher's attitude toward the reward, King Zhao said to his attendants, "So let me meet him!" When the butcher was brought to the king's palace, King Zhao talked about the reward again. And the butcher said, "According to the laws of Chu, the audience of the king is granted only to those who have made great contributions and received great merits. But now my wisdom is not sufficient to keep the state intact, nor is my courage sufficient to kill the invaders. When the army of the State of Wu invaded the capital, I was afraid of the disaster and fled to avoid the enemies. So it was not loyalty that made me follow Your Grace. Now Your Grace wants to see me regardless of laws and social institutions. That is not the way which I would like to see spreading in the world."

Hearing this, King Zhao said to his Minister of War, Ziqi, "Though the butcher comes from a humble status, what he has expressed is very impressive. Go and invite him to take the position of the Three Banners." So Ziqi went to see the butcher. On hearing the minister's purpose, the butcher said, "I know the high position of the Three Banners is much nobler when compared to the job of a butcher, and the salary is much higher than what I earn as a butcher. However, how should I make my king take on the name of mishandling the charity and inappropriately dispensing rewards because of my greed for high position and big money? I dare not accept the position of a high official. Let me return to my butcher's shop instead."

In the end, the butcher still did not accept King Zhao's reward.

Laozi said that Tao turned to the opposite during its evolution, which meant that things would develop in the opposite direction when they came to the extreme. The reason why the butcher declined the reward and stay contented with his humble life was that he knew that though the outside world was colorful and full of temptations, there was always a limit to what one could get from it, and one could only have what rightfully belonged to him. Therefore, one must set down a boundary for one's desires; if one goes beyond the boundary, one ends up with nothing.

19. 一问三不知

　　王倪是尧时的贤人。有一次,王倪的学生啮缺问王倪:"老师,您知道各种事物之间总有共同的地方吗?"王倪说:"我怎么会知道呢!"啮缺又问:"您知道您所以不知道的原因吗?"王倪回答说:"我怎么会知道呢!"啮缺接着又问:"那么世界上各种事物都无法知道吗?"王倪回答:"我怎么知道呢!不过你既然不断地发问,那我就试着来回答你的问题。怎样才能知道我所说的知道不是不知道呢?又怎么知道我所说的不知道不是知道呢?我还是先问一问你:人们睡在潮湿的地方就会腰部患病,甚至酿成半身不遂,泥鳅也会这样吗?人们住在高高的树木上就会心惊胆战、惶恐不安,猿猴也会这样吗?人、泥鳅、猿猴三者究竟谁最懂得居处的标准呢?谁的标准最有道理呢?人以牲畜的肉为食物,麋鹿食草芥,蜈蚣嗜吃小蛇,猫头鹰则爱吃老鼠,人、麋鹿、蜈蚣、猫头鹰这四类动物究竟谁才懂得真正的美味?哪一种食物最好吃?似猿而有狗头的猵狙把雌猿当作配偶,麋喜欢与鹿交配,泥鳅则与鱼在一起游水。毛嫱和丽姬,人人都说她们是少见的美人,可是鱼儿见了她们就深深潜入水底,鸟儿见了她们就展翅飞向高空,麋鹿见了她们撒开四蹄飞快地逃离。人、鱼、鸟和麋鹿四者究竟谁才懂得什么是天下真正的美色呢?依我看来,仁与义的端绪,是与非的途径,无不纷杂错乱,我怎么能知晓它们之间的差别呢!"

啮缺说:"您不了解利与害,这可以理解,但是难道道德修养高尚的至人也不知晓天下的是非与利害吗?"王倪说:"那至人可不一样,进入物我两忘境界的至人实在是神妙不测啊!森林草泽起了大火,也不能使他感到火热;江河中结了厚厚的冰,也不能使他感到寒冷;迅疾的雷霆劈山破岩,狂风翻江倒海,不能使他感到震惊。他可驾驭云气,骑乘日月,在四海之外遨游。这样的人,对生死都无动于衷,还会在乎利与害这些微不足道的事情吗?"

王倪所以一问三不知,是因为他认为天下无是非;所以无是非,是因为天下没有判断是非的统一标准,这就突出了人的认识的多元性问题,对启发人们不要拘泥于一端、不要固执己见是有积极意义的。中国人常讲"和而不同",如果把"和"看作真理,那么没有差异就达不到真理。但如果认识仅仅停留在差异的层面,不扬弃、融化、整合这些差异,形成高一级的认识,就会走向相对主义,从而否定认识的客观性。这将导致许多不可回避又难以解答的问题,例如:毛嫱和丽姬到底是不是美人?

NO TO EVERY QUESTION

Wang Ni was a sage at the time of Yao. Once his student Nie Que asked him, "Do you know, sir, that all things agree with one another at some point?" Wang Ni said, "How should I know?" Nie Que asked again, "Do you know the reason why you don't know?" Wang Ni answered, "How should I know?" Nie Que asked for the third time, "Then is it true that we're unable to know all the things in the world?" "How should I know that?" Wang Ni answered again, "Since you keep on asking questions, let me try to answer them. If I say 'I know', how do you know that it does not mean 'I don't know'? And if I say 'I don't know', how do you know that it does not mean 'I know'? Let me ask you a question first: If people sleep in wet places, then their lower backs will ache and they may even become paralyzed in one side of the body. Will eels be like that? If people live high up in the trees, they will become nervous, tense, and fearful. But will apes react in the same way? Among people, eels and apes, which species know best the standards for living? Whose standards are the most reasonable? People eat the meat of animals, deer feed on grass, centipedes savor snakes, and owls find mice tasty. Among the four creatures, which one knows the best taste? And which kind of food has the best taste? The dog-headed monkey goes in pair with the female gibbon, the elk likes to mate with the deer, and the eel enjoys itself with fish in the water. Mao Qiang and Li Ji are considered by men to be rare beauties, but if fish see them, they will dive into the depths of the water; if birds see them, they will spread their wings and fly high into the sky; and if deer see them, they will speed away as fast as their hoofs can carry them. Among the four creatures, which one knows what the real beauty is in the world? In my opinion, the roots of benevolence and righteousness, and the paths of right and wrong, are all inextricably confused. How should I know how to distinguish among them?"

Nie Que said, "I can understand that you know nothing of benefits and harms. But would the Perfect Man with the highest moral values not know of right and wrong, or benefits and harms?" Wang Ni replied, "The Perfect Man is different. He enters the realm where both material objects and himself are put aside, which is miraculous and unpredictable. If a wetland forest is on fire, it will not make him feel the heat; if rivers and lakes freeze, it will not make him feel cold; if swift lightening strikes and cracks hills and rocks, and howling wind shakes the sea, they will not make him frightened. He rides the cloud and mist, straddles the sun and the moon, and wanders beyond the four seas. For someone who remains impassive even in face of life and death, how would he care about such trivial matters as benefits and harms?"

The reason why Wang Ni said no to every question was because he believed there was no right or wrong in the world, since there was not one single standard to be applied in evaluating right or wrong. This idea brings up the issue about the diversity of human understanding and therefore plays a positive role in encouraging people to break away from arbitrary restraints and to be flexible in understanding the world. Chinese people often talk about "harmony without uniformity". If harmony is seen as truth, one can never reach truth without recognizing differences. But if one stops at recognizing differences only, and doesn't try to develop the useful and discard the useless, thus merging and integrating the differences to reach a higher level of understanding, one will inevitably go to relativism and deny the objectivity of understanding. That will result in many unavoidable but implausible questions, such as whether Mao Qiang and Li Ji are beauties.

20. 夔虫蛇风

　　古代有一种奇兽叫夔,形体像牛,独脚能走,目光如日月,声音如雷。夔爱慕百足虫,百足虫爱慕无脚的蛇,无脚的蛇爱慕无形的风,无形的风羡慕明察外物的眼睛,明察外物的眼睛羡慕内在的心灵。

　　一天,夔对百足虫说:"你看,我依靠一只脚跳跃而行,没有谁比我更方便的了。现在你用上百只脚行走,这又何必呢?"百足虫说:"你这就不对了。不是我要用百只脚行走,而是我天生就有百只脚,自然而然地用百只脚行走。你看见那人吐唾沫的情形吗?喷出的唾沫大的可以像珠子,小的可以像雾滴,大的自然而大,小的自然而小,大小混杂吐落而下,既不可以数计,也难以人为控制。如今我启动我天生的机能而行走,要问其中的原理,我也说不清楚。不过我也并不知道自己为什么能够这样。"

　　百足虫见蛇一只脚都没有,可是爬起来却相当快,常常无声无息就不见踪影，觉得很奇怪，就对蛇说："我用那么多的脚行走，反倒不如没有脚的你，这是为什么呢？"蛇说："仰赖天生的机能而行动，怎么可以改变呢？我行走哪里用得着脚呢！"

风刮起来呼呼地响，席卷大地，一眨眼就从北到南，蛇看到这一景象觉得不可思议，就对风说："我启动我的脊柱和肋骨而行走，还是像有足而行的样子。如今你呼呼地从北海掀起，又呼呼地驾临南海，却没有留下有足而行的形迹，这是为什么呢？"风说："是的，我呼呼地从北海来到南海，从气势上说，你们没有一个可以与我相比。可是你不知道，人们用手来阻挡我而我并不能吹断手指，人们用腿脚来踢踏我而我也不能吹断腿脚。即使这样，折断参天大树，掀翻高大房屋，吹起十丈大浪，却又只有我具备这样的能力。在细小的方面不求胜利才有可能获取大的胜利。而获取大的胜利，只有圣人才能做到。"

风的这种说法也有局限，尽管风承认自己也有软肋。其实，夔、虫、蛇、风虽然各不相同，才能有大有小，但它们都能行走，都可以通过自己的努力达到目标。条条大道通罗马，人们大可不必因为自己是个小人物而放弃自己的追求，不必因为自己力量的微薄而不求作为，不必因为自己职位的低下而抹杀自身的价值。不妨借鉴契诃夫的看法：小狗大狗可以一起叫。

THE MONSTER KUI, THE CENTIPEDE, THE SERPENT AND THE WIND

In ancient times, there was an extraordinary monster called Kui with a body like an ox, shining eyes like the sun and the moon, and a voice much like thunder. It could hop around on one foot. The monster Kui admired the centipede with 100 feet. The centipede admired the serpent with no feet at all. The serpent admired the wind that had no shapes. The wind admired the eyes that could perceive all existence. The eyes admired the inner heart.

One day, Kui said to the centipede, "You see, with this one leg I hop about. Nobody feels more convenient than I do. Now you get around with a myriad of feet. What is the point of that?" The centipede replied, "You are wrong here. It is not that I like to walk on a myriad of feet. I was simply born with them and naturally I walk on them. Have you not seen one spitting? The large drops of saliva spitted out can be big as pearls, while the small drops can be as tiny as mist grains. Large drops are big naturally, and small drops are tiny naturally. They mingle and fall down, countless and beyond the control of the humans. Now I employ my naturally born functions to move, not knowing why if being thus asked. Neither do I know how I am able to do it."

The centipede found it strange that the serpent could move swiftly and often disappeared without making any sounds, even though it didn't have any feet. The centipede said to the serpent, "Though I have a myriad of feet, I can't move as quickly as you. Why is that?" The serpent said, "How can the method of relying on naturally born functions to move be changed? Why would I use feet when I move?"

The wind made a big noise when it blew over the land, and in no time, it traveled from north to south. Seeing this, the serpent was most amazed and said to the wind, "I get about by moving my backbones and my ribs, thus appearing almost like moving on feet. But now you rise with a big howling sound from the North Sea and move on to the South Sea, without leaving any traces of moving on feet. Why is it like this?" The wind said, "Yes. I come howling from the North Sea to the South Sea, and the power is far greater than any of you could possibly possess. But what you don't know is that I can't break people's fingers when they try to stop me with their hands and I can't break their legs when they try to kick and tread on me. Yet it is only I who can break great trees, blow down big houses, and cause huge waves as high as ten *zhang*. Let go of the small things, and it becomes possible to achieve big victories. But it is only the sage who can truly accomplish this."

Though the wind openly admits that it also has its inadequacies, there are still some limitations to what it said. In fact, although the monster Kui, the centipede, the serpent and the wind are different from one another and their abilities are varied, they can all move swiftly, and reach their targets by means of their own efforts. As the saying goes, "All roads lead to Rome." There is absolutely no need for one to give up one's dreams just because one sees himself to be a small potato. Never resort to inaction because of meager strength, and never write off self value for humble position. We may agree with the Russian short-story writer Anton Chekhov that big dogs and small dogs can bark together.

21. 庄子拒绝相位

庄子不喜欢做官，认为高位、权力、名利会扭曲人的本性。庄子有一个习惯，经常在濮水边钓鱼。楚威王早就听说庄子满腹经纶，学问很大，就派遣两位大臣带着几个随从去请他，后来在河边的大树下找到了他。大臣上前向庄子致意，庄子觉得很奇怪，问他们从哪里来，来干什么。大臣回答说："在下从楚国京城赶来。楚王素闻先生的大名，愿将国内政事委托给你，请先生屈就相位。"庄子坐在草地上，手把住钓鱼竿一动也不动。大臣觉得有点尴尬，硬着头皮再说了一遍。这时庄子头也不回，慢吞吞地说："我听说楚国有一只神龟，它已经死了三千年了，楚王用精致的竹器装着它，用漂亮的饰巾覆盖着它，珍藏在宗庙里。你们说，这只神龟，是宁愿死去留下遗骨而显示尊贵呢，还是宁愿活着在泥水里拖着尾巴爬行呢？"两位大臣说："当然愿意拖着尾巴活在泥水里。"庄子说："这就是了，你们走吧！多谢大王的美意，我还是愿意拖着尾巴自由自在地生活在泥水里。"

尽管庄子不屑于做官，但并不是每个人都这么想的，比如他的好朋友惠施。

惠施在梁国做宰相，他的老朋友庄子前去看望他。有人对惠施说："庄子所以来梁国，是想取代你做宰相。"听人这么一说，惠施恐慌起来，连忙派兵在都城内搜寻庄子，整整找了三天三夜。庄子知道后不禁暗自好笑，就闯进宫里去见惠施，他对惠施说："南方有一种像凤凰一样的鸟，它的名字叫鹓雏，你知道吗？鹓雏从遥远的南海出发飞到北海，不是梧桐树它不会停息，不是洁白的竹实它不会进食，不是甘美的泉水它不饮用。一只猫头鹰寻觅到一只腐烂了的老鼠，这时鹓雏刚巧从空中飞过，猫头鹰抬头看着鹓雏，怒吼一声：'嚇！走开，看你敢抢我的死老鼠。'如今你也想用你的梁国来吓唬我吗？"

上帝要让谁灭亡，必先使他疯狂。在庄子看来，能使人疯狂的就是权位、金钱、名声等被称为外物的东西。权位常常置人于死地，金钱常常扰乱人性，名声常常扭曲人格，所以他鄙视惠施的这一作为，说他是捧住死老鼠不肯放手的猫头鹰；他不愿意做没有灵魂、仅存一堆死骨头的神龟，因为人的自由是最珍贵的。他所追求的"曳尾于涂中"的生活态度，不能说是苟且偷生，而是对权贵的藐视，是精神独立的方式。

ZHUANGZI DECLINES THE OFFER OF BEING THE PRIME MINISTER

Zhuangzi disliked entering the government service. According to him, high positions, power, fame and wealth would only distort human nature. Zhuangzi had a habit of going fishing by the Pushui River. King Wei of Chu had long heard that Zhuangzi was a great scholar with profound learning and exceptional talent. So he sent two ministers and several attendants to invite Zhuangzi to government services and later found him under a big tree by the river. Seeing the ministers coming up to him with greetings, Zhuangzi was surprised and asked them where they came from and what their business was. One minister answered, "I came from the capital of the State of Chu. Our King has long heard of you, Master, and wishes to entrust the care of the state affairs to you. Would you please accept the position of the prime minister?" Sitting on the grass and with his hand holding the fishing pole, Zhuangzi remained motionless. The minister felt a bit embarrassed and had to repeat his words once again. Then Zhuangzi, without turning his head, said slowly, "I have heard there is a sacred tortoise in the State of Chu which died over three thousand years ago. The King of Chu keeps it in an exquisite bamboo basket wrapped with fine cloth for decoration and enshrines it in the ancestral temple. Now according to you, would the tortoise rather be dead and leave its bones behind to be honored or would it rather stay alive dragging its tail in the mud?" The two ministers said, "Of course it would rather stay alive dragging its tail in the mud." Zhuangzi said, "That's it. Go away! Please say thanks to the king for his kindness. I would rather be alive dragging my tail freely in the mud."

Zhuangzi disdained to serve in court. But not everyone was like him, for example, his good friend Hui Shi.

Hui Shi held the position of the prime minister in the State of Liang. Once Zhuangzi went to visit him. Somebody said to Hui Shi, "The reason of Zhuangzi's visit to the State of Liang is that he wants to replace you as the prime minister." Hui Shi became worried and sent troops out to search for Zhuangzi in the capital. The search went on for three days and three nights. On hearing this, Zhuangzi laughed to himself and barged into the palace uninvited. He said to Hui Shi, "There's a phoenix-like bird called Yuan Chu in the south. Do you know it? Setting out from the distant South Sea, it flies to the North Sea, not resting but on phoenix trees, not eating but white bamboo, and not drinking but sweet springwater. Once an owl picked up a dead rat when Yuan Chu flew overhead. The owl raised its head and shouted angrily at Yuan Chu, 'Ha! Go away! Don't you dare to take my dead rat.' Now do you wish to frighten me off with your State of Liang?"

If God wishes to destroy somebody, God drives him crazy first. For Zhuangzi, what drive people crazy are the so-called "external things" such as power, high position, money and fame. Power and high position may bring an untimely demise, money may disturb human nature, and fame may distort personality. Therefore, Zhuangzi despised Hui Shi's behavior, comparing Hui Shi to the owl which would not let go of a dead rat. Zhuangzi would not be like a sacred tortoise which was soulless and remained only as a pile of dead bones, because for human beings, the most precious was freedom. What he sought as a lifestyle was to be "dragging tails in the mud", which could not be regarded the same as dragging out an ignoble existence. Instead, such a life attitude implies a disregard of power and high social status, which is the key to achieving spiritual independence.

22. 鼻尖上削泥

　　有一天,庄子的一个朋友死了,他去送葬。半道上看见一座大坟冢,坟前高高地耸起一块墓碑,上面刻着这样几个大字:梁故相惠施之墓。坟上草木茂盛,旁边的小白杨也快有胳膊那么粗了。看到这个墓,庄子回想起昔日与惠施的友情与交往,不禁感慨万分。在一片悲伤的气氛中,庄子对跟随的人讲了一个故事。

　　"相传楚国的都城有个泥匠,手艺高超,干活的时候,常常穿着高领大袖的衣服,随心所欲地仰面涂墙,一天下来,衣服居然会不沾一点泥灰。有一天,泥匠在涂墙。他干得正起劲,忽然觉得鼻端上一阵奇痒,无意中用拿石灰刷子的手抠了一下。后来到了收工的时候,主人惊奇地看着他,他这才知道自己的鼻子上沾上了象蚊蝇翅膀那样大小的石灰。泥匠好为难,正踌躇着,突然灵机一动,叫来了一个颇有名气的石匠,请石匠帮着解决问题。石匠上前仔细看了看,然后后退两步,闭着眼睛,垂着双手,深深地吸了一口气,胸有成竹地抡起石斧,一斧劈去,只见泥匠鼻上的一点石灰被削得干干净净,未留下一丝灰痕。而泥匠则面不改色,若无其事。这时四周看热闹的人已围了一大群,大家瞧得毛骨悚然,伸出舌头连连称奇。后来,这个消息很快就四下传开了,一直传到宋国的宫廷里。宋元王听到后十分惊讶,很想见识一下,于是派了一个使者把石匠召进宫来,一见面就要石匠在自己身上试试,用斧子削去鼻子上的泥。石匠一听连连摇手说:'不行不行,我确实曾经砍削掉人鼻尖上的小白点。但那都是过去的事了,如今与我搭配的伙伴泥匠已经去世很久了,我再也做不成这样的事了。'宋元王有点奇怪,问:'难道就没有人可以替代?'石匠摇摇头说:'很难找到像泥匠那样的朋友,一般的人胆气不壮,看到斧子迎面劈来,他能硬着头皮一动也不动吗?如果他心里稍一慌张,那鼻子就可能保不住了。'"

说到这里,庄子恭恭敬敬地向惠施墓鞠了三个躬,深情地说:"惠兄啊,自从你死后,我再也找不到能够一起讨论、争辩的对手了,我心里的话能够向谁去诉说呢?你怎么走得那么早,害得我有口难开,以后我只能做哑巴了。"

人的一生,要有几个知己朋友,那会增添许多快乐;人的思想,要多几个对手,那将有助于智慧的开发。

CHOPPING PLASTER OFF NOSE TIP

One day, a friend of Zhuangzi died, so he went to the funeral. On his way there, he passed a grand grave with a tall tombstone, on which several words were carved, "The tomb of the late prime minister of Liang — Hui Shi". The grave was covered with a lush growth of trees and grass and the young white poplars nearby were now as thick as arms. Seeing all these and recalling his friendship and his witty arguments with Hui Shi before, Zhuangzi couldn't help but sigh with deep emotion. In a sad mood, he turned to his attendants and told them a story.

"It is said that there was a plasterer in the capital of the State of Chu who enjoyed masterly skills. When at work, he wore clothes with a high neck and loose sleeves. He always carried out his work of plastering walls in a way that he felt like and his clothes would actually remain clean without a speck of plaster on it after a day of work. One day, the plasterer was painting walls energetically when he felt a terrible itch on the tip of his nose and unconsciously scratched it with the hand that held a plaster brush. When it was time to call it a day, he found that the owner of the house was looking at him with an amused look. He asked why and found out that there was a speck of plaster no bigger than a fly's wing sitting on his nose tip. The plasterer felt awkward and when he was hesitating over what to do, an idea hit him. He immediately sent for a well-known stonemason, asking him to solve the problem. The stonemason soon came. He took a good look at the plasterer's face and retreated two steps. With eyes closed, hands hanging by the body, he took a deep breath as if everything was under control, and swung his ax with one go. The speck of plaster was seen to be chopped off clean without leaving any trace. The plasterer remained calm, not turning a hair and not losing his composure. At that time, a crowd of onlookers had gathered in a circle around them, all terror-stricken and with their tongues sticking out: they were marveling about what had happened. The story went out quickly and soon it spread to the royal palace of the State of Song, where King Yuan of Song heard it and was intrigued by the fantastic feat. He wanted to see it for himself, so he sent an envoy to summon the stonemason into the palace. On seeing the stonemason, the king immediately asked the stonemason to have a try on him, helping to chop off a speck of mud on his nose tip. On hearing the king's request, the stonemason waved his hands and said, 'No, no. Once I chopped a small white speck off the plasterer's nose tip indeed. But that was all in the past. My partner, the plasterer has been dead for quite a long time. Now I don't think I am able to do it again.' King Yuan of Song felt a little curious and asked,

'Isn't there anyone to replace the plasterer?' The stonemason shook his head, 'A friend like the plasterer is very hard to find. Ordinary people lack the kind of courage. When seeing the ax coming, is he able to brace himself and remain still? If he gets just a little nervous, it may be difficult to save his nose.'"

Having finished his story, Zhuangzi bowed three times to the tomb of Hui Shi and said with affection, "My brother, after you passed away, I no longer have anyone with whom I can discuss and debate. To whom can I open my heart? Why did you go so early? Now I find it hard to speak out my mind. It seems that I can only keep everything to myself and be like a dumb person from now on."

One needs to have several bosom friends throughout one's life. Friendship will bring about endless joy to one's life. For the intellectual development of one's mind, one needs partners with whom one can match. Friendship will be helpful to the development of wisdom.

23. 废井里的青蛙

　　公孙龙是先秦名家的著名人物,有一次他去请教魏国的公子牟,说:"我小时候学习古代圣王的主张,长大后做符合仁义的事;我能够把事物的不同与相同合而为一,分辨物体的质地与颜色;能够把不对的说成是对的,把不应认可的看作是合宜的;使百家智士困惑不解,众多辩士理屈词穷——我自以为是最为通达的了。但如今我听了庄子的言谈,感到十分茫然。不知是我的论辩比不上他呢,还是我的知识不如他呢?现在我已经没有办法再开口了,你能告诉我其中的道理吗?"

　　公子牟深深地叹了口气,然后仰起头笑了,讲了一个故事:"有一口废井里住着一只青蛙。有一天,青蛙在井边碰上了一只从海里来的大龟,就对海龟夸口说:'你看,我住在这里多快乐!有时高兴了,就在井栏边跳跃一阵;疲倦了,就回到井里,睡在砖洞边休息;或者只留出头和嘴巴,安安静静地把全身泡在水里;或者在软绵绵的泥浆里散一回步,也很舒适。看看那些虾和蝌蚪，谁也比不上我。而且，我是这个井里的主人，在这井里极自由自在，你为什么不常到井里来游赏呢！'那海龟听了青蛙的话，就想进去看看。但它的左脚还没有整个伸进去，右脚就已经被绊住了。它连忙后退了两步，把大海的情形告诉青蛙：'你看过海吗？海的广大，哪止千里；海的深度，哪止千丈。古时候，夏禹时代，十年有九年大水，可海里的水并没涨了多少；商汤时代，八年里有七年大旱，可海里的水也不见得浅了多少。可见大海是不受旱涝影响的。住在那样的大海里，才是真的快乐呢！'青蛙听了海龟的这番话，吃惊地呆在那里，顿时无话可说。"说到这里，公子牟话题一转，说："你公孙龙的才智还不足以知晓是非，却想去察悉庄子的言谈；你的智慧不足以通晓极其玄妙的言论，却满足于那些一时的胜利。庄子的学识、境界不是你能达到的。你这是用竹管去窥视高远的苍天，用锥子去测量浑厚的大地，就像是废井里的青蛙，实在太渺小了！你还是走吧！否则你将一事无成。"公孙龙听了这一番话，目瞪口呆，赶紧就走开了。

从这个故事就引出了成语"井底之蛙"，井蛙没见过大海却认为井外无天，结果这口小井连海龟的一只腿都放不进。看起来，人不管学问有多高，都不能把自己有限的学问当成是无限的。

A FROG IN A DISUSED WELL

Gongsun Long was a famous figure among the Pre-Qin philosophers. Once he inquired of Prince Mou of the State of Wei, "When I was young, I learned the teachings of the legendary emperors of ancient times. I tried to engage in the proper conduct of benevolence and righteousness when becoming a grown-up. I can bring together similarities and differences, distinguish between different qualities and colors, affirm what others deny, and justify what others dispute. I can make all the scholars baffled and render them speechless. I consider myself to have already reached the state of perfect understanding of every subject. But now that I have heard the words of Zhuangzi, I feel bewildered and lost. I don't know whether it is in arguing or in mastering knowledge that I am no equal to him. Now I can no longer open my mouth and express myself. Would you tell me why it is so?"

Prince Mou sighed deeply, and then raised his head and laughed. He told Gongsun Long a story, "There was a frog living down in a disused well. One day at the edge of the well it met a big turtle from the sea and it bragged to the turtle, 'You see, what a great time I am having here! I jump up and down around the rail of the well when I feel happy; I return to the well and have a rest beside the brick hole when I feel tired. Sometimes I soak my body quietly in the water, leaving only my head and mouth above water; sometimes I take a walk in the soft mud, which feels very comfortable. Take a look around me, not one of the crabs or tadpoles here can be my match in enjoyment. Besides, as the one who owns this well, I am as happy as anyone can be. Why don't you come more often to the well and have fun?' Hearing what the frog said, the turtle wanted to go in to see for itself. But it had just put in its left foot when its right foot was stuck fast. It hurried backward for a few steps and told the frog about the sea, 'Have you seen the sea? A thousand *li* is not sufficient to describe its width, nor is a thousand *zhang* sufficient to describe its depth. In the old days of the Yu of the Xia Dynasty, there were nine years of flood out of ten, but it didn't make the sea water to increase visibly; in the days of Tang of the Shang Dynasty, there were seven years of draught out of eight, but it didn't make the sea water to decrease visibly. It's indeed a great joy to live in the sea that is not affected by either flood or drought.' The frog was taken aback in astonishment at the words of the turtle. It didn't know what to say." At this, Prince Mou changed his topic and said, "You don't have the knowledge to understand right and wrong, and yet you attempt to contemplate the words of Zhuangzi; you don't have the wisdom to appreciate mysterious and sophisticated teachings, yet you become satisfied with victories of the current time. The learning, the wisdom and the spiritual level of Zhuangzi are beyond your reach. What you do is like trying to peer at the distant sky through a bamboo tube or to measure the entire earth with an awl. It is just like the frog in the shallow well. What smallness! You might as well take off; otherwise, you will accomplish nothing." Gongsun Long gaped at what he had heard, not able to close his mouth. He slunk away and ran off.

"A frog in a well — a person with a very limited outlook" — this idiom originates from the above story. Having never seen the sea, the frog in the well believes that the well is the entire world, yet the well is actually so small that it's even impossible for a turtle to put in one foot. It follows that one must not take one's limited amount of knowledge as infinite, no matter how learned one can be.

24. 孔子弹琴

　　孔子率弟子周游列国,途经陈、蔡两国交界时被大军包围了,七天中他们没有吃到熟的食品,没有尝过一粒米,完全靠野菜充饥。尽管孔子脸色显得很疲惫,可他却整天呆在屋里不停地弹琴唱歌。有一次,颜回在室外捡菜,子路和子贡在他身边聊起来了:"先生两次被赶出鲁国,在卫国被称为不受欢迎的人,被迫隐匿行踪,在宋国受到羞辱,连上课处那棵用来乘凉的大树也被砍掉了,弄得走投无路,如今又被困陷在陈、蔡之间。那些图谋杀害先生的没有任何罪名,凌辱先生的没有受到处罚,可是先生还不停地弹琴吟唱,不曾中断过乐声,难道君子不懂得羞辱竟能达到这样的地步吗?"

　　颜回听到后也不知怎么回答才好,就进入屋内把他们的谈话一五一十地告诉了孔子。孔子推开琴,长长地叹了一口气说:"子路和子贡真是见识浅薄。叫他们进来,我有话对他们说。"子路和子贡进到屋里,子路说："像现在这样的处境真可以说是太穷困了！"孔子说："话怎么能这样说！君子通达于道叫做一以贯通，不能通达于道叫做穷困。如今我信守仁义之道而遭逢乱世带来的祸患，怎么能算是穷困呢！所以说，善于反省就不会不通达于道，面临危难就不会丧失德行，严寒到来，霜雪降临，才使我真正看到那繁茂不凋的松柏是多么有朝气。所以，这陈、蔡之间的困厄，对于我来说恐怕不是一件坏事！"孔子说完，拿过琴来又弹唱起来。歌声感染着子路，随着阵阵琴声，他也兴致勃勃地拿着盾牌跳起舞来。一旁的子贡感到惭愧，自言自语地说："我真不知道天是那么的高，地是那么的低！怪不得古时候那得道的人，无论是在穷困的环境里还是在通达的情况下，他都十分快乐。看起来，心境快乐的原因不在于境遇的穷困与通达，只要'道'存留心中，那么穷困与通达都像是寒与暑、风与雨那样有规律地变化，根本不能牵制人的心灵。"

　　人生的道路不会那么平坦。当人身处逆境，遇到困难、曲折、危险、痛苦，怎样才能拥有快乐向上的心态，怎样才能坦然处之，这恐怕是每个人都会遇到的问题。庄子的说法是"胸有大道"，有了大道，就不会在意这些困扰，就会把这些困扰看作转眼即逝的小事，看作实现人生发展大道的必经之路，当然我们现在要赋予大道以新的内容。

CONFUCIUS PLAYS MUSIC IN DISTRESS

　　When Confucius was on a tour of visiting various states with his disciples, he was besieged by troops between the State of Chen and the State of Cai. For seven days, they had no food cooked by fire; neither did they have a grain of rice. When they were hungry, all they had was wild vegetables. Though his countenance wore signs of fatigue, Confucius kept playing his lute and singing songs in the house. Once when Yan Hui was picking vegetables outside, Zi Lu and Zi Gong had a conversation right beside him, "The Master has been driven out of the State of Lu twice; he was hiding in the State of Wei for he was pronounced as unwelcome; he was humiliated in the State of Song and driven to a state of despair, until even the tree under which he had sought shade and taught disciples was cut down. And now he was trapped between Chen and Cai. However, those who intended to kill him are free from accusations, and those who humiliated him are not punished. Even so the Master still keeps playing and singing, as not once is the music stopped. Can a virtuous person tolerate shame to such an extent as this?"

After hearing these, Yan Hui didn't know how to answer, and so he went into the house and recounted everything to Confucius. Pushing aside the lute, Confucius took a long breath and said, "What narrow views Zi Lu and Zi Gong are entertaining! Call them in, and I will have something to say to them." Zi Lu and Zi Gong entered the house and Zi Lu said, "The present condition may be called one of extreme distress!" Confucius said, "What words are these! When a virtuous man has a free course toward his principles, we call it success; but when the free course is denied to him, we call it a state of distress. Now I stand by my principles of benevolence and righteousness, but meet the disasters of a troubled age. How can it be regarded as a state of distress? Therefore, a willing exercise of self-examination will make it difficult for one to lose one's course towards principles; with one's course towards principles, one will not lose virtues when encountering difficulties. It is when the cold winter comes and frost and snow fall down that I truly realize the vitality of the lush and evergreen pines and cypresses. Therefore, the trouble we meet between Chen and Cai is not something bad, I am afraid." After this, Confucius picked up his lute and began to play and sing again. Zi Lu, touched by the music, seized a shield and began to dance to the tempo in high spirits. Zi Gong felt ashamed and said to himself, "I didn't know before that the heaven was so high and the earth was so low. No wonder those who got the Tao in ancient times were so happy both when they were reduced to a state of distress and when they had free course towards their principles. It seems that their happiness was independent of the state of distress or free course. As long as they have Tao at their heart, distress and free course are just like the regular changes of winter and summer, or of wind and rain, which are not able to affect their minds."

A man's life is not always a smooth path. When a man is in an unfavorable situation, encountering difficulties, setbacks, dangers or pains, how is he to keep a happy and positive attitude, or to keep calm? This is a problem that everyone might come across. According to Zhuangzi, a man should have the Great Tao at his heart, so he will not be bothered by these hardships and will regard them as some trivia soon gone, as some ordeals in a necessary path towards the development of the Great Tao of his life. Of course we need to add new meanings to the Great Tao nowadays.

25. 人籁、地籁与天籁

　　住在城南的子綦靠着茶几席地而坐，仰首向天不时地叹着气，那无精打采的样子真好像精神脱出了躯体。他的学生颜成子游站在跟前问道："老师，您这是怎么啦？形体诚然可以使它像干枯的树木，精神和思想难道也可以变成死灰那样吗？您今天凭几而坐的样子，跟往昔凭几而坐的情景大不一样呢。"子綦回答说："好啊，你这个问题问得很好。今天我忘掉了自己，你知道这是为什么吗？如果你不明白，说明你只知道'人籁'却不知道'地籁'，即使你知道'地籁'，也一定不知道'天籁'啊！"子游说："请老师告诉我它们的真实含意。"子綦说："大地吐出的气，名字叫风。风不发作则已，一旦发作起来，整个大地数不清的窍孔都怒吼起来。难道你没有听过那呼呼的风声吗？在山林峭壁上生长的百围大树上有无数的窍孔，窍孔千奇百怪，有的像鼻子，有的像嘴巴，有的像耳朵，有的像杯子，有的像脸盆，有的像舂米的臼窝，有的像泥坑，有的像浅池。它们发出的声音，有的像湍急的流水声，有的像迅疾的箭镞声，有的像洪亮的呵叱声，有的像细细的呼吸声，有的像放声叫喊，有的像嚎啕大哭，有的像在山谷里深沉回荡，有的像鸟儿鸣叫叽喳，真好像前面在唱，后面在和。如果是徐徐清风，和声就很细小；如果是阵阵狂风，和声就很高亢；如果迅猛的暴风突然停歇，万般窍穴也就寂然无声。你难道不曾看见万物随风摇晃摆动的样子吗？"

听到这里，子游说："我明白了，地籁是风吹万种窍穴时发出的声音，人籁是吹排列起来的各种不同的竹管时发出的声音。不过，我还有一个问题，究竟什么是天籁？"子綦说："风吹动着不同的孔窍，发出了不同的声音，为什么会这样？那是因为它们自然如此，是由它们自身形成的。那么，究竟谁能够使他们自然如此，发出不同的声音呢？那就是天籁。"

风作为物体只有一个，但却因穿越的孔窍不同，发出的声音也就各不相同。人因生存的环境不同，人生的经历不同，说出的话语也不同。一种舆论、一个传说、一则民谣都可以看作是一种人籁，都是特定历史环境的产物，是社会人际沟通的切入点。当然，切入点不是终点，但如果由此把握时代脉搏的跳动，那也可以说这是一种顺应大道的发展点。

MUSIC OF MAN, EARTH AND HEAVEN

Zi Qi who lived in south city sat on the ground, leaning forward on his tea table. He raised his head up towards the sky and every now and then he sighed gently, looking very listless as if in a trance. His disciple, Yancheng Ziyou who was keeping him company, stood in front of him and asked, "Master, what is it? Body can of course be made to be like a withered tree, but can the spirit and the mind also be made to be like dead ashes? The look you have today leaning forward on your tea table is very much different from the look you had in the same position before." Zi Qi replied, "Good, you did well to ask such a question. Today, I lost myself. Do you know why? If you don't understand, it shows that you have only heard of the Music of Man, not the Music of Earth; or even if you have heard of the Music of Earth, you are yet to hear the Music of Heaven." Ziyou asked, "Would Master please tell me the true meanings of these kinds of music?" Zi Qi said, "The gas emitted by the earth is called the wind. It remains calm when it doesn't rise up. But when it does, numerous cavities on the earth will bellow. Haven't you heard of the angry whistling of the wind? There are so many cavities on the great trees of a hundred spans growing on high mountains and steep cliffs, exhibiting all kinds of strange shapes and forms, like noses, mouths, ears, cups, washbasins, sockets used for husking rice, mud pits, and shallow pools. The sounds made by them are like those of rushing current, of whizzing arrows, of loud brawls, of light breaths, of big shouts, of deep wails, of echoes in valleys, and of chirps of birds. It is like someone taking the lead in singing and others following in chorus. With a gentle breeze, there is a confluence of minor sounds, and with a gust of violent wind, there is a confluence of resounding sounds. When the violent wind suddenly subsides, all the cavities turn silent and still. Haven't you seen the bending and waving of a myriad of things with the wind?"

At this, Ziyou said, "Now I understand. The Music of Earth is the sum of the sounds made by the wind blowing through numerous cavities. The Music of Man come from the various kinds of bamboo pipes lined up in an array. Still I have one more question. What on earth is the Music of Heaven?" Zi Qi answered, "When wind blows, different cavities make all kinds of sounds. Why is it like this? Because they are just like that, which is determined by their own nature. But what makes them to be naturally like that, making different sounds? It is the Music of Heaven."

As an object, the wind is just one item. But because it goes through different cavities, it is able to make different sounds. Owing to different living conditions and different life experiences, people may have different opinions and make different speeches. An opinion, a legend, or a ballad can all be seen as the Music of Man, as they are all the results of a particular historical background and the embodiments of the particular society. All these results and embodiments can hopefully help us understand the tendencies of the times and go along the path towards the Great Tao.

26. 窃贼士成绮

  有一个人名叫士成绮,听说老子的学问很大,就去拜见老子,一见面就说:"我听说先生是个圣人,我便不辞路途遥远而来,一心希望能见到你,走了上百天,脚掌上结了厚厚的老茧也不敢停下来休息一会。如今我观察先生,竟不像是个圣人,和大家说的不一样。从您家的老鼠洞里掏出的泥土中有许多剩余的食物,看来您一点都不注意爱惜粮食,与此同时您却抛弃自己的妹妹而不愿抚养,这不能算合乎仁的要求;您面前的生熟食品很多,吃都吃不完,聚敛财物却没有限度,不停不止。"老子的态度很淡然,好像没有听见似的不作搭理。士成绮自觉没趣,悻悻地走了。

  第二天士成绮再次来见老子,说:"昨日我用言语刺伤了您,今天我已有所省悟,而且改变了先前的看法,这是什么原因呢?"老子说:"世界上有一种人被称为巧智神圣,我自认为早已脱离了这种人的行列。过去你叫我牛我就承认是牛，叫我马我就承认是马。假如存在这样的事实，人们给他相应的称呼他却不愿接受，那他将会错上加错，罪上加罪，第二次受到惩罚。我顺应外物、服从别人总是自然而然，我并不是因为要顺应、要服从才有所顺应、有所服从的。"士成绮看到自己错了，感到十分羞愧，就像雁一样侧着身，蹑手蹑脚地走上前来问道："那么，我应该怎样修身呢？"老子说："你的容颜庄重严肃，你的目光直视前方，你的额头高高突起，你的话语凶猛无情，你的形体高大傲然，好像被拴住的奔马，身虽静止而心犹奔腾。你行为暂时有所牵制，一旦行动就如用机械发射那么迅速；你心思相当机警，观察事物十分精细，自恃智巧而外露骄傲之态，对一切都认为不可相信，疑心重重——凡此种种都不能看作是人的真实本性。边境那里就有这样的人，他们的名字叫窃贼。"

窃是偷的意思，偷与窃两字常常连用，主要意思是偷偷地把别人的东西占为己有。在庄子看来，窃的对象不仅是一般人所理解的某一种物质，还包括精神的、理念的东西。中国有一个成语叫附庸风雅，它是一个贬义词，专指那些不懂装懂、没有内在质量，却通过对外在行为的简单模仿，使大家以为他是在社会所推崇的某一方面颇有造诣的人，士成绮就是一例。他的本性与大道南辕北辙，却拉大道为大旗，追逐时尚，这是窃贼的伎俩。

SHI CHENGQI THE THIEF

A man named Shi Chengqi went to visit Laozi because he knew that Laozi was a man of great learning. As soon as he saw Laozi, he said, "I've heard, Master, that you are a sage. So I come here, setting my heart on seeing you, not complaining about the long hard journey. I have traveled on foot for hundreds of days, not daring to stop and have a rest even though I've developed blisters on my feet. Now

I have had a chance to observe you, and I find that you are not a sage, not like what people have said. There is much leftover food in the mud from the rat hole of your house, which shows that you do not treasure food. You abandon your sister because you are not willing to provide for her, which is not in accordance with the principle of benevolence. All sorts of food, raw or cooked, are placed in front of you, but obviously you cannot consume them all. You keep hoarding without an end." Laozi looked very indifferent and didn't say anything, as if he didn't hear. Shi Chengqi felt snubbed and went away in a sulk.

   The next day, Shi Chengqi returned to see Laozi again and said, "Yesterday I assaulted you with my words, but now I have come to my senses and no longer bear a grudge against you. What is the reason for the change?" Laozi replied, "There are some people in the world who are considered to be clever, knowledgeable, and sagely. But I consider myself not one of them anymore. In the past, if you had called me an ox, then I would have admitted being an ox; if you had called me a horse, then I would have admitted being a horse. If there is truth to the name by which people call him, and he refuses to accept it, then he is making another mistake and is doubly guilty. He is to suffer from punishment a second time. I submit to the external world and obey others because of my nature. I don't submit and obey for the sake of submitting and obeying." Realizing that he had been wrong, Shi Chengqi was very ashamed. He walked up quietly to Laozi, sidling like a wild goose, and asked, "Then how should I cultivate myself?" Laozi said, "You have serious-looking features, a straight and clear gaze, a protruding forehead, and a wicked tongue. You're tall and proud, like a wild horse held by its tether, with its body being restrained but its heart still galloping. Your movement is temporarily deterred but if let go, you will start off as fast as if being launched by machines. When you have an idea, you instantly turn alert and keep a very careful watch for everything around. Believing in your own cleverness and knowledge and therefore appearing to be rather arrogant, you've become distrustful of everything, with a heart heavy with worries. All these are considered not to be the real nature of man.

There are such people over there on the border, who are usually called thieves."

Stealing is the action of taking something without permission, or the secret seizure of other's possessions. According to Zhuangzi, the target of stealing can not only be a certain material property like what people usually believe, but it can cover something spiritual and conceptual as well. There is a Chinese idiom "Mingle with men of knowledge and pose as a lover of culture". It is a derogatory expression, referring to those who though very shallow within pretend to be learned and fool others into believing them to be very accomplished in a certain field that is held in high esteem by the society, through simple imitation of some relevant outward behavior. Shi Chengqi was just one of them, who hoisted the banner of the Great Tao and claimed to be its follower in order to pretend that he was in pace with the trend, though his nature ran counter to the idea of the Great Tao. This is actually a trick played by thieves.

27. 鲁王养海鸟

　　知道自己的学生颜渊要去齐国,孔子显得十分忧虑。子贡看到后就离开坐席上前问道:"学生冒昧地请问,颜渊东去齐国,先生不太高兴,这是为什么呢?"

　　孔子说:"这个问题提得好极了!当年管仲说过这样一句话,我认为说得很好,'小布袋不可能包容大东西,水桶上的绳索太短就不可能汲取深井里的水。'照此说来,我们就应当明白,形体是禀受天命而形成的,他们形状不同,各有用处,全都是不可以随意增减改变的。我担忧颜渊不了解齐侯的性格、想法,却不知深浅地跟齐侯谈论尧、舜、黄帝治理国家的主张,还进一步地推重燧人氏、神农氏的言论。对此,齐侯必将转向自己的内心而苦苦思索,但最终是一无所得,不能理解,而不能理解必定就会产生疑惑,一旦产生疑惑便会迁怒于他人,就要置人于死地。你一定听到过这样的传说:从前,一只海鸟飞到鲁国都城郊外停歇下来,鲁国国君让人把海鸟接到太庙里供养献酒。为了使它高兴，就奏有名的古典乐章'九韶'，杀牛宰羊供它食用。原以为海鸟会感到快乐舒适，谁知它却眼花缭乱，忧心忡忡，不敢吃一块肉，不敢饮一杯酒，三天就死了。这是鲁王在按自己的生活习性、自己的兴趣爱好来养鸟，不是按鸟的习性来养鸟。如果按鸟的习性来养鸟，就应当让鸟栖息于深山老林，在水中沙洲游戏，在江河湖泽浮游，啄食泥鳅和小鱼，与自己的同类在一起，生活得从容逍遥、自由自在。它们最讨厌听到人的声音，却偏偏让它生活在人的环境中。九韶、咸池之类的著名乐曲，如果演奏于广漠的原野，鸟儿听见了腾身高飞，野兽听见了惊惶逃遁，鱼儿听见了潜下水底，一般的人听见了，相互围着观看不休。鱼儿在水里才能生存，人处在水里就会死去，人和鱼彼此间必定有不同之处，他们的好恶因而也一定不一样。所以远古的圣王不强求万物划一，不要求人们做相同的事，只求名副其实，对义的规定要适合人的性情，这就叫条理通达而福祉常在。"

把人的幸福观推广到海鸟，把人的爱好看成是海鸟的追求，虽然出发点很好，但结果是南辕北辙，人做得越多，想得越周全，对海鸟的伤害越大，因为人剥夺了海鸟的自由。看起来己所欲而施于人，并不见得是正确的、合乎道德的。人习惯于把自己的价值观强加于自然界，但结果却常常是招致自然界对人的报复。

THE KING OF LU KEEPS A SEABIRD

When Confucius knew that his disciple Yan Yuan was going to the State of Qi, he wore a very worried expression on his face. Zi Gong, having seen this, left his mat, went forward and asked, "Your humble disciple ventures an inquiry: Why does Master look unhappy about Yan Yuan going east to the State of Qi?"

Confucius said, "What a good question you've asked! In the old days Guan Zhong said something of which I very much approve. He said, 'Small bags won't hold big things, and a short rope on a bucket cannot be used to draw water from deep wells.' According to this, we should know that form and body are determined by destiny and different forms have their respective uses. You cannot change any form or body by adding something or taking away something. I am worried about Yan Yuan who, not knowing the character and the ideas of the Marquis of Qi, will tactlessly discuss with him about the ways of Yao, Shun, and the Yellow Emperor to run states, and go on to recommend the words of the even earlier Suirenshi and Shennongshi. The Marquis will then search hard within himself but will end up finding nothing and understanding nothing, which will in turn cause doubts. Once he has doubts, he will blame people around him and put people to death. You must have heard such a legend. Once upon a time, a seabird flew to the outskirts of the capital of the State of Lu and stopped for a rest. The King of Lu had it escorted to the ancestral temple where it was looked after and served wine. The famous classic music 'Nine Movements of Shao' was played to please it, and ox and sheep were killed to feed it. The king had expected the bird to feel happy and comfortable, but the bird looked dazed and laden with worries instead, not daring to eat a piece of meat or to drink a cup of wine. Three days later, it died. That was because the bird was kept in the way which the king believed to be preferable according to his own habits and interests, but not in the way most suitable for a wild bird. If birds are to be kept in their own way, they should be left to roost in the deep forest, play on banks and islands, float in rivers and lakes, peck loaches and small fish for food, follow its own flock, and live in an unhurried and carefree way which they prefer. They hate to hear the sounds made by men, but the unlucky seabird was forced to live in an environment which was full of men. Try performing the well-known classic music 'Nine Movements of Shao' and 'The Salt Lake' in the open wilds. On hearing them, birds will fly off, wild animals will run away in fright, and fish will dive to the bottom of the water. Only the humans who hear the music will gather around to listen. Fish live in water and thrive, but if men tried to live in water they would die. Men and fish must have differences, hence, their likes and dislikes differ. Therefore, the ancient legendary emperors never required uniformity among all creatures, nor did they make them do the same thing. The only thing they asked for was to make the name match the reality, which meant that the principles of righteousness should be in line with the temperament of man. That is what is called a good command of reasons leading to long lasting blessings."

It is with good intentions that men's ideas of happiness are extended to seabirds, while men's preferences are believed to be the pursuit of seabirds, too. However, the results are far from what's been expected. The more men do and think of, the bigger harm it will bring to the seabirds; for by doing so, men deny the seabirds their freedom. Therefore it does not seem to be always right and moral to do to others what you will do to yourself. Men are used to forcing their own values onto the natural world, but such folly only incurs the nature's brutal revenge upon men.

28. 大葫芦的用处

庄子与惠施是好朋友,经常在一起讨论问题。有一次,惠施对庄子说:"魏王赠给我一粒大葫芦的种子,我把它种上了,葫芦长成之后,里面的种子,足足有六百斤。用大葫芦去盛水浆吧,以它的坚固程度承受不了水的压力;把它剖开做瓢吧,也太大了,没有什么地方可以放得下。这个葫芦不是不大呀,我因为它没有什么用处而砸烂了它。"庄子听了很不以为然,对惠施说:"先生实在是不善于使用大东西啊!"接着就给他讲了一件事情。"宋国有一户善于调制不皲手药物的人家,世世代代以漂洗丝絮为职业。有个游客听说了这件事,愿意用百金的高价收买他们的药方。这家人聚在一起商量,大家认为,'我们世世代代像这样没日没夜地做,到现在所得不过数金,如今一下子就可卖得百金。把药方卖给他,值。'游客得到药方后,去游说吴王。正巧越国发难,吴王派他统率部队,跟越军在水上交战。那时正值冬天,由于使用了这个药,尽管三九严寒,但吴军战士的手足没有受到丝毫影响。结果越军大败,吴王赏了他一片土地。能使手不皲裂,药方是同样的,有的人用它来获得封赏,有的人却只能靠它在水中漂洗丝絮,这是使用的方法不同。如今你有足以容纳六百斤东西的大葫芦,怎么不考虑用它来制成腰舟,浮游于江湖之上,却偏偏担忧葫芦太大无处可容?看来先生你还是心窍不通啊!"

惠施不服,又对庄子说:"我有棵大树,树干疙里疙瘩,不能用绳墨取直,树枝弯弯扭扭,也不能用圆规和角尺取材。虽然生长在道路旁,木匠连看也不看。现今你的言谈,大而无用,大家都会鄙弃的。"庄子说:"先生你没看见过野猫和黄鼠狼吗?它们低着身子匍匐于地,等待那些出洞觅食或游乐的小动物。它们东窜西跳,一会儿高,一会儿低,却不曾想到落入猎人设下的机关,死于猎网之中。再有那牦牛,庞大的身体就像天边的云;它的本事可大了,不过不能捕捉老鼠。如今你有这么大一棵树,却担忧它没有什么用处,你怎么不把它栽种在什么也不长的不毛之地,栽种在无边无际的旷野里,你可以悠然自得地徘徊于树旁,悠闲自在地躺卧于树下。能说它没有用处吗?"

其实,万物存在都有它的价值,事物的大小多少都是相对而言的,大有大的好处,小有小的用处,万万不能走向极端,把某个片面情况当成世界的全部价值,把自己的认识当作不变的真理。

THE USES OF A BIG CALABASH

Zhuangzi and Hui Shi were good friends. They often had discussions together. One day, Hui Shi said to Zhuangzi, "The King of Wei gave me the seed of a large calabash, which I sowed. When the fruit was fully grown, it contained many seeds which weighed a full 600 *jin* (unit of weight). If I used it to hold water or other liquids, it was not strong enough to stand the pressure. If I cut it in two to make ladles, there was no place for them since they were so big. Certainly it was a huge thing, but I had no use for it and so I broke it into pieces." Zhuangzi looked disapproving of these words and said, "Sir, you are indeed not good at handling big things." Then he went on to tell a story, "There was a family in the State of Song who had the skill of making a salve that could keep hands from getting chapped, as the family business had been the washing and bleaching of silk for generations. A visitor heard of this and would like to offer a hundred taels of gold for the formula of the wonderful salve. The family gathered and discussed the offer, 'We have been washing and bleaching silk day and night like this for generations and all we have earned is no more than just a few taels of gold. Now all at once we can sell the formula for one hundred taels of gold. So let's sell it. It's a good bargain.' The visitor, having had the formula, went to give counsel to the King of Wu. It so happened that the State of Yue launched an attack against the State of Wu, so the King of Wu sent him, with the army of Wu under his command, to fight against the army of Yue on water. It was deep winter with a very low temperature, but none of the Wu soldiers had suffered from chapped hands or feet because they all used the salve. As a result, the army of Yue was badly defeated and the King of Wu rewarded that man by giving him a piece of land. It is the same formula of the salve for chapped hands, but when used by some people, it brings the king's rewards, and when used by other people, it just allows them to wash and bleach silk in water to make a living. The difference is due to how the formula is used. Now you are in possession of a calabash which is big enough to hold 600 *jin* of load, why don't you consider making gourd-like boats out of it, which can carry you over rivers and lakes? Instead you worry about it being too big to be put anywhere. It seems that your mind has been closed against all intelligence."

Still unconvinced, Hui Shi said to Zhuangzi again, "I have a big tree. Its trunk is full of knotty lumps and can't be measured with lines and ink, and its branches are twisted and crooked, so disks and squares can't be applied on them. Though it stands right on the roadside, no carpenter would cast it a glance. Now your words are great but useless, not unlike the big tree that everybody ignores." Zhuangzi replied, "Sir, haven't you seen wild cats and weasels? With their bodies crouching low onto the ground, they wait for small animals to go out of their holes for food or for fun. They jump west and east, high and low, never thinking for a moment that they will get caught in traps set by hunters and die in hunting nets. There is the yak with its body as big as a piece of cloud hanging in the sky. It enjoys great abilities, but it can't catch mice. Now you have a big tree but you are troubled that it is useless. Why don't you plant it in a place where nothing else grows, or in the vast and barren wild? There you might saunter beside it, without a care in the world, or lie under it and have a good sleep comfortably. Can you say that the tree is useless?"

Every existence has its value. The size and number of objects are relative. Bigness enjoys its advantages, while smallness has its uses too. Never go to the extreme, mistaking a part as the whole, or one's own knowledge as the facts of the world.

29. 长寿的诀窍

有一个名叫石的木匠去齐国,来到曲辕这个地方,看见一棵被世人当作神社的栎树。这棵栎树其大无比,树荫几乎可以遮蔽数千头牛,用绳子绕着量一量树干,足有近百尺粗,树梢高临山巅,离地面十来丈处才有树枝,大得可用来造船的就有十几根。观赏的人群像赶集似地涌来涌去,而这位匠人根本不瞧一眼,大踏步地往前走。他的徒弟站在树旁看了个够,发现木匠走远了,连忙追上去,对木匠说:"自我拿起刀斧跟随先生,从不曾见过这样好的树木。可是先生却头也不回,不住脚地往前走,为什么呢?"木匠回答说:"算了,不要再说它了!这棵树什么用处也没有的。用它做船,船一定会沉没;用它做成棺材,棺材一定会很快朽烂;用它做器皿,器皿一定会很快毁坏;用它做屋门,屋门会流脂而变形;用它做柱子,柱子一定会被虫蛀。这是一棵不成材的树。它所以能有如此寿命,就因为它没有什么用处。"

晚上木匠回到家，闲聊一阵就睡觉了。后来做了一个梦，梦中见到社树对他说："你能拿什么东西跟我相提并论呢？你打算拿可用之木来跟我相比吗？那山楂树、梨树、橘树、柚子树都属于果树，果实成熟就会被打落在地，打落果子以后枝干也就会遭受摧残，大的枝干被折断，小的枝丫被拽下来。你知道这是为什么吗？其实它们就是因为能结出鲜美果实才苦了自己的一生，结果常常不能终享天年而半途夭折，这是它们自身招来了世俗的打击呀。各种事物莫不如此。后来我用了很久很久的时间，最后终于寻求到了一种长寿的方法，那就是要让自己变得没有什么用处，这才保全性命，这样无用也就成了我最大的用处。假如我果真是有用，还能够获得延年益寿这一最大的用处吗？况且你和我都是'物'，你怎么可以这样看待事物呢？看看你也不过是将近死亡的人，怎么会真正懂得没有用处的树木呢！"

木匠醒后，想起这一天发生的事情，不禁明白了一个道理：社树保护自己的道术与众不同，如果我们用常理来了解它，那就相去太远了；神人应该以无用为大用。

用、无用、小用、大用，都必须有一个参照物。公鸡在稻田里发现了小米与珍珠，它踢掉的是漂亮的珍珠，放在嘴里的是小米，尽管在人看来，珍珠比小米不知要珍贵多少。在庄子看来，在危机四伏的乱世中，人如果要以安全为第一的话，最好的办法是以无用实现大用。

THE KNACK FOR LONGEVITY

A carpenter named Shi was going to the State of Qi. On his way, he stopped at a place called Quyuan, where he saw an oak tree which was regarded as a sacred shrine by the people there. The oak tree was so huge that its shade could cover a herd of thousands of oxen. With a rope going around its trunk, its circumference measured up to nearly one hundred *chi* (unit of length). It rose high up above the top of the mountain, throwing out its branches dozens *zhang* (unit of length) above the ground, among which dozens could be used for building ships. People flocked to see it in crowds as if it was bazaar day. But the carpenter went on without casting a look at it. His apprentice stood beside the tree and had his fill of admiring only to find that his master had gone far away, so he ran forward. When he caught up with the carpenter, he said, "Ever since I picked up an axe and a knife and followed you as my Master, I have never seen such a good tree. But you go on your way without stopping and turning your head. Can you tell me why?" The carpenter replied, "Come on, don't talk about it any longer. This tree is utterly useless. Use it to make boats, and the boats will sink; use it to make coffins, and the coffins will rot soon; use it to make utensils, and the utensils will get damaged; use it to make doors, and the doors will become deformed with saps exuding; use it to make pillars, and the pillars will be worm-eaten. It is a good-for-nothing tree. It manages to live such a long life just because it is useless."

In the evening, the carpenter returned home and after chatting for a while with his family, he soon retired to bed. Then he dreamed of the sacred tree talking to him, "What would you have to compare with me? Would you plan to compare with me the trees which have many uses? Hawthorn trees, pear tree, orange trees, and grapefruit trees are all fruit trees. As soon as their fruits are ripe, they are knocked down onto the ground. After the fruits are gone, the branches' turn comes. The bigger ones are broken into parts, and the smaller ones are torn off. Do you know why? It is because of their ability to grow delicious fruits that they have such a hard life, quite often coming to a premature end without being able to live out their natural lifespans. It is their very nature that has made them suffer at the hands of the common world. And it is the same with everything. It is after spending a long time searching that I managed to find a way to live long, which is to turn myself into a useless tree, thus protecting my life. In this way, being useless becomes my biggest use. Do you think I would be able to enjoy this biggest use of longevity and would have stayed alive till today if I were a useful tree? Moreover, you and I are both 'things', so how could you treat other things like this? You are no more than a mortal who is close to his death, so how can you really understand a useless tree?"

When the carpenter woke up, he went over what had happened that day and understood the intrinsic idea. The practice of Tao used by the sacred tree for its self-protection is exceptional. If we tried to understand it with the help of our common sense, that would be far from the right way. The sacred regards uselessness as great usefulness.

The terms like use, no use, small use and big use are meaningful only when they are used together with their points of reference. Having found a grain and a pearl in the rice field, a rooster kicks away the beautiful pearl and puts the grain in its mouth, though in the eyes of men, a pearl is much more valuable than a grain. According to Zhuangzi, in troubled times when dangers are everywhere, the best way to keep safe is to realize big use through being useless.

30. 伯乐的罪恶

　　有一次,庄子与惠施在街上行走,看到一位牧童牵着一匹老马走了过来。马的颈项与脊背上被拉套和鞍子磨光了毛,长出一块厚厚的硬疤。为了防止丢失,马的屁股上还用烙铁刻了一些印记。马头上套着嚼子和各种各样的金属装饰品。为了不让马逃走,马的前足与后足之间还用结实的麻绳串起来。老马低垂着头,一步一颠地往前走着。牧童嫌马走得太慢了,不时回头在马身上抽几鞭子。

　　庄子走近那匹老马,他出神地注视着老马那忧伤的眼睛,然后回过头来对惠施与牧童说:"马的蹄子可以用来践踏霜雪,皮毛可以用来抵御风寒,饿了吃草,渴了吃水,性起时扬起蹄脚奋力跳跃,这就是马的天性。即使有高台正殿,对马来说没有什么用处。马就应该让它过符合马之真性的生活。谁知后来出了一个伯乐,却改变了这一切。虽然在世人眼里他擅长相马,也擅长驯马,但他用烧红的铁器灼炙马毛,用剪刀修剔马鬃，凿削马蹄甲，烙制马印记，用络头和绊绳把它们拴起来，用马槽和马床把它们围起来，这样一来马便死掉十分之二三了。不仅如此，马饿了不给吃，渴了不给喝，让它们快速驱驰，让它们急骤奔跑，让它们步伐整齐，让它们行动划一，前有马口横木和马络装饰的限制，后有皮鞭和竹条的威逼，这样一来马就死过半数了。所以，那家喻户晓的伯乐实际上是残害马的罪魁祸首。"

看到牧童还不甚明白的样子，庄子又继续说开了："本来马生活在陆地上，吃草饮水，高兴时颈交颈相互摩擦，生气时背对背相互踢撞，马的智慧就只是这样了，它能做的就是这些。等到后来把车轱辘加在它身上，把带有月牙形佩饰的辔头戴在它头上，这时马失去了它们的正常生活，知道自己受到束缚，就会侧目怒视，忍无可忍起来抗争。你们难道没见过，有的马会突然瞪起鼓鼓的眼睛，嘴里发出'嘶嘶'的叫声，曲颈弓背，四蹄乱蹬进行抗拒，或偷偷地咬断缰绳，挣脱头上的马辔，然后逃到深山野林。马的智巧竟能发展到与人对抗，温顺的马会变得像强盗一样，这完全是因为伯乐的罪过。"

伯乐常常受到世人的赞誉，所以有"世有伯乐，然后有千里马"之说。而庄子对伯乐的批评，可以看作是为百姓的一种呼吁，要为百姓提供一种符合人之本性的生活。庄子提出的"提倡仁义、大兴礼乐的圣人是天下大乱的根源，人为的另一面是虚伪做作、强用人意"的说法，是值得人们注意的。

BO LE'S FAULT

Once Zhuangzi and Hui Shi were strolling on the street when they saw a young rancher coming over, pulling an old horse. Because of the constant rubbing of the pulling packet and saddle, the horse was bare in its neck and back, where there were patches of thick and hard scars instead of hair. On its rear end, some marks had been burnt with searing iron to prevent it from being stolen. The horse had a snaffle and other various metal ornaments on its head. In order to keep it from wandering off, there was a thick coarse rope tying the front feet with the hind feet loosely. Hanging its head down, the old horse walked forward in a jerky way. The young rancher didn't like it to be so slow, so he turned and whipped the horse from time to time.

Walking up to the old horse, Zhuangzi gazed intently into its sad eyes. Then he turned his head and said to Hui Shi and the young rancher, "Horses have hoofs to tread on frost and snow, and they have hair to protect them from wind and cold. When they feel hungry, they eat grass; when they feel thirsty, they drink water; and when they feel happy, they fling up their legs and leap high. Such is the nature of horses. Grand towers and houses mean nothing to them. Horses are supposed to live a life which suits their true nature. Then there came a man called Bo Le who changed everything. In the eyes of the common people, he was skillful at picking good horses and training them. However, he burned horsehair with red hot iron, cut horse mane with scissors, trimmed the nails on the hoofs, burned identification marks onto the flesh, tied the horses with bridles and hobbling ropes, and confined them to stables and corrals. As a result, two or three out of every ten horses died. Moreover, horses were denied food and water when they were hungry and thirsty so that they might gallop fast and race rapidly, march in regular steps and move in unison, with the misery of the tasseled bridle on the head and the fear of the knotted whip at the back. Being treated like this, over half of the horses died. So the well-known Bo Le was actually the perpetrator who tortured and killed horses."

Seeing that the young rancher still didn't understand much, Zhuangzi went on, "From the very beginning, horses live on land, eat grass, drink water, intertwine necks and rub one another when pleased, turn back to back and kick one another when enraged. That's all there is to the intelligence of horses and that's all they are capable of doing. But later, when yokes are put on their bodies and bridles with moon-like frontlets are fixed on their heads, they can no longer live their normal lives. Knowing that now they are bound, they will cast vicious looks askance, and rise to struggle and fight out of impatience. Haven't you seen that sometimes some horses suddenly stare with their bulging eyes and make hissing sound? And with their neck bent and their back arched, they kick out their legs to fight or they bite into the rope until it breaks, so that they can get rid of the bridle on their heads and flee into the deep forests and remote mountains. The intelligence of horses can be developed to such a level that they can even fight against men and gentle horses can become as vicious as bandits – all because of the fault of Bo Le."

Bo Le has often been praised by people, thus comes the saying "We have Bo Le first, and one-thousand-*li* steeds second." However, the criticism made by Zhuangzi against Bo Le can be seen as an appeal made on behalf of the common people, who according to Zhuangzi should be provided with a life that suits the human nature. In Zhuangzi's story, the sagely men who advocated benevolence and righteousness and who held ceremonies and provided music were the very cause of disorder in the world. The other side of such deliberate behavior as these was pretentiousness and falseness and the manipulation of human will, which is something people should be wary of.

31. 材与不材

　　有一次,庄子和他的弟子一起出游,来到一座大山,看见山里的一棵大树躯干粗壮,枝叶茂盛,如同一把遮天的大雨伞。有行人经过,多半会停下来,或抬起头向上瞻仰,或用手抚摩着裹着树干的斑斑树皮。山里有一大群工匠正在齐心合力地伐木,他们干得很起劲,周围稍微大一点的树木都被砍倒了,七倒八歪地躺在地上。奇怪的是,他们对近旁的那棵大树却熟视无睹,不屑一顾。

　　庄子看到后觉得很奇怪,就问伐木的人,为什么要保留这棵大树。他们的回答是:"这棵树没有什么用处,它的木质不好,内壁不实,容易发霉受潮,做成的器具容易被虫蛀。它虽然看起来很大,但实在是大而无用,如果是有用之材,这样一棵树早被人砍掉了,哪还会留到现在。"这时庄子恍然大悟,说:"原来这棵树就是因为不成材而能够终享天年啊!"庄子走出山来,来到朋友家中。老朋友相见,主人十分高兴,叫童仆杀鹅款待。童仆问主人:"棚子里有两只鹅,一只能叫,一只不能叫,不知杀哪一只呢?"主人说:"杀那只不能叫的。"第二天,庄子早早就赶路了,路上弟子问庄子:"昨日遇见山中的大树,因为不成材而能终享天年;如今主人的鹅,因为不成材而被杀掉。同样都是不成材,一生一死,结局却如此不同,这是什么道理?如果遇到这类事,先生你将怎样对待呢?"

庄子笑道:"我将处于成材与不成材之间。因为世上的东西不是绝对的,'材'不一定绝对是好,'不材'不是绝对的坏,处于成材与不成材之间,使人有一种适应世界的灵活性。不过,这不是最理想的,因为它好像合于大道却并非真正与大道相合,还不能免于拘束与劳累。假如能顺应自然,自由自在地游乐,那就好了。在这样的境遇中,人不在乎什么赞誉和诋毁,时而像龙一样腾飞,时而像蛇一样蛰伏,随时间的推移而变化,而不偏滞于某一方面;时而进取,时而退缩,一切以顺和作为度量,优游自得地生活在万物的初始状态,役使外物,却不被外物所役使。到那时,没有什么东西能够形成对我的拘束和劳累。这就是神农、黄帝的处世原则。而世界上的万事万物、人事变迁就不是这样了:有聚合就会有分离,有成功也就有毁败;棱角锐利就会受到挫折,有崇高就会有倾邪,有作为就会受到亏损,贤能就会受到谋算,而无能也会受到欺侮,人怎么可以一定要偏滞于某一方面呢!弟子们要记住,要想免除罪累,只有归向于自然。"

庄子对材与不材的这番议论,一方面曲折地再现了人处在乱世中的困境,为人在困境中如何有效地保护自身提供了思路,一方面则强烈地反映了人们追求更高境界自由的一种理想。

USE AND NO USE

One day Zhuangzi and his disciples went traveling. They came to a big mountain where they saw a great tree with huge branches and luxuriant foliage, looking like a gigantic umbrella blocking the sky. When people passed by, they usually stopped, either raising their heads to have a good look with reverence, or touching and rubbing with their hands the mottled barks of the tree. A large group of workmen were cutting woods together. They worked energetically and soon the trees nearby including those which looked just slightly bigger were all cut down, lying here and there in a disorderly way. But the strangest thing was that they turned a blind eye to the great tree close by.

Zhuangzi was curious at this and asked the woodcutters why they had left this great tree alone. Their reply was such, "The tree is of no use for anything. Its quality is not good, and its inside is not solid. It gets damp and moldy easily. Tools made out of it are likely to be worm-eaten. So though it looks big, it is useless indeed. If it had had any uses for anything, it would have been cut down long ago, instead of being left intact until now." Now Zhuangzi was suddenly enlightened and he said, "So this tree has been able to live out its natural lifespan just because it is good for nothing." Walking out of the mountain, Zhuangzi went to his friend's house. Pleased with Zhuangzi's visit, the friend ordered his boy servant to kill a goose and cook it as a treat for Zhuangzi. The boy servant asked his master, "There are two geese in the roost, one can cackle, and the other can't. I don't know which one to kill." The master said, "Kill the one that can't cackle." The next morning, Zhuangzi was off on his way early. One of his disciples asked him, "Yesterday the tree in the mountain was able to live out its natural lifespan because it was useless; now our host's goose was killed because it was useless. Both of them were useless, but one lived, and the other died. Why have there been such different endings? If you come across similar situations, Master, how will you deal with them?"

Zhuangzi smiled and said, "I'd stay somewhere between being of use and being of no use, since there is nothing definite in this world. Being of use isn't necessarily a good thing, while being of no use isn't necessarily a bad thing. Being somewhere between the two offers one a flexibility which is needed in adapting oneself to the world. But it is still not the best place to be, since though it seems to be in line with the Great Tao, actually it is not, therefore it can't free men from restraints and fatigues. It would be ideal if men could go with nature and find their ease and enjoyment in their play with nature. In this condition, without a care about praise or disapproval, men rise high like a dragon in one moment and crouches low like a snake in another, floating and changing along with the passage of time, not willing to be attached to any specific matter. They either move forward or backward, hovering at ease in the original state of everything, with harmony as their only yardstick, neither enslaving others nor being enslaved. By that time, nothing would have been able to restrain and fatigue men. This was way of Shennong and the Yellow Emperor. But such would not be the case with everything in the world and with the vicissitudes of life. For where there is union, there is separation; where there is success, there is failure; where there is progress, there is setback; where there is loftiness, there is evil; where there is achievement, there is loss. The able and virtuous will be plagued by devious schemes, and the weak and incompetent will succumb to bullies. Why should men remain unchanged in a particular aspect? Do remember, my disciples, that the freedom from faults and troubles can only be obtained through a retreat into the nature."

Zhuangzi's comment on being of use and being of no use, on one hand, reproduces in a roundabout way the difficult situation men find themselves in at troubled times and provides some ideas on how to seek effective self-protection in such conditions. On the other hand, Zhuangzi's comment suggests the ideal of pursuing the freedom of a much higher level.

32. 螳螂捕蝉,黄雀在后

有一年夏天,庄子独自一人出外游玩,途中经过了一个名叫雕陵的园子,里面长满了一棵棵茂盛的栗子树,浓荫蔽日,十分凉快。忽然有一只奇异的怪鹊从南方飞来,翅膀宽达七尺,眼睛大若一寸,它飞得很鲁莽,哗啦一下从庄子的脑门上撩过,停歇在果树林里。给这鹊突然一惊,庄子吓了一跳,心里很恼火,嘴里就自言自语地嘀咕起来:"这是什么鸟呀,翅膀大却不能远飞,眼睛大视力却不敏锐?真是有眼无珠。"于是提起衣裳快步上前,拿着弹弓,静静地守候着,一旦时机来临,就准备把它射下来。就在这当口,庄子眼睛突然一亮,一幅奇妙的情景出现在他眼前。

他看见一只蝉,正在浓密的树荫里休息,全身舒展,还不时地唱着歌,欢快中忘记了自身的安危,忘记了周围的世界;而附近有一只螳螂,它用树叶作掩护,虎视眈眈,突然间一个猛扑,把蝉紧紧地压在身下。这时螳螂很得意，琢磨着从何处下手来享用这顿美餐，对怎样保护自己、隐藏形体忘得一干二净；那只怪鹊紧随其后，认为那是极好的时机，于是伸长嘴巴去啄螳螂。它一心一意地盯住螳螂，连手持弹弓正准备射杀自己的庄子都没有看到，不知道自己的生命也危在旦夕。这一情景使庄子十分感叹："啊，螳螂捕蝉，鹊子在后，世上的物类原本就是这样相互牵累、相互争夺的，常常彼此给对方带来麻烦和危险，而互相造成危险的东西往往又有互相利用的一面。见利忘危，人可不能不知不觉地陷入这种境地之中啊！"想到这里，庄子扔掉弹弓转身就走，没料到刚走几步，后面就有人追上来叫住他。原来是看守栗子园的人刚才看见庄子鬼鬼祟祟地东张西望，以为他要偷栗子就来盘问他。

庄子返回家中，整整三天心情很不好。他的弟子蔺且在一旁问道："先生为什么这几天来一直很不高兴呢？"庄子说："我留意外物的形体却忘记了自身的安危，观赏混浊的流水却迷惑于清澈的水潭。而且我从老聃老师那里听说：'每到一个地方，就要遵从那里的习惯与禁忌。'如今我来到雕陵栗园便忘却了自身的安危，只想弄清楚奇异的怪鹊为什么会擦过我的额头，却忘记自己走进了栗子园，违反了栗子园的规定，管园的人不理解我，又进而侮辱我。你说，我怎么会感到愉快？"

成语"螳螂捕蝉，黄雀在后"，就是从这个故事演化而来的。要注意，利益常常会蒙蔽人的眼睛。事实上，为满足高质量、高品位的生命需求，人在追求、实现欲望时，常常会看前不看后，看人不看己，看当下不看将来，从而不知不觉地陷入困境。所以，人生一定要保持几分清醒，拥有几分机警，"得意"千万不能"忘形"。

A MANTIS STALKS A CICADA AND IS STALKED BY AN ORIOLE

On a summer day, Zhuangzi went out traveling on his own. He passed a garden called Diaoling, where a lot of chestnut trees with exuberant leaves blocked the bright sunlight, making the garden very cool. Suddenly a strange-looking oriole flew over from the south. Its wings were seven *chi* in length, and its big eyes were one *cun* wide. It flew recklessly, passing over the head of Zhuangzi, and stopped among the fruit trees. Almost hit on the head by the passing bird, Zhuangzi was shocked and became angry. He murmured to himself, "What bird is this? With such big wings, it still can't fly far and high; with such big eyes, it still can't see clearly. It's as blind as a bat." So he picked up the hem of his long robe, and stepped forward quickly. With his sling in his hand, he waited patiently for the bird, determined to shoot it down once the right time came. Just then, his eyes lit up at a wonderful scene right in front of him.

A cicada was having a rest in the deep shade offered by the trees. With its body fully relaxed, it sang freely now and then, forgetting all about its safety and the surrounding world in its happiness. But a mantis nearby, covered by the leaves of the trees, was eying the cicada menacingly. Suddenly the mantis lurched forward and pressed the cicada hard under it. Feeling very pleased with itself, the mantis was thinking about where to start to enjoy the delicious meal. It forgot entirely about hiding itself and having some self-protection. The strange-looking bird, following the mantis, thought it was good timing. With a jab of its long beak, the bird got the mantis as its prey. But in its full concentration in dealing with the mantis, it didn't see that Zhuangzi, looming large, with a sling in hand, was ready to shoot it, and it didn't know that its life was in danger. Zhuangzi heaved a big sigh at this, "Ah, the mantis stalked the cicada, unaware of the oriole behind. That is how the things in the world thus get involved with one another and fight against one another, bringing troubles and dangers to one another, and at the same time making use of the very things that have brought troubles or dangers. Seeing the advantages and forgetting about the ensuing dangers — that is the situation men should never slip into unwittingly." So he threw away his sling and headed home at once. But no sooner had he made a few steps when someone caught up and stopped him. It was the garden keeper who noticed Zhuangzi's furtive action and took him for a thief of chestnuts.

Zhuangzi returned home, and for three whole days he was in a bad mood. His disciple Lin Qie, who was in attendance, asked him, "Master, why have you been unhappy these past few days?" Zhuangzi said, "I was concentrating on the forms of the external things and forgot my own safety; I was appreciating the turbid water and got confused about the clear pool. Moreover, I have heard from Master Lao Dan (Laozi), 'Wherever one goes, one is to follow the prevailing customs and taboos there.' Now I came to Diaoling, the chestnut garden, and I forgot my own safety. I wanted so much to find out why the strange-looking oriole almost hit me on the head, and I forgot I was in the chestnut garden and therefore broke the rules of the garden; as a result, the garden keeper didn't understand me and insulted me. You see, how am I able to feel happy?"

The idiom "The mantis stalks the cicada, unaware of the oriole behind" originates from the story above. Please remember that benefits often make people blind. In fact, to satisfy the need for a life of higher quality and more cultivated taste, to seek and meet one's desires, one often makes the mistake of looking forward without looking backward, looking at others without looking at oneself, and looking at the present without looking at the future, thus slipping into a dead end unconsciously. So it is important for one to stay cool and sharp somehow. One can be pleased with oneself, but can never be carried out of oneself.

33. 望洋兴叹

秋天一到,山洪开始爆发,大河小河的水都涨起来。水势浩浩荡荡,从各处汇入黄河。黄河河面宽阔,波涛汹涌,人如果站在河岸这边望着对岸,或者从这个沙洲望对面那个沙洲,都难以分辨远处的是牛是马。看到这一景象,河神得意洋洋,认为天下一切美好的东西全都聚集在自己这里。河神顺着水流向东而去,来到北海边,面朝东边一望,看不见大海的尽头。这时河神方才改变先前洋洋自得的样子,面对着海神仰首叹息道:"俗语所说的'听到了上百条道理,便认为天下再没有谁能比得上自己',说的就是我这样的人了。过去曾听说孔丘懂得的东西太少、伯夷的高义不值得看重的话语,开始我不敢相信,总以为孔丘、伯夷是天下第一;如今我来到你的门前,亲眼看到了你是这样的浩渺博大、无边无际,才知道我是多么的孤陋寡闻,如果没遇到你,我必定会贻笑大方。"

海神说:"跟井里的青蛙不可能谈论大海,因它们受到生活空间的限制;与夏天的虫子不可能谈论冰冻,因为它们生存的时间过于短暂;对浅薄的人不可能谈论大道,因为他们接受的教养过于偏执。如今你走出了崖岸,看到了大海,这才知道自己的鄙陋。这样,我就可以与你谈论大的道理了。天下的水,没有什么比海更大的,千万条河川流归大海,根本不知道什么时候才会停止,而大海从来不会溢出来;海底的水不停地泄漏,而海水却从不曾减少。无论是春天还是秋天,看不到海有什么变化;无论是洪涝还是干旱,海也不会有什么知觉。这说明大海远远超过了江河的水流,不能够用数目来计算它的容量。可是我从不曾因此而自满,因为我不过是从天地那里承受到形体,从阴阳中领受到元气,如同存在于天地之间的一块小石子,存在于大山之中的一片小木屑。我的存在是那样的渺小,又怎能够自以为了不起呢?其实你仔细想一想就会明白,四海存在于天地之间,就像一块石头置于大泽中;中原大地存在于四海之内,就像米粒存在于粮仓中;称呼事物类别的名字可以万计,而人类只是万物中的一种;一个人比起万物,不就像是毫毛之末存在于整个马体吗?人们聚集于九州,粮食在这里生长,舟车在这里通行,而每个人只是众多人群中的一员;五帝所续连的、三皇所争夺的、仁人所忧患的、贤才所操劳的,全都包括在里面了!伯夷以辞让而博取名声,孔丘以谈论显示渊博,他们这样自以为了不起;这些不正像你先前在河水暴涨时的洋洋自得吗?"

从此以后,河神不再自以为是了。

河神与海神的这段对话,产生了成语"望洋兴叹"。如果一个人不知道天外有天,大上有大,却以自己之大为天下之大,以自己之高为世界之高,那就犯了同河神一样的错误。如果还固执己见的话,恐怕还达不到河神的水平呢。望洋兴叹其实是一种反思,是视域开阔的产物。

A LAMENT OF SMALLNESS BEFORE THE VAST SEA

The mountain floods began to rush down once the autumn came. Rivers, big and small, rose and poured from all directions into the Yellow River, which was surging with big waves. The Yellow River was so wide that if one looked to the opposite bank or to the other side of the shoal from this side, he could hardly distinguish whether it was a horse or an ox standing in the distance. The River God was very pleased with this, believing that all the good things had been gathered here at his place. The River God walked along the water to the east until he got to the North Sea. He looked out to the east and could not see where the sea ended. With his pleased countenance gone, the River God looked up and said to the Sea God with a sigh, "The old saying 'He who has learnt a hundred truths thinks that no one in the world is equal to him' must refer to someone like me. I have heard in the past the allegations that Confucius knew too little and the high principles of Bo Yi deserved little admiration. At first I dared not to believe, thinking that Confucius and Bo Yi were the best in the world. But now I am here right in front of you and having seen with my own eyes how huge and boundless you are, I know that I was rather ignorant. Had I not come to you, I would have been in danger of making myself a laughing stock."

The Sea God said, "You cannot talk to a frog in a well about the great sea, since it is confined to a limited living space; you cannot talk to insects of summer about ice and freeze, since they live such a short life; and you cannot talk to small-minded people about the Great Tao, since their learning has been too narrow and bigoted. Now that you've emerged out of the cliffs and seen the great sea, you realize your own insignificance. So I can talk about the great truths with you. Of all the waters in the world, there is none as big as the sea. Thousands and thousands of rivers pour into it. Nobody knows when they will stop, and yet the sea never gets filled up; it is constantly draining off at the bottom, and yet the sea never gets decreased. In spring and in autumn, the sea seems to undergo no changes; in floods and in droughts, the sea never seems to notice. It means that the sea far surpasses the waters in rivers and lakes, and its volume is not measurable in quantities. But I have never been conceited because of these, for all I have done is to inherit my bodily form from Heaven and Earth and to receive my energy and vitality from Yin and Yang, just like a small pebble in the world and a tiny piece of wood between the mountains. With such a miniscule existence, how should I make much of myself? Actually if you think hard, you will understand that the existence of the Four Seas lying between Heaven and Earth is just like that of a stone put in a huge marsh; and the existence of the Middle Kingdom in the Four Seas is just like that of a grain in a large barn. There are a myriad of names used to identify different categories of things, and man is only one of them. When compared to the myriad of things, isn't man just like one of the horsehairs compared to an entire horse? People settle down in the Nine Provinces, where foodstuff grow and boats and carriages move, but everyone is just a tiny part among the myriad of crowds. What the Five Emperors succeeded to, what the Three Sovereigns contended for, what the virtuous people worried about and what the good officials toiled for, had all been one part of this. Bo Yi declined the high position to win fame. Confucius lectured to show knowledge. Isn't their overestimation of themselves very much like the self-conceit you just had in the face of the rising water?"

Ever since then, the River God has never thought too much of himself.

The dialogue between the River God and the Sea God gives birth to the Chinese idiom "Lament one's smallness before the vast sea". If a man is not aware that there is a sky beyond the sky and bigness beyond bigness, but mistakes his idea of bigness as the bigness of the world and his height of achievements as the height of the world, he makes the same mistake as the River God did. If moreover he remains unyielding in his opinions, then he falls short of the level of the River God, for "Lamenting one's smallness before the vast sea" is also a kind of self reflection, a product of a broadened horizon.

34. 仁义乱人心

崔瞿子向老子请教,问:"不治理天下,怎么才能使人心向善?"老子回答说:"你千万不要扰乱人心。人心是最不稳定的了,如果受到压抑就会向下消沉颓丧,受到鼓动就会向上趾高气扬。而人的本性是不甘居低下的职位,常为向上爬而绞尽脑汁。要知道,人心的伸缩性很大,柔顺时能软化刚强,尖锐时能雕琢玉器,热时像烈火,冷时如寒冰;其变化极其迅速,转眼间就能到四海之外巡游两周;停下来如同深渊一片寂静,活动时就想腾跃高飞;天地万物中,骄矜不禁而无所拘系的,恐怕就属人的内心吧!其实你看看历史就可以知道了。"

"在古代,黄帝开始用仁义来扰乱人心,后来尧舜疲于奔波,大腿被磨得没有小毛,小腿上没有汗毛,竭力养育天下众多的形体,满心焦虑地推行仁义,并耗费心血来制定法度。然而他们还是未能治理好天下。此后尧将凶人讙兜放逐到南方的崇山,将凶人三苗放逐到西北的三峗,将凶人共工放逐到北方的幽都,这些就是天下不能治理的明证。延续到夏、商、周三代,天下大乱,百姓受到的惊扰更多,下有夏桀、盗跖之流,上有曾参、史鳅之流,而儒家和墨家的争辩又全面展开。这样一来,喜悦的与愤怒的相互猜疑,愚昧的与明智的相互欺诈,善良的与凶恶的相互责难,虚诈的与诚信的相互讥刺,致使天下逐渐衰败;人的基本观念和生活态度如此不同,人类的自然本性被扭曲了,性情也被散乱了,天下都在追求智巧,百姓中纷争迭起,于是就发明了斧锯之类的刑具来制裁他们,建立绳墨之类的法度来规范他们,使用椎凿之类的肉刑来惩处他们。天下相互践踏而大乱,应归罪于人心的扰乱。因此贤能的人隐居于高山深谷之下,而帝王诸侯忧心如焚,在朝堂上担惊受怕。当今之世,遭受杀害的人尸体一个压着一个,戴着脚镣手铐坐大牢的人一个挨着一个,受到刑具伤害的人更是举目皆是,而儒家、墨家竟然在枷锁和羁绊中挥手舞臂地奋力争辩。唉,真是太过分了!他们不知心愧、不识羞耻竟然达到这等地步!我不知道有哪位圣智之人不是在制造枷锁,也不知道有什么仁义不是在做脚镣手铐,也实在不能知道曾参和史鳅之流不是夏桀和盗跖的先导!所以说,'断绝圣人,抛弃智慧,天下就会得到治理而太平无事。'

仁义乱人心,突出的是天下不可治,因为人心的根本是静。内心平静的时候,人会自然而然地随世界运转;内心骚动的时候,会不顾一切独断专行。仁义一类的说教,打破了心灵的宁静,扭曲了人的本性,煽动了人的私欲,引发了人心的阴暗面。所以庄子的看法是,谁能像爱护自己身体那样爱护万事万物的本性,就可以把天下托付给他。

BENEVOLENCE AND RIGHTEOUSNESS DISTURB PEOPLE'S MINDS

Cui Quzi went to Laozi for advice. He asked Laozi, "If you do not rule over the world, how can you influence people's minds and keep them good?" Laozi answered, "Never meddle with people's minds, which are the most unstable things. If suppressed, the minds get low and depressed; if stirred up, they get high and swelled. It is only human nature not to be contented with low position, but to try with all means to get higher. Remember, people's minds enjoy great flexibility. When they are gentle, they can overcome hardness; when they are sharp, they can cut and chisel jade. Sometimes they are hot like blazing fire; other times, they are cold as ice and freeze. They change swiftly and in the twinkling of an eye, they travel twice beyond the Four Seas. When pausing, they are like the stillness of the abyss; when moving, they desire to prance far and fly high. Among the myriad of things between Heaven and Earth, what can remain arrogant and haughty without the slightest restraint? Perhaps only the minds of the people. Take a look at the history and you'll understand what I have said."

"In ancient times, the Yellow Emperor started to meddle with the minds of people with ideas of benevolence and righteousness. Later Yao and Shun ran around and drove themselves so hard in their attempt to take care of the great many people on the earth that even their thighs and calves were bare of fine hairs. They promoted benevolence and righteousness in earnest and worked their hearts out to establish codes of laws and statutes. But they still failed to manage the world well. After that, Yao exiled the villain Huan Dou to Chongshan in the south, the villain San Miao to Sanwei in the northwest, and the villain Gong Gong away to Youdu in the north. These serve as the clear proof that the world is not to be governed. Then it went on to the Three Legendary Dynasties of Xia, Shang and Zhou when the world was plunged into more troubles and the people suffered from more disturbances. At the bottom there were evil people like King Jie of Xia and Zhi the Robber; at the top, there were 'noble' people like Ceng Can and Shi Qiu. At the same time, the contention between Confucianism and Mohism was in full swing. Thus, the happy and the angry were suspicious of one another, the silly and the wise deceived one another, the kind and the vicious rebuked one another, and the pretentious and the sincere mocked one another. As a result, the whole world gradually declined. People's basic concepts and life attitudes became so different that the human nature was distorted, and the human temperament was disoriented. The whole world was after knowledge and skills, and as a result, common people contended and fought among themselves. Then such instruments of torture as ax and saw were invented to punish them; such codes of law as line and ink were established to regulate them; and such corporal punishments as hammers and chisels were used to penalize them. The world fell into great disorder, with people treading on one another, and that should be blamed on people's disturbed minds. So virtuous men sought refuge in high mountains and deep valleys, while emperors, dukes and princes gathered in anxiety and fear in the imperial court. In the present world, those who have been killed are piled high one after another, those who have been put into prison in handcuffs and shackles are pressed tight against one another, and those who have been injured by instruments of torture are seen everywhere. And in the midst of all these chains, fetters and bonds, the Confucians and the Mohists are actually struggling forward with hands and arms waving to argue and to preach. Oh, it is rather too much. How can they be so heartless and shameless to such an extent? I know no sagely man who is not making chains; I know no ideas of benevolence and righteousness which are not used as handcuffs and shackles; and I cannot, for the life of me, know if 'noble' people like Ceng Can and Shi Qiu are actually the forerunners of the evil King Jie of Xia and Zhi the Bandit. So I say, 'Break off with the sages, cast away wisdom, and the world will be cared for and brought to a state of order.'"

The idea that benevolence and righteousness disturb the minds of people suggests that the very nature of people's mind is peace. When the mind is peaceful, man moves naturally along with the rest of the world; when the mind is agitated, man turns reckless and arbitrary. Preaches on benevolence and righteousness disturb the peacefulness of man's mind, distort man's nature, instigate man's desires, and stir up the dark side of man's heart. Therefore according to Zhuangzi, he who cares for the nature of myriads of things like his own body is to be entrusted with the care of the world.

35. 言者不知，知者不言

知向北游历，来到玄水岸边，登上了一座名叫隐弅的山丘，正巧在那里遇上了无为谓。知对无为谓说："我想向你请教一些问题：怎样思索才能懂得道？怎样居处、怎样行事才符合于道？依从什么、采用什么方法才能获得道？"接连问了好几次，无为谓都不回答。他不是不回答，而是不知道怎样回答。知从无为谓那里得不到解答，便返回白水的南岸，登上一座名叫狐阕的山丘，在那里见到了狂屈。知把先前的问题又向狂屈请教，狂屈说："唉，我知道怎样回答这些问题，不过在我想告诉你的时候，却忘记了那些想说的话。"知从狂屈那里也没有得到解答，便转回到黄帝的住所，见到黄帝又问起来了。黄帝说："没有思索、没有考虑才能够懂得道，没有安处、没有执守才能安于道，没有依从、没有行动才能获得道。"

知又问黄帝："我和你知道这些道理，无为谓和狂屈不知道这些道理，那么，谁是正确的呢？"黄帝说："无为谓是真正正确的，狂屈接近于正确，我和你则远着呢。言者不知，知者不言，所以圣人施行的是不用言传的教育。道不可能靠言传来获得，德不可能靠谈话来达到。仁是可以施行的，义是可以谈说的，而礼仪的推行只是相互欺骗。所以说，'失去了道而后能获得德，失去了德而后能获得仁，失去了仁而后能获得义，失去了义而后能获得礼。礼是对道的伪饰，是乱的祸首。'所以说，'体察道的人每天都得清除伪饰，清除而又再清除以至达到无为的境界，达到无所作为的境界也就无所可为了。'如今我们已化为一种物体，想要再返回根本是很困难的；要说容易，恐怕只有得道的人才能做到。"

知又对黄帝说："我问无为谓，无为谓不回答我，不是不回答我，是不知道回答我。我问狂屈，狂屈内心里正想告诉我却没有告诉我，不是不告诉我，是心里正想告诉我又忘掉了怎样告诉我。现在我想再次请教你，你懂得我所提出的问题，为什么又说回答了我便不是接近于道呢？"黄帝说："无为谓他是真正了解大道的，因为他什么也不知道；狂屈他是接近于道的，因为他忘记了；我和你终究不能接近于道，因为我们什么都知道。"

后来狂屈听说了这件事，认为黄帝的话很有见地。

知的这番经历反映了中国古人对语言的看法。"言意之辩"是中国人经常讨论的话题，历史上就有"得意忘言"之说：鱼抓住了，鱼笼就扔掉了；意思明白了，言语就可以忘掉。所以中国古人喜欢用最精练的话语来表达深刻的话题，喜欢用一句话，甚至一两个字来概括自己的思想，最好的是不说话，"双目一击道存焉"。人们常说的雄辩是银，沉默是金，实际上就是言者不知、知者不言的另一种表述。

THOSE WHO TALK DON'T KNOW AND THOSE WHO KNOW DON'T TALK

The Knowledgeable One traveled north to the bank of the Dark Water, and climbed onto a hill called Hidden Mound, where he happened to meet the Indifferent One. The Knowledgeable One said to the Indifferent One, "I would like to ask for your advice. How do we meditate and contemplate in order to know Tao? How do we live and behave to be in line with Tao? What do we rely on and what approach do we take to attain Tao?" He repeated his questions several times, but the Indifferent One gave no reply. It was not that the Indifferent One didn't want to reply, but he didn't know how to reply. Having gotten no answers from the Indifferent One, the Knowledgeable One returned to the south bank of the White Water and climbed onto another hill called Fox's End, where he met the Crazy One. The Knowledgeable One asked the Crazy One the same questions as he asked the Indifferent One. The Crazy One replied, "Oh, I knew how to answer these questions, but just when I was about to tell you, I forgot what I wanted to say." Having gotten no answers from the Crazy One, the Knowledgeable One turned around and went to the place of the Yellow Emperor. Upon seeing the Yellow Emperor, the Knowledgeable One asked again the same questions. The Yellow Emperor said, "Without meditation and without contemplation can we know Tao; without a place to live and without a code of conduct to follow can we be satisfied with Tao; and without reliance and without action can we attain Tao."

The Knowledgeable One asked the Yellow Emperor again, "You and I understand these, but the Indifferent One and the Crazy One don't. Then, who is right?" The Yellow Emperor said, "The Indifferent One is truly right, the Crazy One is close to being right, while you and I are far from being right. Since those who talk don't know and those who know don't talk, what the sagely men teach are not expressed in words. Tao cannot be attained through words, and virtue cannot be reached through discussions. Benevolence can be practiced, righteousness can be talked about, while the promotion of rituals and ceremonies is just mutual deceits. So it is said, 'One gets virtue when Tao is lost; one gets benevolence when virtue is lost; one gets righteousness when benevolence is lost; and one gets rituals when righteousness is lost. Rituals are nothing but phony floral adornments of Tao and the source of great disorder in the world.' So it is said, 'Those who understand Tao eliminate phony adornments every day. They work hard at it until they reach the State of Inaction. By reaching such a state, there are no more reasons for them to take actions.' Now we have already been turned into beings, and if we desire to return to our original state, it would be very difficult. Only those who have attained Tao would find it easy to accomplish that task."

The Knowledgeable One said to the Yellow Emperor again, "I asked the Indifferent One and he gave me no reply. It was not because he didn't want to reply, but he didn't know how to. I then asked the Crazy One, and though at the bottom of his heart he wanted to tell me, he didn't. It was because when he was thinking about giving me the answer, he forgot how to. So I have to seek your advice. Now that you understood the questions I asked, why did you say that you were far from Tao by answering them?" The Yellow Emperor answered, "The Indifferent One truly understands Tao, for he knows nothing; the Crazy One is close to Tao, for he forgets; but you and I are indeed not able to get even close to Tao, for we know everything."

Later the Crazy One heard of this and he thought that the Yellow Emperor's remarks were quite sensible.

This experience of the Knowledgeable One reflects the view of the ancient Chinese philosophers toward language. The gap between spoken words and the hidden meaning has been a favorite topic with Chinese people. Beginning from the ancient times, there has been a saying about "Meaning grasped, words forgotten", which is like "Fish caught, fish basket thrown away". The meaning is understood, and the words can be forgotten. Therefore the ancient Chinese philosophers preferred to use the most laconic language to express the most profound meanings, to use one sentence, or even just one or two words to describe one's ideas. The most ideal state was to "take just one look to find out Tao, without saying a single word". A popular saying goes that "Speech is silver and silence is gold." It is in fact another version of "Those who talk don't know and those who know don't talk."

36. 机器与机巧

子贡到南边的楚国游历,返回晋国,经过汉阴时,见一老翁正在菜园里整地开畦。只见他凿了一条水沟直通到井边,抱着瓦罐从井里打水灌地,气喘吁吁,显得相当吃力,但功效不大。子贡就对老人说:"如今有一种机械,每天可以浇灌上百个菜畦,用力很少而效率很高,老先生你何不去试试?"老人抬起头来看着子贡问:"应该怎么做呢?"子贡说:"有一种机械叫做桔槔,是用木料加工而成的,在木头上凿个洞,它后面重而前面轻,提水就像从井中抽水似的,速度之快就像沸腾的水向外溢出一样。"老人听了脸色一变,讥笑说:"我听我的老师说过这样的话,有了机械之类的东西必定会出现机巧之类的事,有了机巧之类的事必定会出现机巧之类的心思。机巧之心存留在胸中,那纯洁的不曾受到世俗浸染的心境就不完整齐备;纯洁的心境不完备,精神就不会专一安定;精神不能专一安定的人,他是不可能修成'道'的。其实,你说的这种方法,我不是不知道,只不过是不愿这样做,这让人感到羞辱呀。"听了这番话，子贡满面羞愧，低下头半天不作一声。

隔了一会儿，种菜的老人问："你是干什么的呀？"子贡说："我是孔丘的学生。"老人说："你不就是那具有广博学识并处处仿效圣人，用浮夸妄诞压过众人，自唱自和周游天下去卖弄名声的人吗？如果你能抛弃你的精神，废置你的形体，恐怕就可以逐步接近于道了吧！可你自身都不懂得如何修养和调理，哪里顾得上去治理天下呢！你走吧，不要在这里耽误我的事情！"

子贡神色大变，怅然若失而不能自持，走出三十里外方才逐步恢复常态。子贡的弟子问道："先前碰到的那个人是干什么的呀？先生为什么见到他后顿然失色，一整天都心事重重的？"子贡说："起初我总以为天下圣人就只有我老师孔丘一人，不知道还会有刚才碰上的那样的人。老师常说，办事要寻求可行，功业要寻求成就。用的力气要少，获得的功效要多，这就是圣人之道。如今听到的却截然不同，认为持守大道的人德行才完备，德行完备的人形体才完整，形体完整的人精神才健全，精神健全才是圣人之道。这样的人内心世界深不可测，淳厚质朴而又德行完备，从不把功利机巧放在心上。他们这样的人，不同于自己的心志就不会去追求，不符合自己的思想就不会去做，天下人的非议和赞誉，他们也无动于衷，这就叫做德行完备的人啊！而我只能称作心神不定，为世俗尘垢所沾染的人。"

把机械与心灵的机巧联系起来，颇有点唯物论的味道，表明人的思维能力、思维特性与一定的物质生产活动水平相关。只是中国传统重的是伦理，所以，在庄子那里，聪明、智慧、技巧就常常与狡猾、虚伪、做作联系在一起了，说"有大智必有大伪"就是一例。

MACHINE AND ADROITNESS

Zi Gong, a disciple of Confucius, traveled to the State of Chu in the south. On his way back to the State of Jin, he passed a place called Hanyin where he saw an old man plowing and digging in his vegetable garden. The old farmer dug a ditch to the well, and with a pitcher in his hand, he was bringing water from the well to irrigate his garden. He was breathing hard, looking very tired, but had very little to show for his efforts. Zi Gong said to him, "Now there's a machine which can irrigate hundreds of vegetable gardens every day. It needs very light work, but enjoys high efficiency. Sir, why don't you have a try?" The old farmer looked up at Zi Gong and asked, "What should I do?" Zi Gong said, "There is a machine called well-sweep, made of wood on which a hole is drilled. It is light in front and heavy behind. If you use it to get water, it will be like pumping water from a well, and the water comes out as fast as if it were boiled and just bubbled outside." At this, the old farmer looked angry and said with a sneer, "I have heard from my teacher that where there are contrivances as machines, there is sure to be tasks accomplished with adroitness; and that where there are tasks accomplished with adroitness, there are sure to be desires for adroitness. But when such desires are harbored within, the pure mind which hasn't been tainted by worldly affairs becomes incomplete. With the mind being incomplete, one's spirits are no longer focused and settled, which makes it impossible for him to reach Tao. Actually, the method you mention has not been unknown to me. I just don't want to use it. It would only make me feel ashamed." Having heard what the old man said, Zi Gong was abashed, and he hung down his head and remained silent for quite a while.

After some time, the old farmer asked, "Who are you?" Zi Gong answered, "I am a disciple of Confucius." Then the old farmer said, "Are you not the scholar who has great learning but tries to compare to a sage in every aspect, who puts himself above all others with boasting and exaggeration, and who sings tunes with his own accompaniment and travels all over the world to show off his fame? If you had abandoned your spirit and neglected your bodily form, you would have been getting closer to Tao. Yet, as you don't have any ideas about nourishment and regulation for yourself, how can you be so sure of bringing order to the world? Go away! Do not interrupt my work here!"

Zi Gong turned pale and felt lost and bewildered. It was not until he was 30 *li* away that he gradually regained his composure. His disciple asked him, "Who was the old farmer we met before? Why did Master turn pale and look preoccupied with worries for a long time after meeting him?" Zi Gong said, "I used to believe that Confucius, my Master, was the only sage in the world. I didn't expect that there were people who were like the old farmer we met just now. My Master has often said that practical means are to be found for the completion of a task, and that success is to be desired for the attainment of one's achievements. It is the Tao of the sages to seek better results with less effort. But what I have heard today is different. Those who hold fast to Tao are perfect in their virtues. With perfect virtues, they are complete in their bodily forms. Complete in bodily forms, they reach a state of integrity in their spiritual world. And only spiritual integrity is the Tao of the sages. The inner world of such people is deep as to be immeasurable, yet simple without any pretentiousness, where desires for success, benefits and adroitness are not to be found. They don't seek anything which runs counter to their will or do anything that their mind doesn't approve. They heed no praises nor blames from the world. Such people can be regarded as being perfect in both virtues and conducts, while I can only be called the one who is tainted by the worldly affairs and who drifts along with the tide in both mind and heart."

It sounds a bit like materialism to connect a piece of machine with the adroitness of human mind. But it suggests that both the thinking capability of human mind and the characteristics of human thoughts are related to a certain level of material production. It is a Chinese tradition to put a high value on moral ethics. Therefore, according to Zhuangzi, adroitness, wisdom and skills often mix with craftiness, hypocrisy and affectation. The saying that great wisdom comes with great hypocrisy is a good example.

37. 做老师的学问

　　春秋时，鲁国有个隐者名叫颜阖，他将被请去做卫国太子的师傅。颜阖听说那个卫国太子是个有凶德的人，所以一到卫国，就去拜访贤者蘧伯玉，用曲折的方式向他求教如何教太子："假定有这样一个人，他的德行生就凶残嗜杀。跟他朝夕与共的过程中，如果不符合法度与规范，就会去做不好的事，从而势必危害自己的国家；如果合乎法度和规范，那就会引起他的不满，从而危害自身。他很聪明，其智慧足以了解别人的过失，却不了解自己的错误，不了解自己为什么会出现过失。面对这样的情况，你说我该怎么办呢？"

　　蘧伯玉说："你这个问题问得好啊！要警惕，要谨慎，首先要端正你自己的态度，明确自己的位置！表面上你要表现为顺从依就的样子以示亲近，而内心则要顺其秉性暗加疏导。不能以为这种做法就完美了，因为其中还有隐患，还有危险。亲附他时关系不要过于密切，疏导他时心意不要太显露。关系过密，会招致颠覆毁灭，招致崩溃失败；顺性疏导太露,自己可能会获得不少好名声,但人怕出名猪怕壮,它也会招致祸害。所以,他如果像个天真的孩子一样,你也姑且跟他一样像个无知无识的孩子;他如果同你做没有分寸的事,你也就跟他一起做有失分寸的事;他如果做没有理性的事,你也就姑且跟他一起,无拘无束——然后才可以慢慢地将他思想引入正道。如果你明白了这个道理,就不会有什么过失了。你知道那螳螂吗?它会奋起它的臂膀去阻挡滚动的车轮,不明白自己的力量全然不能胜任,还自以为很有力量。你一定要警惕,要谨慎!如果经常在他面前夸耀自己的才华,劝诫他应该怎样做事而触犯了他,那就危险了!你不了解那养虎的人吗?他从不敢用活物去喂养老虎,因为他担心扑杀活物会激起老虎凶残的怒气;他也从不敢用整个的动物去喂养老虎,因为他担心撕裂动物也会诱发老虎凶残的野性。要知道老虎饥饱的时刻,要通晓老虎暴戾凶残的秉性。老虎与人本不是同类的,但它却向饲养人摇尾乞怜,原因就是养老虎的人能顺应老虎的性子,而那些受到老虎伤害的人,是因为触犯了老虎的性情。有一个爱马的人,喜欢用精细的竹筐装马粪,用珍贵的漆器接马尿,有一次他看到一只牛虻叮在马身上,出于爱惜马上随手一击,没想到马儿受惊便毁断笼头就跑,把头也撞伤了,胸口也撞破了。你看,爱马之心却导致伤马之果,人处理事物能够不谨慎吗?」

这个故事,后来就引出了成语"螳臂当车", 用来比喻不自量力,其深层涵义说的是人不能逆流而行,这个"流"就是规律、本性。其实做老师也是这样,一个老师如果只认为自己所传授的知识是如何的重要,而不考虑学生的可接受性,那这种知识再好也是没有意义的,皮之不存,毛将附焉?

THE ART OF TUTORING

During the Spring and Autumn Period, there was a hermit named Yan He. He was invited to be the tutor of the prince of the State of Wei. Having heard that the prince had a vicious disposition, Yan He went to consult the virtuous sage Qu Boyu as soon as he got to the State of Wei. In a roundabout way, Yan He sought advice from Qu Boyu on how to teach the prince. He asked, "Suppose there is a man whose natural disposition is vicious and prone to kill. In his company, if taking no heed of the rules and codes, one is sure to do something bad which are detrimental to one's country; but if insisting in observing the rules and codes, one is sure to displease him, bringing harm to oneself. He is clever, having wits enough to see faults in others, but not enough to see his own, nor to understand how he makes mistakes himself. What do you suggest I should do in a situation like this?"

Qu Boyu said, "You've asked a good question indeed! Be on guard and be cautious. First you should get your attitude rightly adjusted and your position clearly defined. Outwardly you behave in a compliant and obedient way to show your goodwill, while inwardly you try to lead him in a way that is in harmony with his disposition. And yet don't regard this as a perfect solution; there are hidden troubles and dangers. In showing him your compliance, don't get too close; in leading him, don't get too obvious. If you get too close, you will fall and ruin yourself, before failing in the end. If you are too obvious with your leading in harmony with his disposition, you may be rewarded with good reputation. But just like the old saying goes that 'Fame portends trouble for men just as fattening does for pigs', good reputation may bring you troubles and harms. So if he acts like an innocent child, you just play with him as an ignorant child; if he asks you to do something inappropriate with him, you just join him; and if he does something irrational, you just humor him in being irrational. Then you will be able to gradually lead him back to the right track. If you understand these, you will be free from faults. Have you heard of the mantis which in its rage extends its arms to stop the rolling wheels of a carriage, not knowing that its meager strength is not up to the job, but putting blind faith in its own power? So be cautious and be on your guard. If you often show off your learning in front of him by providing him with cautionary advice on how to deal with things, you are going to offend him, which will be very dangerous. Have you not heard of the man who keeps and tames tigers? He dares not feed living animals to the tigers, for fear that the killing will stimulate the tigers' vicious rage, neither does he dare feed whole animal bodies to the tigers, for fear that tearing them apart will also incite the viciousness in the nature of the tigers. He knows exactly when the tigers are hungry or full, and he manages to have a good understanding of their vicious nature. Tigers are different species from men, but they can be made to fawn on those who feed them, because the trainers understand how to keep in harmony with the nature of tigers. Some people are hurt by tigers because they have acted against that nature. There is a man who loves horses. He goes so far as to put horse dung in exquisitely made bamboo baskets and keep horse urine in valuable lacquer jars. Once he saw a mosquito bite a horse, and out of his care for the horse, he shot out his hand to slap it away. But what he didn't expect was that the horse was startled; it broke free its bridles and bolted, breaking its head and skinning its chest. You see, good intentions result in the horse being injured. Therefore one can't be too cautious when dealing with things."

Later from the above story derives the idiom "A mantis tries to stop a chariot with its raised arms," which is used to describe someone overrating himself. It means that one can't go against the inevitable trend, i.e. the laws of nature. It is the same with being a tutor. If a tutor considers only how important his knowledge is and pays no attention to the acceptability on the part of the students, then even the best knowledge is meaningless. When the skin is gone, what can the hair adhere to?

38．列御寇与拍马

有一个人名叫列御寇，有一天，他到齐国去，走到半路突然改变主意，慌慌张张地往回走。半路上列御寇遇上了他的老师伯昏瞀人。伯昏瞀人问道："怎么往回走了，什么事情让你走得急急忙忙的？"列御寇说："我刚才吃了一惊，感到惊惶不安。"伯昏瞀人又问："到底怎么啦？看你脸色都白了，究竟是什么原因使你惊惶不安？"列御寇说："我来到一个小镇，因为口渴我想买水喝，小镇上有十家卖水浆的店子，其中有五家事先就把水给我送来了。"伯昏瞀人说："像这样的事，你怎么会惊惶不安呢？"列御寇说："我与店主素不相识，但却无缘无故地向我敬献水浆，原因可能是我肚子里有了点文章，平时不知不觉地显现出来，好像与众不同，鹤立鸡群，眉宇之间总有一股庄严之气，使百姓产生了一些恐惧感，趋炎附势的人开始拥上来了。他们内心虽然忠诚，却又未能从流俗中解脱出来，喜欢在外表上显示自己，用外在的东西镇服人心，信奉拍马胜于敬老，对我的尊重胜过对年长者的尊重，这就必然会招致祸患。那卖水浆的人只不过是小本经营，没有多少钱财，他们的赢利是很微薄的，施行的计划很小，可是还如此地对待我，不用说，那些大国的国君见了我一定会千方百计地拖住我。为国君亲身操劳，将使我身体劳累、才智耗尽。国君把重任托付给我，为了取得成果而叫我去效力，要我不断做出功绩。我正因为这个缘故才惊惶不已，所以当时连水浆都顾不上喝，就赶紧走了。"听完这话，伯昏瞀人连连点头说："你的观察与分析实在是好啊！你安处自身吧，人们一定会归附于你了！"

过了没多久，伯昏瞀人前去看望列御寇，看见门外摆满了鞋子。伯昏瞀人面朝北方站着，竖着拐杖撑住下巴，站了一会儿，一句话也没说就走出去了。接待宾客的人员告诉了列御寇，列御寇提着鞋子，光着脚就跑了出来，赶到门口，说："先生已经来了，为什么竟不说一句药石之言呢？"伯昏瞀人说："算了吧，我本来就告诉你说人们将会归附于你，现在果真大家都归附你了。这并不是说人们归附于你是对你的肯定，而是说你不能做到让人们不归附于你。你何必因此感到愉快而表现得与众不同呢！必定是内心有所触动方才会动摇你的本性，但这又无可奈何。依附你的人没有谁会告诫你，他们细巧迷惑的言辞，全是毒害人的，怎能互相审视、互相觉察、互相解悟呢！"

常可以听到这样的话：你很漂亮，像仙女下凡；你很有学问，听君一席话，胜读十年书。对诸如此类的话千万要保持几分清醒。庄子就提醒说，"好面誉人者，亦好背而毁之。"意思是喜欢当面说好话的人，也喜欢背后说人坏话。拿破仑讲的更明确，"善于阿谀奉承的人精于恶意中伤。"列御寇开始是清醒的，认为拍马猛于虎，所以逃得远远的，但后来列御寇就犯糊涂了，整天沉醉于他人的依附。看来，人总喜欢听好话，因为好话听了让人舒服。

FLATTERIES ARE POISONOUS

One day, a man named Lie Yukou went to the State of Qi. When he was half way there, he suddenly changed his mind and went back in a hurry. On his way back, he met his teacher Bohun Maoren, who asked him, "Why have you come back? What put you in such a hurry?" Lie Yukou said, "I had a shock just now, and was very frightened." Bohun Maoren asked again, "What happened? You look pale. What on earth made you so frightened?" Lie Yukou said, "I stopped at a small town to buy some water because I was thirsty. There were about ten shops selling water, but five of them sent me water for free before I even went to their shops." Bohun Maoren asked, "How would such things make you so frightened?" Lie Yukou answered, "The shop owners and I are total strangers, but they sent water to me without being asked to. The reason might be that I show my difference and superiority in front of others without being conscious of doing so, as I know a thing or two about the worldly goings-on. I might have worn a serious and important look in my face, which inspired a sense of awe in the common people and drew in the social climbers. By nature these are loyal people, but they are not free from the bonds of common fashions. They like to show off with their appearances and curry others' favors with exterior things. They believe in sucking up to the superior more than respecting the old. Their way of treating me with more deference than treating the elderly is sure to cause troubles. The water sellers are in small business, with not much money in it. If with meager profits and humble plans, the water sellers still manage to treat me like this, then the kings of the big states will do everything possible to keep me in their service. Serving those kings in running their states will make my body worn out and my wisdom exhausted. Those kings will entrust me with huge tasks and, expecting success, they will urge me to work hard and to make progress constantly. That was what made me so frightened that I left in a hurry without having any water." Having heard these, Bohun Maoren nodded his head several times and said, "Very good insight and very good analysis! Carry yourself as you do now, and the world will still gather around you."

Shortly afterwards when Bohun Maoren went to pay a visit to Lie Yukou, he saw many shoes lined up outside Lie Yukou's door. Bohun Maoren stood facing north, with his chin resting on the top of his walking stick, and after a while, he left without saying a word. After being informed of Bohun Maoren's arrival from the usher, Lie Yukou rushed out to the door bare-footed, with his shoes still in his hands, and said, "Now that Master has come, why don't you offer me instructive advice like medicines and stone needles?" Bohun Maoren said, "Forget about it! I told you that the world would gather around you. It is exactly what has happened. I am not saying that the world gather around you because you encourage them to. What I am saying is that you are not able to keep them from doing so. Why should you feel pleased with it and behave as if you are different from the rest? Inwardly you must have been stirred up, so the core of your nature is now agitated. But it cannot be helped. Since none of those who gather around you would admonish you and their enchanting and polished words are nothing but poison, how can you examine each other, warn each other and enlighten each other?"

We often hear people say that "You are so beautiful, like an angel descending to the earth" or "You are so learned that I gained more from talking to you than from ten years of reading". We must keep a level head when we hear flatteries like these. Zhuangzi warned, "He who likes to praise men to their face also likes to speak ill of them behind their back." Napoleon put it in a more specific way: "He who is good at flattering excels in malicious slandering." Lie Yukou was clear-headed at first. He believed that flattering was more deadly than ferocious tigers, so he fled. But later he lost his good sense and indulged in the headiness of being looked up to. So it seems that people all like to hear words of praise, which make them feel comfortable and contented.

39. 子贡求教老子

　　孔子拜见老聃回来后,好像总在思考什么问题,整整三天没讲一句话。弟子们觉得很奇怪,就问:"先生见到老聃,对他作了什么规劝?"孔子说:"可以说,通过与老聃的交谈,我才算见到了真正的龙!那龙,合在一起便成为一个整体,分散开来又成为华美的篇章,乘驾云气而养息于阴阳之间。那老聃就像一条龙,见到了他,我张大着嘴久久不能合拢,哪能对老聃作什么规劝呢!"子贡说:"照老师的说法,人难道会像尸体一样安稳不动,像飞龙一样显现,像疾雷一样震耳,像渊水那样沉寂,一举一动像天地那样运动变化的吗?我也想见见他,看看到底是怎么一回事。"看孔子没有反对,子贡就以孔子的名义去拜见老聃。

　　到了老聃的住处,老聃正伸腿坐在堂上,得知子贡的来意后,他轻声轻气地说:"我已经年老体迈,你打算用什么来告诫我呢?"子贡说:

"远古时代三皇五帝治理天下各不相同，然而却都有好的名声，唯独先生您不认为他们是圣人，这是为什么呢？"老聃说："年轻人，你稍稍近前些！你凭什么说他们各自有所不同？"子贡回答："尧让位给舜，舜让位给禹，禹用人力兴修水利，而汤用兵力征夏桀，文王顺从商纣不敢有所背逆，武王背逆商纣而不顺服，所以说各不相同。"老聃说："年轻人，你再稍微靠前些！我对你说说三皇五帝治理天下的事。黄帝治理天下，使人民心地淳厚保持本真，百姓有谁死了双亲而不哭泣，人们也不会加以非议。尧治理天下，使百姓敬重双亲，百姓为了敬重双亲，减去了一些繁琐的礼仪，人们也没有说这有什么不对。舜治理天下，使百姓心存竞争，怀孕的妇女十个月生下孩子，孩子生下五个月就张口学话，不等长到两三岁就开始识人，于是开始出现夭折短命的现象。禹治理天下，使百姓心怀狡诈，人人存有机变之心，因而动刀动枪成了理所当然之事，杀死盗贼不算杀人，人们各自结成团伙而肆意于天下，所以天下大受惊扰，儒家、墨家都纷纷而起。他们初始时也还有一点道理，可是时至今日就形同妇女，越来越离谱了，还有什么道理可言呢！我告诉你，三皇五帝治理天下，名义上叫做治理，而扰乱人性和真情没有什么比他们更严重的了。三皇五帝的智慧只不过是，对上遮掩了日月的光明，对下违背了山川的精粹，就中毁坏了四时的推移。他们的智慧比蛇蝎的尾巴、横冲直撞的野兽还毒狠，这些害人者失去了纯朴的天性，还自以为是圣人。不觉得可耻吗？他们太无耻了。"子贡听了惊惶不定，心神不安地站着。

　　中国有一个成语叫画蛇添足，意思是多此一举，反而坏事。蛇本来没有脚，画画的人却自以为聪明，加上几个脚，结果蛇不像蛇。儒家的仁义以及被称为经典的诗、书、礼、易、乐、春秋，在庄子看来就是蛇脚，用庄子的话来说，它扰乱人的本性，毒害人的真情，使人变得昏聩糊涂，智慧与大伪、智慧与大害就被捆绑在一起了。

ZI GONG SEEKS ADVICE FROM LAOZI

After a visit to Lao Dan (Laozi), Confucius returned home. For three days, he looked as if he was thinking about something important and didn't say a word. His disciples felt curious and asked, "What did Master say to admonish Lao Dan when Master saw him?" Confucius said, "I may say that after talking with him, I have actually seen a real dragon. When it solidifies itself, it forms a complete body; but when it dissipates, it seems to turn into splendid parts, riding on floating clouds, and nourishing on Yin and Yang. Lao Dan is just like a dragon. When I saw him, I kept my mouth open and was not able to shut it, let alone saying anything to admonish him." Zi Gong remarked, "Then according to Master, a man can be still like a corpse, and then make a sudden appearance like a flying dragon; a man can be loud like a flashing thunder and then be silent as a deep abyss, with every movement undergoing changes like Heaven and Earth, can't he? I would, too, like to go and visit him and see for myself what he is like." With no objections from Confucius, Zi Gong went to visit Lao Dan in the name of Confucius.

Having reached Lao Dan's place, Zi Gong found Lao Dan sitting in the hall, with legs stretched forward. After learning what Zi Gong had come for, Lao Dan said in a light and gentle voice, "I am old and weak. How do you plan to admonish me?" Zi Gong said, "The Three Sovereigns and the Five Emperors of the ancient times ran the world in their different ways, but they all enjoyed good reputation. Sir, you are the only one who doesn't regard them as sages. Can you tell me why it is so?" Lao Dan said, "Young man, come closer! On what ground do you say that they ran the world in different ways?" Zi Gong replied, "Yao passed the throne to Shun, and Shun passed it to Yu. Yu exerted himself in building irrigation works, while Tang deployed troops to conquer the evil King Jie of Xia. King Wen was obedient to the cruel King Zhou of Shang, not daring to rebel, while King Wu went against King Zhou of Shang, not willing to submit. So I say they employed different methods." Lao Dan said, "Young man, come still a little closer! Let me tell you how the Three Sovereigns and the Five Emperors ran the world. When the Yellow Emperor ran it, he made people pure and kind in both mind and heart. So if one didn't weep for his deceased parents, nobody blamed him. When Yao ran the world, he made people respectful of their parents. To show respect to his parents, one might eliminate some complicated rituals and ceremonies and nobody blamed him. When Shun ran the world, he made people think about competing against one another all the time. Pregnant women gave birth to their babies in the tenth month of their pregnancy. The babies started to learn to talk only five months after birth. Not after the babies reached the age of two or three did they learn to get involved in worldly affairs. So that was when people started to die young. When Yu ran the world, he made people's minds full of guile. Everybody began to think about scheming and plotting. They used weapons at will and killing robbers was not murder. People formed respective groups and roamed wild in the world. Therefore the world was scared and that was when the Confucians and Mohists all arose. At first, what they advocated sounded reasonable somehow. But by now, they have behaved like petty women and their preachings have become more and more ridiculous. What else is there to say? Let me tell you: What the Three Sovereigns and the Five Emperors did with the world was described as 'running the world', but that was only nominal. Nothing was greater than the disorder they brought to the human mind and heart by their so-called 'running the world'. The wisdom of the Three Sovereigns and the Five Emperors was just something to block the brightness of the sun and the moon above, to depart from the essence of the mountains and rivers below, and to disrupt the movement of the four seasons in between. Such 'wisdom' was more fatal than the poison of serpents and scorpions, or the marauding beasts of prey. Those who inflicted harms on people already lost their innocence in their nature, and yet they regarded themselves as sages. Was that something to be ashamed of? And they were shameless." At this, Zi Gong looked shaken, standing there ill at ease.

There is a Chinese idiom "Draw a snake and add feet to it", which means "to ruin a good work by adding something superfluous." A snake has no feet, but the painter thinks he knows better and adds a few feet, making the snake not like a snake. The ideas of benevolence and righteousness of Confucianism, the so-called Confucian classics like *Poetry*, *History*, *Changes*, *Music*, *Rites* and *Spring and Autumn*, are just like the snake feet in Zhuangzi's opinion, and in Zhuangzi's words, they disrupt people's nature and corrupt people's minds, making people confused and foolish. Great wisdom and downright hypocrisy, great wisdom and grave danger are thus bundled together to become the two sides of a coin.

40. 庄子卖鞋

庄子的名声很大,各国的诸侯、学者、名人,对庄子及其高深的学问几乎无人不晓,但他由于他的清高和固执,生活状况越来越差,主要靠抓鱼维持生计,收入不多,也不稳定,有时还会吃了上顿没有下顿。

一天,庄子和他的学生去河边钓鱼,钓了半天,鱼钩一动不动,就是不见鱼儿上钩。庄子两眼盯着水面,一言不发,琢磨着如何解决吃饭问题。忽然,学生用手指着一望无际的茫茫葛草说:"先生,这葛草取之不尽,用之不竭,我们何不靠采葛编织来养家呢?"庄子一听,连声称好,二人说干就干,采了两大捆葛草背上回家了。一到家,两家就开始一起动手,很快就编织了不少鞋子。第二天一早,庄子就提着鞋子到市场叫卖,虽然是小生意,但由于人人都用得上,再加上庄子名气大,又务实,没有什么虚荣心,因此只要他去卖,许多人都慕名去买,供不应求,生意越做越红火,两家人的生活渐渐地好起来。

大学问家庄子在家乡卖鞋的事不久就传开了,宋王听说后,觉得很不光彩。因为爱士是当时的时尚,庄子卖鞋就等于往他脸上抹黑。

于是宋王就派官员装载了一车食品,去慰问庄子,一路上招摇过市以示礼贤下士。那官员来到庄子家,对前来迎接的庄子说,"国君听说庄周先生生计艰难.特派我送上一车粟,请先生笑纳。国君还说,如先生愿意,国君可以委你以要职,也可任原来的漆园吏。"说着就送上了国君的亲笔邀请信。庄子接过信,看也没看就说:"庄周老矣,难以胜任任何之职,也决不取无功之粟,谢谢了,请君返回吧!"说完就转身回屋了。那官员听了目瞪口呆,想不到当今世界上竟有这样的事——对送上门来的人们趋之若鹜的东西,他都弃之不要。

后来,庄子的一个老同学鲁商衣锦还乡,特来拜访庄子。他看到生活艰难的庄子,神气活现、洋洋自得地说:"庄周兄,你看到我的成片的马车了吗?我作为宋国使者去见秦王,凭三寸不烂之舌,我曲意逢迎,秦王待我为上宾,并与我同寝同食,寸步不离,我离开时,秦王破例赐我百乘马车。像我这样,一见万乘之主,就得百乘之车,这就是我的长处。要说身居偏僻狭窄的里巷,贫困到要靠自己编织麻鞋,脖颈干瘪面色饥黄,这我可比不上你。"

面对鲁商的浅薄,庄子慢吞吞地说:"听说秦王有病,召请属下的医生,凡破出脓疮溃散疖子的人可获得车辆一乘,舔治痔疮的人可获得车辆五乘,凡是疗治的部位越是低下,所能获得的车辆就越多。你难道给秦王舔过痔疮吗?要不然,秦王奖赏给你的车辆会这么多吗?算了吧,你还是走吧!"

不为五斗米折腰,可说是庄子人格的写照。不是我的,送给我的我都不要,我要的只是本来就应该属于我的东西。人如果有了分外之想,就会做出舔痔得车的丑陋之举。社会上总有一些人,是不以舔痔为丑的,因为舔痔好像也是一种水平、一种能力,今天他替别人舔痔,是为了以后别人替他舔痔。社会应该铲除产生形形色色"舔痔"一类丑恶现象的土壤。

ZHUANGZI SELLS SANDALS

Zhuangzi enjoyed great fame. Dukes and princes, scholars and celebrities all knew about him and his sophisticated learning. But because of his aloofness and stubbornness, he suffered from worsening destitution. He had to live on fishing, which brought in a small and unstable income. Sometimes he even had to worry about where the next meal was coming from.

One day, Zhuangzi and his disciple went fishing by the river banks. But after quite some time, the fishing rod still remained motionless, without even one fish taking a bite. Zhuangzi fixed his eyes on the water, and instead of saying anything, he was thinking about the food problem. Suddenly, his disciple pointed at the hemp field stretching endlessly ahead and said, "Master, the hemp field is inexhaustible. Why don't we pick some and make a living on weaving?" Hearing the suggestion from his disciple, Zhuangzi replied with a chorus of "good". They immediately took action and set about picking the hemp. Then they carried two bundles of hemp on their back and returned home. Once back, the two families got together to weave sandals. Soon they had made many. Early next morning, Zhuangzi took the sandals to the market. Zhuangzi was very pragmatic in doing business, which, together with his big fame, brought him many buyers. A lot of people went to buy his sandals out of admiration for him. Small though the business was, it was doing very well and sometimes even could not keep up with the demand. As a result, the life of the two families was getting better gradually.

Soon the word got around that Zhuangzi, the great scholar, was selling sandals at his hometown in the State of Song. The King of Song heard of it and felt that he had lost his face, for it was the fashion at that time for the monarchs to appreciate talents. So the fact that Zhuangzi was selling sandals brought shame on the king. Therefore, the king sent an official to visit Zhuangzi with a cartload of food. The government procession went over the streets ostentatiously to show that they treated talented people with courtesy. Having got to Zhuangzi's house, the official said to Zhuangzi who was coming towards him, "Our king has heard that Master Zhuang Zhou lives a hard life. So he asked me especially to send you a cartload of grains. Please kindly accept. Our king also said that if Master so willing, you would be entrusted with an important post, or you could take up once again the position as an official in the garden of lacquer trees." With this, the official presented the letter of invitation written by the king himself. Zhuangzi took it over and without taking one look at it, he said, "Zhuang Zhou is old now, and no longer competent to hold any official positions. Nor is Zhuang Zhou able to take the grains which Zhuang Zhou has done nothing to earn. Thank you. Please go back to the king." After this, Zhuangzi turned and went into the house. The official was dumbfounded, unable to believe that there was such thing in the present world – saying no to something that people scrambled for but that was handed to him in a platter.

Later, Lu Shang, a former schoolmate of Zhuangzi, returned to his hometown in silk robes after acquiring wealth and power. He went to visit Zhuangzi. Having seen Zhuangzi's hard living conditions, he glowed with pride and said complacently, "Brother Zhuang Zhou, have you seen the great many carriages of mine? I was sent as an envoy of the State of Song to pay a formal visit to the King of Qin at his court. I acted obsequiously and offered flatteries. The king was so pleased with my silver tongue that he regarded me as his distinguished guest and spent most of his time with me, having meals and even sharing sleeping chamber with me. When it was time for my departure, the King of Qin made an exception and bestowed on me a hundred carriages. Now look at me: I paid a visit to a king of ten thousand carriages, and left with a hundred of my own. This is what I call my advantage. As for living in a narrow and obscure lane, reduced to such poverty as surviving on making sandals, with a shriveled neck and a yellow and hungry look, this I cannot compare with you."

In face of the shallowness displayed by Lu Shang, Zhuangzi said slowly, "I have heard that the King of Qin was ill and he summoned doctors to cure the illness. He who cut open an ulcer and squeezed out a boil would get a carriage; he who licked the king's piles would get five. The lower the parts being treated, the bigger the number of carriages would be given as a reward. Have you licked the piles of the King of Qin? How else should he have bestowed on you so many carriages? All right, you'd better go away."

"Not bowing for five *dou* (a measure unit) of grains" can be regarded as the portrayal of Zhuangzi's personality: I refuse to accept what is not rightly mine, even if it is handed to me in a platter; what I want is only what I am entitled to. If one has inordinate ambitions, one is likely to be reduced to performing such ugly acts like getting carriages by licking piles. There have always been some people in the world who believe there is nothing disgraceful with licking piles, for it represents a certain level and ability. Licking other's piles today is to make others lick his in the future. We believe that such a practical environment which encourages vices like licking piles should be absolutely eliminated.

41. 徐无鬼相面

徐无鬼是魏国的隐士,经魏国女商的引荐去晋见魏武侯,武侯慰问他说:"先生居住在山林,吃的是橡子,满足于葱韭之类的菜蔬,而谢绝与我交往,已经很久很久了!如今是上了年岁吗?还是为了寻求酒肉之类的美味呢?抑或有什么治国的良策而造福于我的国家吗?是不是需要我的慰问?"徐无鬼说:"我出身贫贱,不敢奢望能够享用国君的酒肉美食,我是来慰问你的。君王如果充满了嗜好和欲望,增多了喜好和憎恶,那么你的心灵就会疲惫不堪,性命就会受到损害;你想要废弃嗜好和欲望,退却喜好和憎恶,那么耳目声色的享用就会受到妨碍。我本来是慰问君王来了,君王又有什么要慰问我的!"武侯听了怅然若失,一时回答不上来。

不一会儿,徐无鬼转了一个话题,他对武侯说:"我会相面,会替狗相面,替马相面。"武侯眼睛一亮,马上要了解个究竟。于是,徐无鬼就细细地说开了,"我善于观察狗的体态以确定它们的优劣。下品的狗只求填饱肚子,有吃就可以了,这是跟野猫一样的禀性;中品的狗心志高昂,总是凝视上方;上品的狗精神镇定,不在意自身的存在。其实,我相狗的技艺不如我相马的技艺高明。我观察马的体态,应该平直的地方要像拉紧的墨线一样,应该弯曲的地方要像钩子一样,应该方正的地方要像矩尺一样,应该圆的地方要像圆规画出来一样,这样的马就是国马,不过还比不上天下最好的马。天下最好的马具有天生的材质,或若有所思地缓步,或神采奕奕地奔跑,总像是忘记了自己的身体,超越马群,疾如狂风,把尘土远远留在身后,却不知道这样高超的本领从哪里得来。"魏武侯听了高兴得笑了起来。

　　徐无鬼走出宫廷,女商问:"先生究竟是用什么办法使国君高兴的呢?我用来使国君高兴的办法是,从远处说,向他介绍诗、书、礼、乐,从近处说,向他谈论太公兵法。侍奉国君而大有功绩的人不可计数,而国君从来没有笑过。如今你究竟用什么办法来取悦国君,竟使国君如此高兴呢?"徐无鬼说:"我只不过告诉他我怎么相狗、相马罢了。"女商觉得不可思议,问:"就是这样吗?"徐无鬼说:"你没有听说过那被流放到远方的人的故事吗?离开都城几天,见到故交旧友便十分高兴;离开都城十天整月,见到在国都中所曾经见到过的人便大喜过望;等到过了一年,见到好像是同乡的人便欣喜若狂;不就是离开故人越久,思念故人的情意越深吗?那逃亡在山洞里的人,丛生的野草堵塞了黄鼠狼出入的路径,他在洞里住久了,听到人的脚步声就高兴起来,更何况是兄弟亲戚在身边说笑呢?国君能够开心地说笑,是因为很久很久没有听到'真人'纯朴的话语了!"

　　中国有一个成语叫对牛弹琴,人们一般用来批评牛的愚蠢,因为它听不懂琴声。其实,牛听不懂琴声的原因是多方面的,至少与弹琴的主体有关,否则就不会有乱弹琴之说。徐无鬼的相面术所以成功,就在于他知己知彼。解决人的问题,一定要具体分析他的身份、地位、教养、性格、情感等,对不同的人采取不同的方法。

XU WUGUI READS APPEARANCES

Xu Wugui, a recluse of the State of Wei, went to pay a formal visit to Marquis Wu of Wei on the recommendation of an official Nü Shang. The marquis said to Xu Wugui in sympathy, "Master has been living in wooded mountains for a long time, all the while declining my association and being content with acorns as main food and vegetables as onions and chives. Now is it because you are getting on with your years, or because you wish to have good wine or delicious meat, or because you have some good strategies on governing which can benefit my country, or because you desire my sympathy and comfort, that you are here today?" Xu Wugui replied, "I was born in a poor and humble state, and have never dreamed of enjoying your lordship's good wine and delicious meat. I am here to offer my sympathy and comfort. If your lordship has many addictions and desires, and has developed more likes and dislikes with the passage of time, you will feel exhausted in both your body and your mind, and your life will be harmed as a result. If you want to get rid of the addictions and desires, and to reduce the number of likes and dislikes, the enjoyment brought by your senses of perception will be hindered. Therefore I come to offer my sympathy and my comfort. What does your lordship have to comfort me for?" At this, Marquis Wu looked lost and didn't say anything.

After a while, Xu Wugui said to Marquis Wu on another topic, "I can read people's characters by looking at their faces. I can do it for dogs and horses too." The eyes of Marquis Wu suddenly lit up. He wanted to find out everything about it at once. So Xu Wugui explained slowly, "I am good at observing the postures of dogs to determine their worthiness. The inferior type seeks only a full stomach. It goes as far as where the food is and stops – the same attributes found in wild cats. The medium type is high-spirited and high-minded, always staring up at the sky. The superior type looks very composed, not caring about its self-existence. In fact, I don't size up dogs as well as I do horses. I observe the postures of horses. The straight parts of a horse should be like an ink line stretched tight, the curvy parts should be like hooks, the square parts should be like squares, and the round parts should be like circles drawn by bow compasses. These are the horses of the state. But they are still not equal to the best horses of the world, which, with their naturally born qualities, now saunter as if worried, and then gallop in high spirits, always looking as if they have forgotten their mortal beings. They race as a gust of wind to overtake other horses, leaving thick dust far behind, and doesn't know at all where such superb abilities come from." Marquis Wu was greatly pleased at this and laughed.

After Xu Wugui walked out of the court, Nü Shang asked him, "What did Master do to cheer up the marquis? When I was with the marquis, I discussed ancient times with him, introducing books of *Poetry*, *History*, *Rites* and *Music*. The topic on more recent times would be Lord Jiang's *Art of War*. I have never seen the marquis laugh before, though many of those who wait on him have been rewarded for their notable good deeds. Now what exactly have you done to please the marquis, to make him so delighted?" Xu Wugui replied, "I simply told him how I size up dogs and horses by observing their appearances." Nü Shang found it unbelievable and asked, "That was it?" Xu Wugui said, "Have you not heard of the story about the man who had been exiled to faraway places? Just a few days away from the capital, he was very pleased when he met anyone he had known before. Ten days or one month away from the capital, he was very happy when he saw anyone he had seen before. One year away, he was beside himself with joy when he saw anyone who looked like a fellow countryman. The longer he was away, the more affectionately he thought of his own people. Isn't it like that? Those who fled and took refuge in caves, where clusters of wildly-grown weeds were so thick that they blocked out the paths of weasels, became happy when they heard the footsteps of men, because they had been living in caves for so long. What if it was their brothers and relatives talking and laughing by their side?

Today the marquis laughed heartily while he was talking. That is because he hasn't heard the honest words from a True Man for such a long time."

"Playing the lute to a cow" is a Chinese idiom, used by people to ridicule the foolishness of the cow, for it can't understand the music played on the lute. In fact, there are many reasons why a cow can't understand the music. At least the lute player has to be more careful in selecting his audience, otherwise he will be called "playing the lute like a fool". The reason why Xu Wugui succeeded with his theory of reading appearances was because he understood the importance of knowing himself and his audience. When dealing with matters of people, we must analyze the people's identity, status, breeding, personality and emotional states, etc. Different solutions should be applied to different people.

42. 孔子求道

孔子活了五十一岁还没有听说过什么叫大道,于是就去南方的沛地拜见老聃(老子)。老子说:"你来了?我听说你是北方的贤者,你恐怕已经领悟了大道吧?"孔子回答说:"到现在还没有呢。"老子问:"那你是怎样寻求大道的呢?"孔子说:"从上下贵贱的等级到法律条文的制订,从百官依次行事的各级条款到具体的制度措施,所有这些方面我都花了很大的力气,千方百计地在寻找道,但用了五年的功夫依然没有得到。"老子说:"那后来你又是用什么方法来寻求大道呢?"孔子说:"我想可能是我的做法不对,后来改从阴阳的变化来寻求道,但找了十二年还是未能得到道。"老子说:"是这样的。假使道可以用来晋献,那么谁都会向国君晋献大道;假使道可以用来传授,那么谁都会向自己的双亲传授大道;假使道可以告知他人,那么谁都会告诉给他的兄弟;假使道可以给与,那么谁都会用来给与他的子孙。但这都是不可能的。所以不可以这样做的原因，不是别的，就是内心没有主宰就不能自持，不能自持大道就不能停留；外界没有辅助，就不能产生共鸣，没有共鸣大道就不能推行。从内心发出的东西，倘若不能为外者所接受，圣人也就不会有所传教；从外部进入内心的东西，倘若心中无所领悟而不能接受的话，圣人也不会放在心上的。名声，乃是人人都可使用的器物，不可过多猎取；仁义，乃是前代帝王的馆舍，可以临时住上一宿但不可以久居，老是沉醉于名誉仁义之中必然会生出许多责难。"

"古代道德修养很高的人，借助于仁作为自己的道路，义也只是暂时居住的处所，而游乐于自由自在、无拘无束的境域，生活于马虎简单、朴实无华的境地，立身于粗茶淡饭、自给自足的田园。自由自在、无拘无束，便是无为；马虎简单、朴实无华，就易于生存；粗茶淡饭就容易服养，自满自足就不需要输出。古代把这种情况叫做本色全真的遨游。把富足看作人的价值，就不会推让利禄；把追求显赫看作人的价值，就不会推让名声；把权势地位看作人的价值，就不会授权于人。掌握了利禄、名声和权位，就唯恐丧失而整日惶惶不安；丢弃这些东西，又会悲伤痛苦。而对上述利害一无察觉，眼睛只盯住自己不断追求的权势名利，这样的人无异于自杀，是大自然所要刑戮的人。怨恨、恩惠、获取、施与、谏诤、教化、生养、杀戮，这八项全是用来整治天下的工具，只有遵循自然的变化而无所滞碍的人才能够运用。所以说，所谓正，就是使人端正。如果内心里认为不是这样，那么心灵的门户就永远不可能打开。"

孔子求道，牵涉到价值观的问题。儒家入世，说的是修身、齐家、治国、平天下，而利禄、名声、权位则是入世成功与否的标准，是人生的归宿。而庄子与此不同，他要人追求的是安贫乐道、自由自在、朴实无华的生活，与人的内在本性相一致的生活。附带说明的是，孔子求道这个故事，可以看到百家争鸣、互相渗透的痕迹，庄子虽然认为阴阳、度数、仁义这些法家、墨家、儒家的理论是不可取的，但作为实现大道的工具，还是可用的。

CONFUCIUS SEEKS TAO

When Confucius reached the age of fifty-one, he still had not learned what was called Tao. So he went south to a place called Pei to visit Lao Dan (Laozi). Lao Dan said, "So you have come. I hear that you are considered a wise person in the north. You must have already gained the understanding of Tao." Confucius answered, "So far I have not." Lao Dan asked, "Then how have you been looking for it?" Confucius replied, "From the ranking of social status to the establishment of laws and statutes, from the arrangement of responsibilities for different official positions to the employment of detailed systems and measures, I had been looking for the understanding of Tao. But five years had passed, and I still hadn't gained it." Lao Dan asked again, "Then after that, what have you been doing to seek Tao?" Confucius said, "I thought that my way of searching might not be the right one. So I later changed to searching for Tao from the changes of Yin and Yang. But twelve years have passed, and I still haven't found it." Lao Dan said, "It is like this. If Tao could be presented as an offering, then anyone would offer it to their kings. If Tao could be taught, then anyone would teach it to their parents. If Tao could be told to others, then anyone would tell it to his brothers. If Tao could be given, then anyone would give it to his offspring. But all these are impossible. The reason is simple: one can't be self-possessed if one is not in control of one's heart, and without self-possession, one is not able to stay on the Way (Tao); with no external assistance, one is not able to find an echo in one's heart, and without an echo, one is not able to proceed on the Way (Tao). If what's put forth from the inside isn't received by those on the outside, the sage won't pass it on. If it enters from the outside but isn't understood and received within, the sage won't bother about it. Fame is a tool to be used by everybody, but it can't be sought for in excess. Benevolence and righteousness are palaces of former sovereigns and emperors, where one can spend one night but not for long stay. If one is addicted to fame, benevolence and righteousness, one is sure to incur many reproaches."

"In ancient times, people of high moral levels took benevolence merely as their path, and regarded righteousness as a temporary place where they stayed briefly. They traveled in the realm of freedom and complete ease, leading a life of simplicity without any luxuries or glories, dwelling in self-reliant gardens and living on plain food. Being free of restraints means non-action; simplicity without luxuries or glories makes it easier to survive; plain food makes it easy to feed; self-reliance makes output unnecessary. In ancient times, this was called 'traveling freely with the true nature'. If affluence is regarded as the value of man, then one will not decline wealth and ranks; if prestige is regarded as the value of man, then one will not decline fame. If power and status are regarded as the value of man, then one won't entrust others with his authority. With wealth, fame, power and status, one would be worried and restless, afraid of losing all; but without the above, one would feel grieved and painful. If one is unaware of the above harms, he will fix his eyes on wealth, fame, power and status, and never stop until he gets his hand on them; such behavior is no different from committing suicide and such people are whom the nature is out to kill. The eight items, hatred and favor, receiving and giving, criticizing and teaching, and life and death, are all the tools of governing the world, available only to those who are able to follow along the changes of nature without being tied down. So it is said that the so-called correction is making others correct. If one doesn't believe so in his heart, then the gates of the soul will never open for him."

Confucius's pursuit of the understanding of Tao touches upon the issue of moral values. A relatively "practical" school, Confucianism preaches about cultivating morals, regulating the family, governing the country and establishing peace throughout the world. Wealth, fame, power and status are regarded as the standards against which one is to measure one's success in the world and as the ultimate goal of one's life. But Zhuangzi thought differently. He wanted people to seek a simple and free life with enjoyment found in Tao, a life in harmony with one's nature, and be content with it. By the way, from the story of Confucius seeking Tao, we can identify traces of "100 Schools of Thought" contending and influencing one another. Zhuangzi believed that although such Legalist, Mohist and Confucian theories as Yin and Yang, measurements and numbers, and benevolence and righteousness were not advisable, they were usable as tools in achieving Great Tao.

43. 鲁太师谈孔子西游

孔子要带弟子到西边的卫国去游说,颜渊去请教鲁国的金太师,问:"您认为我老师此次卫国之行怎么样?"太师说:"可惜呀,你先生一定会遭殃!"颜渊问:"为什么呢?"太师说:"用草扎成的狗还没有用于祭祀时,一定会用竹制的箱笼来装着,用绣有图纹的饰物盖着,由祭祀的主持斋戒后迎送着。等到祭祀结束,它的用处已经没有了,行路人会随便踩踏它的头颅和脊背,拾草的人捡回去用于烧火煮饭。如果有人再把它取回来,拿竹筐装着它,拿绣有图纹的饰物披着它,像祭祀的时候那样跪在它的下面,即使他不做恶梦,也会一次又一次地感受到梦魇似的压抑。这是因为事情已经过去了,已经不是原来的那个时间了。如今孔子如同拿着先王已经用于祭祀的草扎之狗,并聚集众多弟子向它跪拜。所以宋人砍伐了他讲习礼法的大树,在卫国游说受到阻止,在殷地和东周游说遭到围困,这不就是在做那样的恶梦吗?在陈国和蔡国之间遭到围困，整整七天没有能生火就食，让死和生成了近邻，这又不就是那压得人喘不过气来的梦魇吗？如今他还要宣传他的那套仁义，不是在自寻烦恼吗？大家都知道，水上通行船是最快的了，陆地上行走车是最好的了，如果把水中划行的船放在陆地上推着走，那么一辈子也走不了多远。古今的不同不就像是水面和陆地的差异那样吗？周和鲁的差异不就像是船和车的不同吗？如今一心想在鲁国推行周王室的治理办法，这就像是在陆地上推船而行，徒劳无功，自身也难免遭受祸殃。他们不懂得运动变化是不固定的，必须顺应无穷事物的道理。"

"况且，你没有看见那吊杆汲水的情景吗？拉起它的一端，另一端便俯身临近水面，放下它的一端，另一端就高高仰起。那吊杆的起降，是因为人的牵引，并非它牵引了人，所以不管怎样都归罪不了它。三皇五帝时代的礼义法度之所以受到推崇，不在于古今相同上，而是在于它们都适合当时的情况进行治理。如果要拿三皇五帝时代的礼义法度来打比方，就像柤、梨、橘、柚这四种酸甜不一的果子，它们的味道彼此不同，然而都很可口。"

"所以，礼义法度，都是顺应时代而有所变化的东西。如今捕捉到猿猴，给它穿上周公的衣服，它必定会咬碎或撕裂，直到全部剥光身上的衣服方才心满意足。观察古今的差异，就像猿猴不同于周公。从前西施心口疼痛而皱着眉头在邻里间行走，邻里的一个丑女人看见了认为皱着眉头很美，回去后也在邻里间捂着胸口皱着眉头。邻里的有钱人看见了，紧闭家门而不出；贫穷的人看见了，带着妻儿子女远远地跑开了。那个丑女人只知道皱着眉头好看，却不知道皱着眉头好看的原因。"

说到这里，鲁太师摇摇头，又重复了前面说过的话，"可惜呀，你的先生一定会遭殃啊！"

如果有人要你回答：下雨是好事还是坏事？你是回答不上来的，因为好与坏离不开特定的条件。任何事物都是在一定的空间与时间中运动发展的，如果以不变应万变，不讲主客观的条件，不讲具体的历史环境，不管你的出发点是好是坏，就一定会碰钉子。故事中讲的东施，犯的就是这种错误，据此，就有了"东施效颦"的成语。

A COMMENT ON CONFUCIUS'S TRAVEL TO THE WEST

Confucius was about to take a tour to the State of Wei in the west in the company of his disciples. Yan Yuan, one of the disciples, went to seek advice from the prime minister of the State of Lu. Yan Yuan asked, "What do you think of my Master's trip to the State of Wei?" The prime minister said, "What a pity that your Master is going to suffer!" "How is it so?" Yan Yuan asked. The prime minister answered, "Before a straw dog is offered in sacrifice, it is put in a bamboo box and covered with embroidered cloth. Then it will be presented by the master of the sacrifice after a period of fasting. When the sacrifice is over, the straw dog has no use at all. Passers-by may tread carelessly on its head and back, and grass-pickers may pick it up and throw it in fire for cooking. If someone should once again put it in a bamboo box, cover it with embroidered cloth, and kneel under it like at the time of sacrifice, he would be plagued or burdened by nightmares again and again. That's because the event of the straw dog's sacrifice is now over and it is no longer the right time. Now what Confucius does is just like keeping the straw dog used by the former kings in the sacrifices and making many disciples kneel before it in worship. No wonder the tree under which he preached rituals and ceremonies was cut down by people in the State of Song. He was interrupted in his teaching in the State of Wei, and he was surrounded in Ying and East Zhou. Aren't these like nightmares? When besieged between the State of Chen and the State of Cai, he had not been able to light a fire for cooking for seven days, making death a close neighbor to the alive. Isn't that like the suffocating burden of nightmares? Now he still wants to preach his theories of benevolence and righteousness. Isn't he asking for trouble? It is known that for traveling on water, nothing is faster than a boat; for moving on the land, nothing is better than a cart. But if you put a boat on the land and push it forward, then for all your life you won't get far. Isn't the difference between the ancient times and the present world just like that between water and land? Isn't the difference between the Zhou Dynasty and the State of Lu just like that between a boat and a cart? Being bent on teaching the ways of running the world used by the Zhou Dynasty to the State of Lu is like pushing a boat on dry land – futile and sure to cause troubles for themselves. What they don't understand is that the movements and changes are unpredictable, so men must adapt themselves to myriads of things."

"Furthermore, haven't you seen the contraption called well-sweep drawing water? When one end is pulled up, the other end is lowered to the water; when one end is lowered, the other is raised high. The well-sweep is manipulated by men, not the other way round. Therefore, whatever happens, the well-sweep itself is not to be blamed. The canons of propriety, righteousness, laws and measures of the Three Sovereigns and the Five Emperors are held in high regard not because they are applicable both in ancient times and now, but because they had ways of governing which fitted the situation at that time. If the canons of propriety, righteousness, laws and measures of the Three Sovereigns and the Five Emperors are to be explained in an analogy, they are just like four different fruits — the cherry-apple, the pear, the orange, and the pomelo, different in taste but equally delicious."

"So it follows that propriety, righteousness, laws and measures should change in accordance with the time. If we catch a monkey and dress it in the robes of the Duke of Zhou, it will bite and tear at the robes; it will not be satisfied until it strips off every piece of clothing on itself. If we take a look at the difference between the past and the present, we will find that it is as great as the difference between the monkey and the Duke of Zhou. When the famous beauty Xi Shi walked in the neighborhood with her brows knitted because she was suffering from chest pains, an ugly woman saw it and concluded that knitted brows looked beautiful. So after she returned home, she knitted her brows and put her hands on her chest when she walked in the neighborhood. When the rich people saw her, they shut their doors fast and would not go out; when the poor people saw her, they ran away with their wives and children. The ugly woman knew only that knitted brows looked beautiful but not why it was so."

At this point, the prime minister of the State of Lu shook his head and repeated what he had said before, "What a pity! Your Master is going to suffer."

If someone asks you whether it is good or bad to rain, surely you are not able to give an answer, for whether a rain is good or bad cannot be determined without the relevant conditions. Everything moves and develops within a particular space and time period. If you cope with every changing situation by relying on a fixed set of principles regardless of the relevant subjective and objective conditions or the specific historical environment, you are bound to encounter troubles, no matter how good your intentions might be. The mistake made by the ugly woman in copycatting Xi Shi belongs to this kind, and from that story derives the idiom "The ugly woman copycats Xi Shi's knitted brows", meaning "bad imitation with ludicrous effect".

44. 被砍去一只脚的人

鲁国有个被砍掉一只脚的人,名叫王骀,他虽然身体残疾,可是跟从他学习的人却跟孔子的门徒一样多。孔子的学生常季向孔子问道:"王骀是个被砍去一只脚的人,在鲁国跟从他学习的人数却和先生的弟子相当。他站着不能上课,坐着不能议论大事;学生们去的时候空空而来,回去时满载而归。难道确有不用说话就能使学生无形中从内心领会的吗?这又是一种什么样的人呢?"孔子回答说:"王骀先生是一位圣人,我的学识和品行都落后于他,只是还没有前去请教他罢了。我都把他当作老师,何况那些学识和品行都不如我孔丘的人呢!何止是鲁国,我将引领天下的人跟从他学习。"

常季说:"他是一个被砍去了一只脚的人,而学识和品行竟超过了先生,跟平常人相比距离就更大了。像这样的人,他运用心智是怎样与众不同的呢?"孔子回答说:"人的死生都是人生变化中的大事了,可是死或生都不能使他随之变化；即使天塌地陷，他也不会因此而丧失、毁灭。他通晓天地的运行不息，但并不随物变迁，他明察天地万物的无穷变化，因而信守自己的根本。"常季说："这是什么缘故呢？"孔子说："从事物差异的角度去看，邻近的肝胆虽同处于一体，但也像楚国和越国那样相距很远；从事物相同的角度去看，万事万物又都是同一的。这样的人，不知道耳朵眼睛最适宜何种声音和色彩，而让自己的心思自由自在地遨游在和顺的道德境域中。对于外物，看到了它同一的方面就看不到它所失去的，这样，丧失了一只脚就像是丢失了一块泥土一样。"

常季说："王骀运用自己的智慧来认识自己的心灵，提高自己的道德修养，他运用自己的心灵来领悟天道。如果这是一种自我修养，并非专门教人，那么，众多的弟子为什么还追随他，聚集在他的身边呢？"孔子回答说："一个人要照见自己的身影，不能面向流动的水面，而必须是静止的水面，只有本身是静止的，才能使别的事物也静止下来。各种树木都受命于大地而生，但只有松树、柏树得天地的真性，无论春夏秋冬都郁郁青青；每个人都受命于天而生，但只有虞舜得上天的真性，道德品行最为端正，故成为万民之首。幸而松柏、虞舜都善于使自己的品行端正，因而能端正他人的品行。那些能够保全本初的人，具有无所畏惧的品格，即使勇士一人，也敢直冲敌人千军万马之阵。为了追求功名而要求自己的人尚且能够这样，更何况那主宰天地、包藏万物，只不过把躯体当作寓所，把耳目当作外表，掌握了自然赋予的智慧，精神世界又一直充满活力的人呢！不久他将选择一个好日子升登最高的境界，人们将紧紧地跟随着他。他哪里肯把世俗的琐屑当作一回事呢！"

一个外貌丑陋的人，可以是心灵美丽的人；一个身体残废的人，可以是人格高尚的人。外表与内心、现象与本质的联系常常是多样的、复杂的，有时甚至是相反的。这就要求我们区分什么是现象，什么是本质，怎样才能透过现象抓本质。

THE MAN WITH ONE FOOT CUT OFF

In the State of Lu, there was a man called Wang Tai, who had had one of his feet cut off. However, his disciples were as many as those of Confucius. Chang Ji, one of Confucius's disciples, asked Confucius, "Wang Tai, whose one foot was cut off, has as many disciples in the State of Lu as you, Master. When standing, he cannot teach; when sitting, he cannot discuss. His disciples go there empty-handed but return home full and content. Is there such kind of teaching which has no need for words but communicates through hearts imperceptibly? What kind of master is that?" Confucius answered, "Master Wang Tai is a sage, whose learning and moral integrity are superior to mine. It is just that I have been late in seeking his advice. And even I regard him as my Master, let alone those whose learning and moral integrity are far inferior to mine! It is not just the people in the State of Lu; I shall lead all the people in the world to learn from him."

Chang Ji said, "He is a man with one foot cut off and yet his learning and moral integrity are superior to you, Master. How great will the gap be when he is compared with ordinary people? How do people like him manage to employ their mind and heart in ways that make them extraordinary?" Confucius answered, "Life and death, though big considerations in a lifetime, are not able to make him change accordingly. Even if the sky and the earth were to crash and fall, he would not be damaged and lost. He is familiar with the constant and forever-lasting circulation of Heaven and Earth, and yet he does not drift with the changes of things. He is perceptive of the infinite changes of the myriads of things between Heaven and Earth, yet he keeps a fast hold of his very core." Chang Ji asked, "What is the reason for that?" Confucius said, "In so far as there are differences among things, the liver and the gall bladder, though in one body and close to each other, are as far apart as the State of Chu and the State of Yue; in so far as things are similar, the myriads of things and matters are one and the same. People like Wang Tai don't know what sound and color suit their ears and eyes the best, but let their mind float freely along with the harmonious environment of virtues. As for external things, they look at the unity of all, not paying attention to what is missing. So it follows that losing one foot is just like losing a piece of mud."

Chang Ji said, "With the help of his wisdom, Wang Tai perceives his mind and improves his moral cultivation; with the help of the perception of his mind, Wang Tai gains an understanding of the Tao of Heaven. If it is a kind of self-cultivation, not to be taught to others, then why are so many disciples still following him and gathering around him?" Confucius answered, "One sees one's reflections not in running water, but in still water. For only what is still in itself is able to still others. Of all the trees which owe their lives to the earth, only the pine and the cypress have obtained the essence from Heaven and Earth, staying green regardless of the changes of seasons. Of all the men whose lives are decided by Heaven, only Shun has obtained the essence from Heaven, being perfect in his virtues and conducts, therefore becoming the leader of all people. It is fortunate that they were good at perfecting their own conducts and therefore were able to help perfect the conducts of others. Those who can remain true to their original endowments are blessed with qualities as courage and fearlessness. Even when left on his own, he is brave enough to charge into a whole army of thousands of soldiers and horses. If a man who seeks fame can make demands of moral improvement upon himself like thus, how much more can come from a man who is in control of Heaven and Earth, who takes myriads of things in his stride, who regards the bodily form as the dwelling place and the ears and eyes as external appearance only, and who acquires the wisdom endowed by the nature and has a busy and energetic spiritual world? Soon he is going to pick a good day when he will ascend onto the higher realm and people will flock to follow him closely. For such a man, why would he concern himself with the trivia of the world?"

An ugly man may have a beautiful heart; a deformed man may be blessed with noble qualities. The relationship between the exterior and the interior, between the phenomenon and the nature, is often diversified and complicated instead of straightforward. What is implied beneath may sometimes run completely counter to what is perceived outwardly. Therefore, it is necessary for us to distinguish between the phenomenon and the nature and to grasp the nature amid a plethora of phenomena.

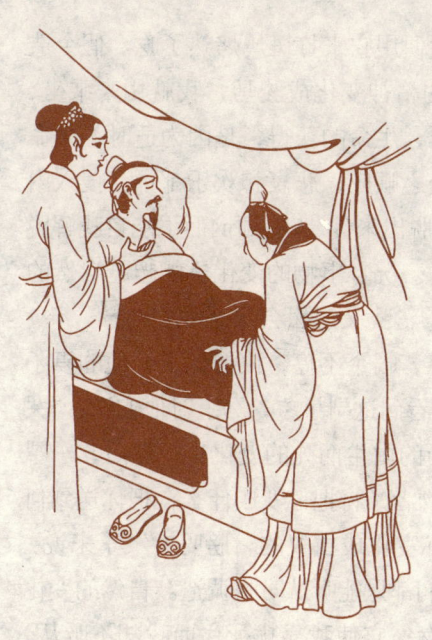

45. 四大奇人

有一次,子祀、子舆、子犁、子来四个人聚在一起交谈起来,后来大家不约而同地说道:"无论是谁,只要他能够把无当作头,把生当作脊柱,把死当作屁股,通晓生死存亡浑为一体的道理,我们就可以跟他交朋友。"说完四个人相视而笑,心有灵犀,大家相互交往成了好朋友。

不久子舆生了病,子祀前去探望他。子舆对子祀说:"伟大啊,我的造物者!居然把我变成这个样子!"只见子舆腰弯背驼,有五根脊椎露出在头顶之上,下巴隐藏在肚脐之下,肩部高过头顶,发髻朝天直上。虽然阴阳二气不和酿成如此灾害,可是子舆的心里却十分闲逸,就好像没有生病一样。他摇摇晃晃地来到井边,对着井水照看自己,说:"哎呀,这造物者又要把我变成如此曲屈不伸的样子啊!"

子祀说:"你讨厌这种样子吗?"子舆回答:"没有,这有什么可以讨厌的!假令造物者逐渐把我的左臂变成公鸡,我便用它来报晓;假令造物者逐渐把我的右臂变成弹弓，我便用它来打斑鸠烤熟了吃。假令造物者把我的屁股变化成车轮，把我的精神变化成骏马，我就用来乘坐，还省得我去更换别的车马嘛！更何况，生命的获得，是因为适时，生命的丧失，是因为顺应；安于适时而处之顺应，悲哀和欢乐都不会侵入内心，这就是古人所说的'从倒悬中解脱出来'。人有烦恼而不能自我解脱的原因，就是因为受到了外物的束缚。况且事物的变化不能超越自然的力量，现在既然天把我变成这个样子，我又怎么会厌恶呢？"

不久子来也生了病，他胸闷气急，喘个不停，快要死了，他的妻子儿女围在床前哭泣。子犁前往探望，看到这副景象，马上对他们说："哭什么，快走开！不要惊扰他正在经历的由生而死的变化！"然后，子犁靠着门跟子来说："真是伟大啊！造物者又将把你变成什么，把你送到何方？把你变化成老鼠的肝脏吗？把你变化成虫蚁的臂膀吗？"子来说："子女对于父母，无论在哪方面，他们都只能听从吩咐调遣。自然的变化对于人来说，则不啻于父母对于子女；它使我靠拢死亡而我却不听从，那么我就太蛮横了，阴阳变化从来就没有什么过错！天地自然用形体铸造了我，用生存让我劳苦，用衰老让我闲适，用死亡让我安息。所以我的存在可以看作是好事，我的死亡也可以看作是好事。现在如果有一个高超的冶炼工匠铸造金属器皿，金属熔解后跃起说'我必将成为良剑莫邪'，冶炼工匠必定认为这是不吉祥的金属。同样的道理，如果人一旦承受了人的外形便说'我成人了'，造物者一定会认为这是不吉祥的人。如今我把整个浑一的天地当作大熔炉，把造物者当作高超的冶炼工匠，又有什么不适宜的地方呢？"说着说着，子来就安安静静地睡着了，一会儿又自然而然地醒过来了。

迎生拒死，追求外物，追求无穷欲望的满足，人会活得很累，也没有什么意义，因为自由才是生命的本质。历史上有多少人想成仙，千方百计地寻找长生不老之术，但没有一个成功，因为他违背了自然。庄子说的"从倒悬中解脱"，不仅要把倒挂的头脚再倒过来，更重要的是把斩断物欲作为解脱倒挂的根本。后人说的无欲则刚，这个刚也是自由的表现。

FOUR EXTRAORDINARY MEN

Once four men, Zi Si, Zi Yu, Zi Li and Zi Lai, got together to talk freely when simultaneously they said, "Whoever can take inaction as head, life as back, death as bottom and understand that living, dying, surviving and perishing are one and the same, will be a friend of us." After that, they looked at one another in the eyes and laughed, knowing that they had reached mutual affinity without the need for more words. Later they mingled and became good friends.

Not long after, Zi Yu got ill and Zi Si went to see him. Zi Yu said to Zi Si, "How great! My Creator! He has reduced me to such a state!" Now Zi Yu was stooped and hunched, with five backbones protruding over the top of his head, and his chin hiding below his navel. His shoulders were higher than the top of his head and his bundle of hair pointed to the sky. Though such illness had been caused by the discordance between Yin and Yang, Zi Yu was at ease in his mind, as if he was not ill at all. He went to the well shakily and looked at his own reflection in water. He said, "Alas, the Creator once again has turned me into such a crooked and hunchbacked shape."

Zi Si asked, "Do you hate this look?" "No," answered Zi Yu, "there is nothing to hate about. If the Creator were to gradually turn my left arm into a rooster, I would use it to tell the approach of morning; if He were to gradually turn my right arm into a sling, I would use it to shoot down a turtle sparrow and roast it for food; if He were to turn my bottom into wheels, and my spirit into a fine horse, I would mount them for a ride. There would not be any need for me to get a new carriage! Furthermore, life was obtained because it was the right time, and life will be disappearing in accordance with the time, too. Be content with both, and neither sorrow nor joy will be able to invade the mind — that is what the ancients called 'the release from being suspended in the mid-air upside-down'. In endless trouble but without a release, that is because one is bound by the external things. What's more, changes of the world can never surpass the force of the nature. So now that the Creator has turned me into this, why would I hate it?"

Some days afterwards, Zi Lai fell ill too. He was short in breath, gasping and dying. His wife and children stood around his bed, weeping. Zi Li went to pay him a visit, and on seeing this, he said to them immediately, "Hush! Get away from him! Don't disturb him. He is undergoing the change from life to death." Then leaning against the door, he said to Zi Lai, "How great it is! What will the Creator turn you into and where will the Creator send you? Will He turn you into the liver of a rat or the arms of an ant?" Zi Lai said, "Children follow every order of their parents without question. The changes of nature matter to the human beings the same way as parents matter to children. Nature makes me get closer to death and if I don't follow, I will be too rebellious and unreasonable, because the changes of Yin and Yang will never go wrong. Nature has shaped me into this shell, made me toil through surviving, allowed me to enjoy comfort through aging, and finally it will put me to rest through death. Therefore my existence can be regarded as a good thing, and so is my death. Suppose here was a master founder who was casting metal utensils and the boiling metal suddenly jumped up and said, 'I am destined to become the famous sword Mo Ye.' The master founder would believe that it was a piece of metal which would bring ill fate. It follows that if a man said immediately when put into the man's shape, 'I am made into a man!', the Creator would also dismiss him as uncanny. Now that I regard the whole universe as the big casting cauldron and the Creator as the master founder, how can there be anything inappropriate?" With that, he fell into a peaceful sleep and after a while he woke up naturally.

Men welcome life and fear death, pursue material things and seek satisfaction of endless desires. Thus they live a hard and also meaningless life, for the very essence of life is none other than freedom. In the past, there were so many people who in order to become immortal left no stone unturned in their search for methods of maintaining life indefinitely. Yet not a single one of them could claim success, because what they tried to do is against the nature. According to Zhuangzi, "the release from being suspended in mid-air upside-down" is realized not only by turning the head and feet back to normal, but what's more important is to take the severance of desires for material things as the very basis for any kind of release. Later generations say that one is the strongest when one is without desires. Here being strong is a manifestation of having freedom.

46. 黄帝求道

黄帝做了十九年天子,诏令通行天下,可以说是国泰民安,但他并没有满足。他听说广成子通晓宇宙大道,特意前往广成子居住的崆峒山拜见。黄帝对广成子说:"我听说先生已经通晓至道,冒昧地请教什么是至道的精华。我一心想获取天地的灵气,用来帮助五谷生长,用来养育百姓。我又希望能主宰阴阳,从而使众多生灵遂心地成长。对此我将怎么办?"广成子回答说:"你所想询问的,是万事万物的根本;你所想主宰的,却又伤害了事物的根本,两者是互相背离的。自从你治理天下,天上的云气不等到聚集就下起雨来,地上的草木不等到枯黄就飘落凋零,太阳和月亮的光亮也渐渐地晦暗下来。你是用歪门邪道来引诱人心的见识短浅的小人,有的只是小鸡肚肠,怎么能够谈论大道!"黄帝听了这一席话便退了下来,回去后就弃置朝政,筑起一个小房子,地上铺着洁白的茅草,他谢绝交往,闭门养性,反复体会广成子的那番话。

过了三个月，黄帝再次登山求教。来到广成子的住所，只见他头朝南正躺着，黄帝小心翼翼地顺着下风，双膝着地匍匐向前，深深地拜了两拜，然后问道："听说先生已经通晓至道，冒昧地请教，修养自身怎么样才能长寿？"广成子急速挺身而起，说："问得好啊！来，我告诉给你至道。至道的精髓，虚无缥缈；至道的至极，晦暗沉寂。什么也不看什么也不听，持守精神保持宁静，形体自然会端正。一定要做到寂静和清明，不要使身形疲累劳苦，不要使精神动荡恍惚，这样就可以长生。眼睛什么也没看见，耳朵什么也没听到，内心什么也不知晓，这样你的精神定能持守你的形体，就能获得长生。小心谨慎地摒除一切思虑，封闭起对外的一切感官，知识多了就会坏事。只要你明白了这一点，我就来帮助你走向最光明的境地，直达那盛阳的本原；我帮助你进入到幽深渺远的大门，直达那盛阴的本原。天地自有管理天地的法则，阴阳自有规范阴阳的规矩，不妨小心地守护你的身体，万物会自然地成长。我持守着浑一的大道而又处于阴阳二气调和的境界，所以修身至今已经一千二百年，容貌还从不曾有过衰老。"听到这里，黄帝再次拜了两拜说："先生真可说是跟自然混而为一了！"

广成子又说："来，我告诉你。宇宙间的事物是没有穷尽的，然而人们却认为有个尽头；宇宙间的事物是不可能探测的，然而人们却认为有个极限。掌握了我所说的道的人，在上可以成为皇帝，在下可以成为王侯；不能掌握我所说的道的人，在上只能见到日月的光亮，在下只能化为黄土。如今万物昌盛，无不生于土地又返归土地，所以我将离你而去，进入那没有穷尽的大门，从而遨游于没有极限的原野。我将与日月同光，与天地共存。朝我而来，我无所觉察！离我而去，我无所在意！人们恐怕都要死去，我还是独自存在。"

黄帝求道可以给人一个启示：人的生命是有限的，茫茫宇宙是无限的，人要做到与日月同光，与天地共存，重要的是拥有宁静的心灵和宽人的胸怀，宁静要的是心清、心静，宽大要的是接纳百川、容纳天地。那种计较于个人得失，得意于计谋得逞，满足于些微智巧的人，实在是不值一提。作茧自缚，搬起石头砸自己的脚，都是对这类人的一种写照。

THE YELLOW EMPEROR SEEKS TAO

The Yellow Emperor had been sitting on the throne for nineteen years. His imperial orders were in operation all through the prosperous kingdom where people lived in peace. But he was not satisfied. When he heard that Guang Chengzi had a good understanding of the universe and the Great Tao, he went to Mount Kongdong to pay a visit to Guang Chengzi. On meeting Guang Chengzi, the Yellow Emperor said, "I hear Master has a good understanding of the perfect Tao. May I venture to ask what the essence of the perfect Tao is? I set my mind on obtaining the essence of Heaven and Earth, so that I can help with the growth of crops to feed my people. I again wish to have a control over Yin and Yang so as to help with the free development of many living souls. So what shall I do?" Guang Chengzi replied, "What you want to know is the essence of myriads of things but what you want to control is against the very nature of them. The two are contradictory. Ever since you've been governing the world, the vapors of the clouds drop in rain before they are gathered thick, and the grasses on the ground wither before they turn yellow. The brightness of the sun and the moon has paled slowly. What crooked means and dishonest methods have you employed to tempt people's mind? You narrow-minded small person, what you have are only petty concerns. How are you able to talk about the Great Tao?" At this, Yellow Emperor withdrew and after returning home, he gave up the throne and declined all visitors. He built a small hut for himself where he put a white grass mat on the floor and practiced self-cultivation in solitary, all the while going over and over the words of Guang Chengzi. Three months later, he climbed up the mountain and went for advice again.

At Guang Chengzi's place, the Yellow Emperor found him lying with his head to the south. Entering from the north in deference, Yellow Emperor went forward on his knees. He bowed low twice with his head to the floor before he asked, "I hear that Master has gained an understanding of the perfect Tao. May I venture to ask how I should cultivate myself to maintain a long life?" Guang Chengzi pushed himself up in haste and said, "What a good question! Here let me tell you about the perfect Tao. Its essence is the deepest obscurity; its highest level is the darkness and the silence. See nothing and hear nothing; keep your spirit and maintain the peacefulness, then the body will naturally take the correct shape. Do keep your quietness and purity; do not let the body toil and the spirit wander. In following these, you live long. The eyes see nothing, the ears hear nothing, and the mind knows nothing, thus your spirit is able to keep guard of your body; in doing so you will lead a long life. Take care to eliminate all the worries within; shut up all the sensory organs connecting to the outside, for too much knowledge is bound to interfere. Once you understand this, I shall help you travel to the brightest realm to reach the ultimate source of the great Yang; I shall help you enter the gate of the deepest obscurity to reach the ultimate source of the great Yin. Heaven and Earth have their way of governing, so do Yin and Yang. So keep watch of your body, as myriads of things grow naturally. Keeping to the homogeneous Great Tao and dwelling in the harmony of Yin and Yang, I have been cultivating myself for one thousand and two hundred years without having any changes in my appearance." Hearing this, the Yellow Emperor once again bowed twice and said, "Master and the nature have indeed become one and the same!"

Guang Chengzi added, "Come, let me tell you something. Things in the universe are inexhaustible, though people believe there is an end to everything; things in the universe are impenetrable, though people believe there is a limit to everything. He who understands the Tao I talk about can make his way to a monarch or, if unlucky, a prince at the least. He who does not understand the Tao I talk about can only see the light from the sun and the moon or, if unlucky, be reduced to a pile of loess. Nowadays all things in their prosperity grow from the land and will finally return to the land, so I shall leave you to enter the door of no ending and roam in the open fields of no limit. I shall share the brightness with the sun and the moon, and exist side by side with Heaven and Earth. I shall not perceive the things that come my way, nor shall I pay attention to things that depart. People may perish, but my existence lasts alone."

The revelation in the story of the Yellow Emperor seeking Tao is that there is an end to human life, while the universe is infinite. In order to share the brightness with the sun and the moon, to exist together with Heaven and Earth, the most important is to be in possession of a peaceful mind and a big heart. A peaceful mind requires purity and quietness; a big heart holds a capacity as vast as the cosmos itself. A person lives a worthless life if he is preoccupied with his gains and losses, pleased with schemes being carried out, and content with petty cleverness. Idioms such as "get enmeshed in a web of one's own spinning" and "shoot oneself in the foot" give a good portrayal of such people.

47. 庄子论剑

　　从前，赵文王喜好剑术，击剑的人蜂拥而至，有剑客三千余人，他们在赵文王面前日夜比试剑术，死伤的剑客每年都有百余人，而赵文王喜好击剑的兴趣却从来就不曾得到满足。像这样过了三年，赵国国力日益衰退，各国诸侯都在谋算怎样攻打赵国。对此，太子悝十分担忧，他不断考虑用什么样的方法让赵王回心转意，最后决定请庄子前去劝说赵王。庄子接受了太子的邀请。

　　几天后，庄子穿上剑士的服装，跟太子一道拜见赵王。赵王把宝剑拔出剑鞘，露出利刃正等待着庄子。庄子不急不忙地进入殿内，见到赵王也不行跪拜之礼。赵王说："你让太子作引荐，想用什么话来开导我呢？"庄子说："我听说大王喜好剑术，特地用剑术来参见大王。"赵王说："你的剑术有多高超，可以遏阻剑手、战胜对方呢？"庄子说："我的剑术，十步之内可杀一人，行走千里也不会受人阻留。"赵王听了非常高兴，说："这样你就是打遍天下无对手了，这其中的奥秘是什么？"庄子回答："击剑的要领是，有意把弱点显露给对方，用有机可乘之处引诱对方，后发制人，同时要抢先击中对手。如果不信，我愿意找个机会试试我的剑法。"赵王说："先生暂回馆舍休息休息，我来安排一个击剑比武的盛会，到时请先生前来比武。"

于是，赵王用了七天的时间让剑士们比武较量，死伤六十多人，从中挑选出五六人，让他们拿着剑在殿堂下等候，这才召见庄子。

赵王说："今天可让剑士们跟先生比试剑术了，先生习惯使用长剑还是短剑？"庄子说："我的剑术用长短剑都可以。不过我有三种剑，任凭大王选用，比试前能否让我先作些说明？"庄子的这种说法，赵王很感兴趣。于是庄子作了详细的说明。他说剑有三种：天子之剑、诸侯之剑、平民之剑。

天子之剑，拿燕谿的石城山做剑尖，拿齐国的泰山做剑刃，拿晋国和卫国做剑脊，拿周王畿和宋国做剑环，拿韩国和魏国做剑柄；用中原以外的四境来包扎，用四季来围裹，用渤海来缠绕，用恒山来做系带；靠五行来统驭，靠刑律和德教来论断；遵循阴阳的变化而进退，遵循春夏的时令而持延，遵循秋冬的到来而运行。这种剑，向前直刺一无阻挡，高高举起无物在上，按剑向下所向披靡，挥动起来旁若无物，上可割裂浮云，下能斩断地纪。它匡正诸侯，使天下人全都归服。这就是天子之剑。

诸侯之剑，拿智勇之士做剑尖，拿清廉之士做剑刃，拿贤良之士做剑脊，拿忠诚圣明之士做剑环，拿豪杰之士做剑柄。这种剑，对上效法于天而顺应日月星辰，对下取法于地而顺应四时序列，居中则顺和民意而安定四方。一旦使用，就好像雷霆震撼四境之内，没有不归服而听从国君号令的。这就是诸侯之剑。

而平民之剑，使用者全都头发蓬乱，鬓毛突出，帽子低垂，帽缨粗实，衣服紧身，瞪大眼睛而且气喘语塞。他们相互在人前争斗刺杀，上能斩断脖颈，下能剖裂肝肺，跟斗鸡没有什么不同，最后无不命尽气绝，对于国事却什么用处也没有。庄子最后对赵王说："如今大王拥有夺取天下的地位，却喜好百姓之剑，我私下认为大王显得微不足道了。"

听了这番话，赵文王感到十分惭愧。后来他三月不出宫门，开始考虑治国的方略，剑士们也死的死，走的走。

剑是取胜的武器。但是，胜有大胜小胜之分，人如果能够大胜却弃大胜而不为，不能说是一个真正的成功者。

ZHUANGZI TALKS ABOUT SWORDS

King Wen of Zhao was fond of swordplay. Swordsmen flocked to his place, amounting to a total number of over three thousand. In the presence of the king, they fought one another with real swords day and night, which led to a casualty of over one hundred swordsmen every year. Even so, the king's interest in swordplay was never completely satisfied. Things went on like this for three years and the state started to decline, while dukes and princes of other states were plotting to attack the State of Zhao. Prince Kui of Zhao was worried about it and considered what possible measures could be taken to persuade the King of Zhao to change his mind. Finally he decided to entrust Zhuangzi with the task of persuading the King of Zhao. Zhuangzi accepted the invitation from the prince.

Several days later, dressed in the outfit of a swordsman, Zhuangzi went with the prince to see the King of Zhao. The king sat there waiting for Zhuangzi with his sword unsheathed, baring the sharp edge. Without any haste, Zhuangzi walked into the hall and when he saw the king, he did not bow or fall on his knees. The King of Zhao said, "Now that you are here on the recommendation of the prince, what do you have to teach me?" Zhuangzi said, "I have heard that Your Majesty is fond of swordplay. So I come with my skills in swordplay to pay you a visit." The King of Zhao said, "Are your skills in swordplay so high that you can overpower an opponent and defeat him?" Zhuangzi said, "My skills in swordplay allow me to kill one within ten steps and not to be stopped on a journey of one thousand *li*." The King of Zhao was very happy about that and said, "So that means you have no match in the world. Then what is the secret behind it?" Zhuangzi answered, "The important thing with swordplay is to show your opponent your weakness on purpose, and to try to tempt him with an apparent opening which he wants to take advantage of by thrusting. Only after he has made his thrust will he realize that you have made yours and what's more, you have gotten him first. If you don't believe me, I would like to have an opportunity to show you my swordsmanship." The King of Zhao said, "Master, please go back to your lodging to have a good rest. Meanwhile I shall arrange for a grand gathering for swordplay and you'll be invited to take part in it."

So for seven days the King of Zhao ordered his swordsmen to compete among themselves in swordplay. During that time, over sixty of them were either killed or wounded. Finally he selected five to six swordsmen and ordered them to bring their swords and wait in the audience hall. Then he summoned Zhuangzi.

The king said to Zhuangzi, "Today will be the time for Master and swordsmen to compete in swordplay. What type of sword is Master more used to? The long sword, or the short sword?" Zhuang replied, "My swordsmanship is thus that any length will suit me fine. But I have three swords, one of which I shall ask Your Majesty to pick for me. Before the swordplay, allow me to make some explanations about them." The King of Zhao was very much interested in this, so Zhaungzi explained in detail. He said that there were three kinds of swords: the sword of the heaven's son, the sword of the princes and the sword of the people.

The sword of the heaven's son has Mount Stonewall of Yanxi as its point, Mount Tai of the State of Qi as its blade, the states of Jin and Wei as its back, the capital of Zhou and the State of Song as its loop, and the states of Han and Wei as its hilt. It is enclosed by four wild tribes outside the Central Plains, wrapped by the four seasons, surrounded by the Bohai Sea, and belted with Mount Heng. It is governed by the Five Elements, and regulated by laws and teachings of virtues. It evolves with the changes in Yin and Yang, goes on in the seasons of spring and summer and operates in accordance with the arrival of autumn and winter. The sword of this kind, when thrust forward, is stopped by nothing in front; when held high, it is topped by nothing above; when pointed downward, it is interrupted by nothing beneath; and when slashed about, it is deterred by nothing around. It cuts through floating clouds above and penetrates into the core of the earth below. It sets the princes right and makes the world submit willingly. That is the sword of the heaven's son, or the emperor.

The sword of the princes has wise and brave people as its point, honest and upright people as its blade, able and virtuous people as its back, loyal and sagely people as its loop, and heroic and eminent people as its hilt. Above, it models itself on the heaven to conform to the sun, the moon and the stars; below, it follows the laws of the earth to be in accordance with the sequence of the four seasons; in the middle, it follows the wishes of the people to bring peace to all parts of the world. Once it is used, it resounds like the roaring claps of thunder within the four quarters of the world, where there is not a single one who doesn't submit and obey his ruler's orders. That is the sword of the princes.

As regards the sword of the people, its users are those who have unkempt hair and protruding whiskers, who wear their hats low with coarse tassels and their clothes tight, whose eyes are opened wide, whose breathes come out short and whose words are jumbled. They fight and kill each other in public. Above, this sword can cut heads and throats; below it can slash livers and lungs. It is no different from a rooster fight. Their lives are snapped off in the end, but it is of no use to the management of state affairs. In the end, Zhuangzi admonished the King of Zhao, "Now Your Majesty enjoys the position of potentially taking the whole world, and yet delights in the sword of the people, which I venture to believe has made Your Majesty seem to be insignificant."

Hearing Zhuangzi's word, the King of Zhao felt very ashamed. After this, he stayed in the palace for three months without going out, and he started to think about strategies of governing the state. As for the swordsmen, some of them died, and some of them went away.

Sword is a weapon used to prevail upon others. But there are different kinds of victories, small ones and big ones. If one is able to acquire a big victory but gives it up by taking no action, one cannot be regarded as a victor in its real sense.

48. 宜僚替鲁侯解忧

居住在城南的熊宜僚去拜见鲁侯,见鲁侯闷闷不乐,就问:"国君面呈忧色,为什么呢?"鲁侯说:"我学习先王治国的办法,承继先君的事业;我敬仰鬼神,尊重贤能,身体力行,没有片刻的休止,可是仍不能免除祸患,我正为此忧心忡忡。"

宜僚听后摇摇头说:"你消除忧患的办法过于浅陋!你看那皮毛丰厚的狐狸和斑斓花纹的豹子,栖息于深山老林,潜伏于岩穴山洞,可以说是相当静心了;夜里出来活动,白天在洞里休息,可以说是相当警惕了;即使饥渴也隐形匿踪,小心翼翼地到江湖上觅求食物,这可以说是相当镇定了。然而即使如此,还是不能逃脱猎人设置的罗网和机关。为什么这两种动物会遭受这些灾祸,它们有什么罪过呢?原因就是它们自身的皮毛,就是这些珍贵的皮毛给它们带来了灭顶之灾。如今鲁国的权位不就是为你鲁君带来灾祸的珍贵皮毛吗?我希望你能剖空身形,舍弃皮毛,虚静内心，摈除欲念，进而逍遥于没有人迹的原野。在遥远的南方有个城邑，名字叫建德之国。那里的人民纯厚质朴，很少有私欲；知道耕作而不知道储备，给与别人却从不希图酬报；不明白怎样实现义，也不懂得怎样合乎礼；虽然随心所欲任意而为，却能各自行于大道，身心与自然融化为一；他们生时自得而乐，死后安然而葬，这样的境遇会有什么灾祸呢？所以，我希望国君你不如剥下君王这张世人眼红的皮，舍去国政，远离世俗，从而跟大道同步而行。"

鲁侯说："你说的那条道路遥远而又艰险，又有江河山岭阻隔，我没有可用于渡河的船，也没有用于行路的车骑，怎么办呢？"宜僚说："国君如果不高傲自大，不停步不前，这种态度就可以作为你的车子。"鲁侯又说："你说的那条道路遥远偏僻又无人居住，我跟谁做伴？我没有粮食，饿了怎么办？又怎么能够到达那里？"

宜僚说："减少你的耗费，节制你的欲念，虽然没有粮食也能感到充足。你渡过江河，浮游大海，一眼望去无边无际，越向前行便越发不知道它的穷尽。送行的人都从岸边回去，只有你一人越走越远，最后远离人世！所以说统治他人的人必定受劳累，受制于别人的人必定会忧心。而唐尧从不役使他人，也从不受制于人。我希望你能减除劳累，除去忧患，而独自跟'道'一块儿遨游于虚空的王国。现实生活中，如果你坐着一条船去渡河，突然有条空船碰撞过来，即使心地最褊狭、性子最火爆的人也不会发怒；但如果那条船上有人，哪怕是一个人，人们就会大声呼喊，叫他或者改道或者靠岸，如果呼喊一次没有回应，呼喊第二次也没有回应，就会喊第三次，那时必定会骂声不绝。人们刚才不发脾气而现在发起怒来，那是因为刚才船是空的而今却有人在船上。谁都知道，对着空船骂声再大也无济于事。由此看来，虚空的事物最能抵御世俗的骂声，一个人倘能割断外界的一切牵累，虚心地与'道'自由自在地遨游于世，又有谁会去伤害他！"

宜僚替鲁侯解忧，谈到了君权、王位、荣辱以及吃穿住行等人的需求、欲望等，它们都可以归之于利益，利益在很大程度上支配着人的活动，如同"无所不能的魔术师，他能在众目睽睽之下改变任何事物的形象"。但利益不能支配一切，因为人的价值观也可以左右人的行为。马克思有一个说法：如果有希望获取百分之三百的利润，资本家就敢犯任何罪行，甚至冒绞死的危险，这实际上还是对资本家价值观的批判。而庄子在谈利益的时候，反映的则是一种"我不累人，人不累我，无所牵挂，独立自由"的精神价值。

REMOVAL OF MUNDANE WORRIES

Xiong Yiliao who lived in south city went to pay a visit to the Marquis of Lu and found him looking down-hearted. Therefore Yiliao asked the marquis, "Your Highness looks worried. Why is that?" The Marquis of Lu said, "I have studied the ways of the former kings to run a state and have inherited their cause. I honor the spirits of the dead, respect the able and the virtuous, and I am engaged in what I advocate without taking any breaks. And yet I'm still not without troubles and disasters, for which I am burdened with worries."

Yiliao shook his head, "The way for you to remove worries is superficial. Look at the thickly furred fox and the striped leopard. They dwell in deep mountains and thick forests, and lurk in caves among rocks — so quiet and still, it can be said. They go out at night, and rest at day in their caves — so vigilant and cautious, it can be said. They lie hidden even in hunger and thirst, venturing out to the outside world for food — so calm and cool, it can be said. But even so, they are still not able to escape from the nets and traps set up by hunters. Why do these two animals suffer from these disasters? What have they done wrong? It's their skins which are so valuable that have brought them the fatal calamity. Now isn't your status in the State of Lu the precious skin that has brought disasters to you? I wish Your Highness will put away the form, rip off the skins, cleanse the mind and the heart, and get rid of the desires so as to enjoy yourself in the wilderness where there are no traces of human presence. There is a city in the far south named 'the State of Established Virtues' where people are simple and honest, rarely having personal desires. They know how to cultivate but not preserve. They give without expecting returns. They don't know how to achieve righteousness, nor do they understand what is in line with the rituals and ceremonies. Though guided only by their will and carrying on as they please, they are each on the way of the Great Tao, with their minds and bodies becoming one with the nature. They rejoice for their birth and are buried in peace at the time of their death. In circumstances like these, what disasters can ever come to unsettle them? So I should wish Your Highness to relinquish the status as the king which is the precious skin attracting all the envy in the world, and distance yourself from the state politics and the worldly affairs, so as to be in pace with the Great Tao."

The Marquis of Lu said, "The Way (Tao) you are talking about is far away and full of hardship and dangers. There are also rivers and mountains to cross. But I have neither the boats that ferry in water, nor the carriages that move on land. What do I do then?" Yiliao said, "If Your Highness can get rid of self-importance and arrogance, and move ahead with determination, such attitude is good enough to be a carriage for yourself." The Marquis of Lu again said, "The Way (Tao) you are talking about is remote and uninhabited. Who shall I have for my companions? What shall I do when I am hungry? Without food, how shall I be able to get there?"

Yiliao said, "Limit your expenditures, lessen your desires, and then even though you are without the provision of food, you will feel full and content. When you wade through the rivers and float along on the sea, only the boundlessness meets your eyes. The farther you go ahead, the less you know about the end to your journey. Those who go to the shore to see you off now turn their backs to leave. Only you are left to go farther and farther away, until you finally part with the world. Thus it is said that he who rules others is tired by others, and he who is bound to others is to suffer from worries. Yao never ruled others nor was he thereby enslaved by others. I should wish you to lessen your burdens, get rid of your worries and roam with Tao alone in the kingdom of the great void. In real life, if one is crossing a river in a boat, and suddenly a boat with nobody on it crashes against him, then be he of the smallest mind and the hottest temper, he is not going to get angry this time. But if there is someone on that impacting boat, even just one, then people on the impacted boat will shout at him to get out of the way or to pull into the shore. If there is no response the first time, or the second time, either, then what follows will be an endless flow of curses and swears. People remain cool in the first case but become angry in the second case because then it is an empty boat but now it is occupied. And it is known to all that it is futile to hurl abuses at an empty boat. So it seems that it is the 'void' that has the best capacity to hold the abusive shouts of the common world. Therefore if one can break free of all the ties with the external world, and roam freely in humbleness with the Tao, who would be able to harm him?"

To help remove the worries of the Marquis of Lu, Yiliao talked about the royal rights, the throne, honor and disgrace, and also such human desires as food, shelter, clothing and transportation, all of which can be termed as interests. Like "an omnipotent magician who can change the form of anything even under the watchful eyes of everybody", interests determine human activities to quite a large extent. But interests cannot control all, since moral values influence behavior too. Karl Marx said that the capitalists would commit any crimes, even running the risks of being hanged, to get a potential profit of 300%. But his ideas have been more of a criticism against the values held by the capitalists. However, when Zhuangzi talked about interests, he actually suggested a way of getting spiritual independence and freedom by detaching oneself from the worldly concerns, not troubling others and not being troubled by others.

49. 宰牛的功夫

  据说魏国梁惠王有个专门掌管宰牛的厨夫,人称其为"庖丁"。庖丁大抵懂一点导引气功之道,宰牛有绝活。他通常不用绳索捆绑,只是让牛悠悠然在场地上随意吃草,然后意守丹田,宁神运气,接着操起一刀向牛飞起,刀光在牛前牛后牛上牛下牛左牛右飞快闪烁,如同浪里的白鲛,神出鬼没,寒气逼人,又见他手在这里一抓,肩在那里一顶,脚随之一踩,膝随之一抵,身手步法,形同闪电。但听"哧啦"一声——仿佛东墙塌了半壁——一大片的牛肉随着刀尖纷纷向四面八方滑落下去,刹那间,场地上只剩下一个光秃秃的牛骨架完整地矗立在那里,而牛眼睛还在转,牛尾巴还在甩呢。

  更加奇妙的是,庖丁解牛时左右闪动的步法,忙而不乱,腾挪有序,如同商代王宫里取名"桑林"的莲花舞步;而刀刃在牛肉与牛骨间伸展运行时所发生的"吱吱"声,抑扬顿挫,宛转动听,完全符合帝尧宫廷内名叫"咸池"乐章的韵律。

当时，梁惠王在一旁目睹了庖丁解牛的全过程，不禁脱口称赞道："啊，妙极了，你宰牛的技术怎么会达到如此出神入化的地步呢？"庖丁放下刀，双手抱拳对梁惠王作了个揖，回答道："宰牛仅仅是一门粗糙的技术，而小臣往往喜欢研究能够贯通万事万物的大道，然后再以这种大道来指导宰牛的技术，就能得心应手，挥洒自如。刚开始宰一头牛时，小臣看上去无非是浑沌一团，宛如一堵铜墙铁壁横在眼前，令人不知从何处下手。经过长期的琢磨与实践，三年之后，当拉过一头牛预备宰杀时，小臣一眼望去，何处有骨，何处有筋，以及五脏六腑灿烂分明，其可说是'目无全牛'了！"

"二十多年过去了，至今小臣宰起牛来，闭着眼睛操起一把刀，只是凭着一种感觉。在牛身上前后左右持刃运行，势如破竹，如同一把铁犁在松软的泥土中所向披靡。小臣的刀刃是按照牛身上的自然纹理，进入筋肉的间隙，进入骨节的空隙，完完全全是顺着自然结构去行动，这样刀刃连经络相连的地方都不会遇到，怎么会撞在大骨头上呢？好的厨子，据说是一年更换一把刀，因为他们是用刀去割筋肉的，刀刃磨损得慢。而普通的厨子呢，据说一个月就要换一把刀，因为他们是用刀去砍骨头，刀刃损坏很快。现在小臣这把刀已经用了十九年了，用它宰杀的牛也已达几千头，可是它的刀刃似乎刚从磨刀石上磨出一样，银光闪闪，锋利异常。小臣的看法是：牛骨节虽然紧密，总是有间隙的，而刀刃呢，几乎没有厚度；以没有厚度的刀刃切入稍有间隙的骨节，当然是游刃恢恢而宽大有余了。尽管如此，每当遇到筋骨盘结的地方，小臣也知道不容易对付，于是全神贯注，手脚稍慢，找到间隙，刀刃微微一动，整条牛就哗啦一声解体了。大块牛肉如土散落，牛本身还来不及感受疼痛就死了。这时候，小臣才感到如释重负，提刀站立，顾盼自如，觉得大功告成，心满意足。随后把这口刀擦拭干净收藏好，以备后用。"

梁惠王听了庖丁这一番"宰牛经"，不禁深受启发，赞扬说："好啊，听了庖丁这一席谈论，从中亦可悟到不少养生的道理。"

成语"庖丁解牛"就是从这个故事来的，但庖丁的故事实际上谈到了人的认识过程和规律。看来任何一门功夫都可以分为高低不同的境界，功夫的形成就是从较低的层面走向较高的层面，用西方的术语说是感性、知性和理性，功夫如果到了炉火纯青的地步，那就"从心所欲不逾矩"了。

SKILLS OF CATTLE BUTCHERING

King Lianghui of Wei was said to have a cook in charge of butchering cattle, whose name was "Ding the Cook". Somehow familiar with Qigong, the traditional exercise that involved controlling breaths and moving limbs, Ding the Cook had unique skills in cutting up cattle. Usually he didn't have the cattle tied with ropes, but let it graze on the grass freely. Focusing his mind onto the deep breath in the diaphragm, he controlled and directed it through his concentration. Then he took up a knife and wielded it at the cattle. The knife was seen flying quickly up and down, right and left on the body of the cattle, just like a white shark in the waves, appearing and disappearing mysteriously, bringing about a cold nip in the air. With a touch of his hand here, a thrust of his shoulders there, followed by a stamp of his foot and a bend of his knees, he maneuvered his body stance and his footwork as quick as flashlights. With a sound like a wall collapsing in half, a great many slices of meat fell into all directions with the tip of his knife. In a split second, what was left on the ground was only a bare yet intact skeleton of the cattle standing there, even with its eyes still turning and its tails still wagging.

What was even more marvelous was that when Ding the Cook was cutting up the cattle, his busy yet orderly steps with the unpredictable ups and downs were like the lotus-like moves in the dance named "Mulberry Groves" popular in the palace of the Shang Dynasty, and the "chi, chi" sounds made by the blade of knife flowing between meat and bones, melodious and enchanting, now rising now falling, were rhythmical with the famous musical score "The Salt Lake" in the palace of Emperor Yao.

Witnessing the whole process, King Lianghui could not refrain from exclaiming, "Ah, how wonderful that your skills in cutting up cattle should have reached such a superb state!" Ding the Cook put down his knife and, bowing slightly with both of his hands folded in front, he replied, "Cutting up cattle is no more than a vulgar skill. What your servant loves is to study the Great Tao which provides a thorough knowledge of the myriads of things. With the knowledge of the Great Tao, I have become skillful and proficient in cutting up cattle. At the time when I first began to butcher cattle, all of them looked none other than a complete wholeness, towering before me like a range of iron bastions, and I didn't know where to put my knife. I studied and practiced for a long time. Then, three years later when a cattle was pulled over for butchering, your servant took one look at it, and instantly saw the bones, the tendons, and all the vital internal organs in clear patterns. It can be said that in my eyes, a cattle ceases to be a whole cattle."

"Twenty years have passed. Now, when I deal with a cattle, I take up a knife and with my eyes closed and relying on just a hunch, I wield my knife on the body of the cattle freely, front and back, right and left, with irresistible force like an iron plough working its way ahead in soft mud. Following the natural patterning, the blade of my knife slides into the niches between meat and tendon, and cuts into the gap among bones. Moving in complete accordance with the natural structuring, the blade is able to steer clear of the interconnected channels and points, let alone big bones. A good cook is said to replace his knife once a year, for he uses it to cut meat and tendon, and therefore it wears out slowly. An ordinary cook replaces his knife once a month, for he uses it to hack bones, and therefore it wears out much more quickly. This knife of mine has been in use for nineteen years on several thousand cattle, and yet its blade remains sharp and shiny as if it has just been ground on a whetstone. My explanation is that though the bones are closely knitted, there are niches and interstices, while the blade has almost no thickness.

So when the blade with no thickness slides into the bones with niches and interstices, it has plenty of room to move about. But even so, when I come across complicated joints which I know is difficult to deal with, I concentrate my mind, slow down a bit until I find the niche and with a slight thrust of the knife, the joints all come apart. Like clods of earth, big pieces of meat fall down and the cattle is dead before it even feels the pain. Then I stand there with my knife in hand and look around in a leisurely manner, enjoying my success, with a sense of relief washing all over me. I clean my knife and put it away for future use."

Hearing Ding's "art of butchering cattle", King Lianghui was deeply impressed and enlightened. He said, "Excellent! From the words of Ding the Cook, I have learned quite a few truths on the nourishment of life."

The Chinese idiom "Ding the Cook butchering cattle" derives from the above story. It is in fact about the rules and processes of human cognition. Every skill seems to have high levels and low ones. The development of skills is about moving from the lower level to the higher one or, in terms used by the Westerners, evolving from perception to understanding and then to reasoning. If skills have reached the degree of excellence, they can be applied at one's pleasure, regardless of all the rules and processes.

50. 心斋

颜回准备去卫国,就向孔子辞行。孔子问:"去卫国干什么?"颜回说:"我听说卫国的国君年轻气盛,办事专断,行为孤僻。他随意动用国家的力量,却看不到自己的过失;他轻率地让百姓为他卖命,死人遍及全国不可称数,就像大泽中的草芥七倒八歪,百姓都弄得走投无路。我曾听老师说:'治理得好的国家可以离开它,昏乱的国家却要投奔那里',就好像医生门前病人多一样。我希望根据先生的这些教诲思考治理卫国的办法,卫国也许还有救!"

孔子听了不以为然,摇摇头说:"哎呀,你这样恐怕是去送死!很危险呀!"颜回问:"如果我严肃谦虚,勤奋努力,始终如一,这样可以吗?"孔子说:"这怎么可以呢!卫君脾气暴烈,刚愎自用,喜怒无常,人们都不敢有丝毫违背他的地方,他也借此压抑人们的真实感受和不同观点,放纵他的欲望。让他每天积些小德都不会干,更不用说积大德了,你如果固守己见，表面上赞同他，而内心不敢对他的言行提出指责，这怎么行得通呢？"

颜回说："如此，我采用内直外曲、与古人做比较的方法行吗？内直就是与自然交朋友。跟自然交友的人，可知国君与自己都是上天养育的子女，那又何必希望人们赞同自己的言论，反对别人的言论呢？这样做，人们会说未失童心，跟自然融为一体。外曲就是与世人交朋友。与世人交友的人，这就叫与人融为一体。拱手、鞠躬、下跪、磕头，这是做臣子的礼节，别人都这样去做，我敢不这样做吗？做一般人臣都做的事，人们也就不会责难了吧。上比古代贤人，是跟古人交友。自己的言论虽然是在教导别人，但这种说法实际上不是从我才开始的，古人早就这么说了。像这样，虽然正直不阿却也不会受到伤害，这就叫跟古人融为一体。这样做是不是可以了？"

孔子说："唉，怎么可以呢？虽然这样做不会给你带来灾难，但作用不过如此。其实这种做法很繁琐，让人无所适从，而且也难以感化别人。你好像还是太执着于自己的内心成见了。"颜回说："我实在没有更好的办法了，还是请老师指点一下。"孔子说："你先去斋戒吧，等你斋戒完了，我就告诉你。"颜回马上回答说："我颜回家境贫穷，不饮酒浆、不吃荤食已经好几个月了，这可以说是斋戒了吧？"

孔子说："不一样，这是祭祀前的斋戒，并不是'心斋'。心斋时你必须摒除杂念，专一心思，不用耳去听而用心去领悟，不用心去领悟而用虚无淡漠去把握！要知道，耳的功用仅在于聆听，心的功用仅在于跟外界事物交合，虚无淡漠的心境才是对待宇宙万物的主宰，大道汇集在虚无淡漠之中，虚无淡漠就叫'心斋'。"颜回说："在我接受'心斋'教诲之前，我感到确实存在一个真实的颜回；在接受'心斋'教诲之后，我感到并不存在我这个人。这可以叫做虚无淡漠吗？"孔子说："你对'心斋'的理解十分透彻。我告诉你，假如你能够进入到卫国，又不为名利地位所动，卫君能采纳你的观点你就说，不行就不说，如同进入不得已而为之的境域，这就差不多了。看那空旷的宇宙，自己的心境就会虚空生辉，吉祥就进入心田。如果人不能虚一而静，那就是'坐弛'，表面上看你安静地坐着，实际上却心猿意马，奔驰不息；倘若让耳目的感观向内通达而又排除心智于外，那么鬼神将会前来归附，何况是人呢！"

"斋"有打扫干净的意思，最初可能出于巫术，古人在祭祀的时候，常常要先沐浴，后更衣，表明自己是干净之人。心斋就是要把自己的心灵打扫干净。打扫干净了，心灵才有空间，才能心域宽广，才能接纳万物，才能与天地融为一体。中国传统文化很多都带有心斋的特点。道教讲得道成仙，斋醮就是成仙的一个途径。后来的禅学、宋代的心学都可以看到心斋的痕迹。

THE FAST OF THE HEART

Yan Hui, a disciple of Confucius, was going to the State of Wei and he came to say goodbye to his Master. Confucius asked, "What are you going to do there?" Yan Hui said, "I have heard that the King of Wei is young and aggressive, who consults nobody but himself and behaves in an incommunicable manner. He employs state resources carelessly without seeing his own faults. In an irresponsible manner, he forces the people to toil for him; as a result, a great many people died throughout the state, and the dead bodies were left everywhere like weeds in a marsh. People are driven to their last shifts. I remember Master once said, 'You may leave a country that is well-run, but you should go to a country that is in disorder.' That is the same idea as why many sick people gather at the doctor's door. I wish to learn from Master's teachings and think about ways to put the State of Wei in order. Perhaps it can still be saved."

Confucius shook his head in disapproval and said, "Alas, I am afraid what you do will only bring harm to yourself. It is too dangerous." Yan Hui asked, "If I become serious and humble, devoting studious efforts and being single-minded

220/221

in my purpose, will it do?" Confucius said, "No, it won't do. The King of Wei, a man of moods, is hot-tempered and self-willed. Ordinary people dare not oppose him at all, and he takes advantage of that and tramps on people's true feelings and different ideas to seek more satisfaction of his own desires. He won't even engage in the everyday practice of small virtues, let alone greater ones. If you stick to your ideas and agree with him only outwardly, while inwardly you still dare not put forward charges against his conducts, how will it do?"

Yan Hui said, "Well then, will it do if I am outwardly bent and inwardly straight, and compare myself with the ancient people? To be inwardly straight means to make friends with nature. He who is a friend of nature knows that the king and he are all sons of the Heaven. Thus there is no need to seek other's approval of his ideas, nor is there any need to disapprove other's ideas. In so doing, he is said to be an innocent child, merging as one with the nature. To be outwardly bent means to make peace with the world. He who is in peace with the world is said to have been merged with the people. Folding hands, making bows, kneeling down and kowtowing are the rituals performed by subjects. When others are all doing so, how should I dare to act differently? Do what other subjects do, and I won't be in fault. To compare with the people in the ancient times means to make friends with them. Although I am trying to give instructions and guidance to others, the ideas are not mine, but have long been advocated by the ancient people. In this way, though straightforward, I will not be harmed. That is what is said to be merged with the ancient people. If I go in this way, will it do?"

Confucius said, "Alas, it will never do. Though going in this way will not bring you harm, it will do no more than that. Loaded down with too many trivial details, this way of yours makes it hard for people to follow, and therefore it is difficult to produce in people the kind of transformation that you desire. You still seem to be too obsessed with your preconceived ideas." Yan Hui said, "I don't know what else to do. I venture to ask for some advice." Confucius said, "Go on a fast. Then I shall tell you." Yan Hui answered immediately, "My family is in straitened circumstances and I haven't had any wine or meat for several months. Can this be regarded as fasting?"

Confucius said, "No, it is different. What you have done is the fasting before sacrifices, not the fasting of the heart. When you are on a fast of the heart, you must banish all the distracting thoughts from your mind and concentrate. You listen not with your ears but with your heart; you understand not with your heart but with nothingness and nonchalance. You know, ears are used just for listening and heart is used just for communication with the external things, while nothingness and nonchalance of the mind is the king in control of the myriads of things in the universe. The Great Tao accumulates in nothingness, which is considered the 'fast of the heart'." Yan Hui said, "Before the teachings on the 'fast of the heart', I perceived the existence of my individuality — the real Yan Hui; but after the teachings, I perceive the nonexistence of my individuality. Can this be considered nothingness?" Confucius said, "Now your understanding of the 'fast of the heart' is thorough enough. Let me tell you: if you are able to enter the State of Wei and are not affected by desires of fame, interests and positions, you go ahead when the King of Wei listens to and accepts your ideas and when he doesn't, you stop. If you manage to enter the realm where you have no alternatives but to let him hear your consultations, then you've almost made it. When you look at the vast universe, your mind enters the void and your heart is blessed with peace and happiness. If one cannot enjoy peace through being void, it is called 'galloping while sitting', which means being restless as having a heart like a capering monkey and a mind like a galloping horse. If you allow what is perceived by the eyes and ears to reach the internal world, but keep the knowledge and wisdom out of it, then even supernatural beings would be drawn to you, let alone human beings."

The word "fast" carries the meaning of making something clean. Perhaps influenced by some sort of witchcraft, ancient people bathed and changed clothes before the sacrifices to show that they were clean. The "fast of the heart" is to make one's heart clean. Only when it is clean will the heart enjoy bigger space.

Only when the heart is broad and vast will it be able to have the capacity to hold the myriads of things and to merge with Heaven and Earth. Much of Chinese traditional culture takes on the characteristics of the "fast of the heart". Taoism talks about becoming immortal with the ascendence in Tao. According to Taoism, fasting before sacrifices is one way to becoming immortal. Besides, traces of fasting can also be found later in Zen, a Chinese sect of Buddhism, and the neo-Confucianism of the Song Dynasty.

51．季咸看相

　　郑国有个算命十分灵验的巫师，名叫季咸，他能预测人的生死存亡和祸福寿夭，算起期限来就像神仙那样，无论年、月、旬、日都准确应验。郑国人见到他，都急忙跑开，但列子见到他却被迷住了。

　　列子回来后，把见到的情况告诉老师壶子，并且说："起先我总以为先生的道行最为高深，看来还有更为高深的人了。"壶子说："我教给你的全是表面的东西，还没有深入到实质，你难道就已经得道了吗？只有众多的雌性却无雄性，又怎么能生出受精的卵呢！你用所学到的皮毛就跟世人相抗衡，必然轻信别人，让人给你相面。你明天试着跟他一块儿来，把我介绍给他，让他给我看看相。"

　　第二天，列子陪着季咸来见壶子。季咸走出门就对列子说："哎呀！你的先生快要死了！活不了了，超不出十天了！我观察到他临死前的怪异形色，神情像遇水的灰烬一样难以复燃。"列子进到屋里，泪水打湿了衣襟，伤心地把季咸的话告诉壶子。壶子说："刚才我显露给他看的是大地阴静的气象，表现我寂然不动的心境，茫茫然既没有震动也没有生长。这样恐怕看不到我的生机。你试试明天再跟他来看看。"

第三天，列子又陪着季咸来见壶子。季咸一出门就对列子说："幸亏你的先生遇上了我！症状减轻了，完全有救了，我已经观察到闭塞的生机中有神气微动的情况。"列子进到屋里，把季咸的话告诉壶子。壶子说："刚才我显露给他看的是天地相合的气象，把名声和实利等一切杂念都排除在外，而生机从脚跟发至全身。这样恐怕已看到了我的一线生机。你试试明天再跟他来看看。"

第四天，列子再陪着季咸来见壶子。季咸走出门来就对列子说："你的先生没有斋戒，我不可能给他看相。什么时候斋戒了，我再来给他看相。"列子进到屋里，把季咸的话告诉壶子。壶子说："刚才我显露给他看的是阴阳二气调和的太冲之象，这样恐怕看到了我平衡气息的机能了。大鱼盘桓逗留的地方叫做渊，静止的河水聚积的地方叫做渊，流动的河水滞留的地方叫做渊。渊有九种称呼，这里只提到了三种。你试试明天再跟他来看看。"

第五天，列子又陪季咸来见壶子。季咸还未站定，自己就觉得没有立脚的地方，马上拔腿就跑。壶子说："快，追上他！"列子没能追上，回来问老师其中的缘故，壶子说："前几次我显露给他看的始终未脱离我的本源。这次我跟他随意应付，他弄不清我的究竟，我好像对他百般顺从，又好像随波逐流，所以他逃跑了。"

这下，列子深深感到自己并没有什么道术，就回到了自己的家，三年不出门。他帮助妻子烧火做饭，喂猪就像侍候人一样，对于各种世事不分亲疏没有偏私，过去的雕琢和华饰已恢复到原本的质朴和纯真，像大地一样木然忘情地生存着，封闭自己的心窍不染尘世，就这样走完了人生。

神巫季咸给壶子看相的故事，反映了庄子对预测的看法，他把预测作为世俗的智慧，认为通过外部现象来预测世界的本质是测不准的，社会不能把这种智慧才能作为治理国家的工具。这个问题牵涉到认识的不确定性。由于现象界是在不断变化的，进入人视域的只是现象界的一部分，包括主体在内的接纳现象的各种条件不断发生变化，人的认识就具有一种不确定性。测不准原理就说，当你观察到事物的时候，你已经在不可避免地改变着你的观察对象了。当然庄子夸大了这种不确定性，忽视了认识所具有的确定性。

JI XIAN TELLS FORTUNE

In the State of Zheng, there was a wizard called Ji Xian whose predictions were said to be very accurate. He could predict births and deaths, disasters and good fortunes of men. Like a supernatural being, he could be precise with the year, the month, the week and the day of a future event. People of Zheng all ran away from him every time they met him, but Liezi was fascinated by him instead.

Liezi returned and told his master Huzi what he had seen about Ji Xian. He said, "Before I had always considered your practice of Tao, my Master, to be the most perfect. But now it seems there are others who are superior to you." Huzi said, "I have only taught you all the exterior parts of the practice, not yet the essentials. You don't think that you have already achieved the Tao, do you? When there are many hens but not a rooster among them, how can eggs be produced? When you confront the world with what little you have learned, you are sure to take people's words at face value and ask others to tell fortune for you. Try to bring him with you tomorrow. Introduce me to him and ask him to tell my fortune."

On the next day, Liezi brought Ji Xian with him to see Huzi. As soon as they were finished with the meeting and got out, Ji Xian said to Liezi, "Alas, your Master is dying! He is not going to live any longer, not more than ten days. I saw the strange pre-death countenance on his face. It is like ashes in water, no longer flammable." Liezi went into the room, and with tears wetting the front of his cloths, he told Huzi sadly what Ji Xian had said. Huzi said, "Just now I showed him the patterns of shadows and the stillness of the earth as a reflection of my peaceful and still state of mind, which is blank with neither motion nor growth. That's why he seemed unable to see my vigor of life. Try to bring him here again tomorrow."

On the third day, Liezi brought Ji Xian to see Huzi again. As soon as they were out, Ji Xian said to Liezi, "What good fortune that your Master has met me! The symptoms have lessened. He is now saved. I have detected signs of stirring life in the blocked growth." Liezi went into the room and told Huzi what Ji Xian had said. Huzi said, "Just now I showed him the patterns of Heaven and Earth being merged into one. I discarded all the distracting ideas such as fame and interests, so as to let the vigor of life sweep over me, from the heels to the whole body. Thus he has seen a gleam of hope. Try to bring him with you tomorrow."

On the fourth day, Liezi came to see Huzi with Ji Xian again. As soon as Ji Xian went out, he said to Liezi, "Your Master has not been on a fast. So I cannot read his fortune. I shall come back when he has fasted." Liezi went into the room and told Huzi everything. Huzi said, "Just now, I showed him the patterns of the harmony of Yin and Yang. He seemed to have seen my ability to balance my breaths. The place where big fish gather and linger is called an abyss; the place where still rivers converge is called an abyss; and the place where flowing water is held up is called an abyss too. There are nine abysses with different names. Here I have just mentioned the above three. Try to bring him here with you tomorrow."

On the fifth day, Liezi brought Ji Xian to Huzi again. Before Ji Xian had settled himself, he found that there was no place for him and he took to his legs at once. Huzi said, "Hurry! Catch him!" But Liezi was unable to catch up with him. So Liezi returned and asked his Master why the wizard had run off. Huzi said, "In his previous visits, what I showed him had never been far away from myself. This time I dealt with him indifferently, so he was not able to find out about me. Sometimes it was like complete submission, while at other times it was free as flowing water.

So that is why he ran away."

After this, Liezi felt strongly that he hadn't made much achievement in Tao. So he returned home and stayed in for three years. He helped his wife light the fire for cooking and feed the pigs, as if he was waiting on people. He was unbiased towards the worldly affairs, irrespective of degree of intimacy. The trimmings and ornaments of the past were restored to the original naturalness and purity. Like a clod of earth, he indulged in his own existence, shutting up his mind and heart, remaining uncontaminated amid the confusions of the mortal life. In this way he continued to the end of his life.

The story about the wizard Ji Xian telling Huzi's fortune reflects the views Zhuangzi had on making predictions about the future. Regarding this kind of prediction as worldly wisdom, Zhuangzi believed that it was impossible to make accurate predictions on the essentials of the world by relying on the external signs and the society should never view prediction as a proper tool for the governing of the world, since it involved the uncertainties in the process of cognition. In the world of external phenomena, everything is under constant change. What enters people's observation is just one part of the whole. And what's more, every condition of the received phenomena, including the receptor, is constantly changing. Therefore, the human cognition involves uncertainties to some degree. The primary reason why the predictions are inaccurate is that the instant you perceive something, you are changing the object of your perception inevitably. Of course Zhuangzi overstated the uncertainty of this kind and overlooked the certainties in human cognition.

52. 小鸟与大鹏

　　北方的大海里有一条鱼,它的名字叫做鲲。鲲的体积很大,后来变成为鸟,它的名字叫鹏。鹏的脊背说不清有几千里长;当它奋起而飞的时候,那展开的双翅就像天边的云。这只鹏鸟,随着海上汹涌的波涛迁徙到南方的大海。南方的大海是个天然的大池。有一部书名叫《齐谐》,专门记载怪异事情,书中叙述了鹏鸟迁徙时的情景:翅膀拍击水面激起了三千里的波涛,海面上急骤的狂风盘旋而上直冲九万里高空,整个迁徙用了六个月的时间方才停歇下来。当鹏鸟在空中飞行时,昔日在林泽原野上漂浮的云气如野马奔腾,如尘埃飞扬,都是大自然里各种生物的气息吹拂所致。地面上的人向上眺望时看到的是蓝天白云,这就是它真正的颜色吗?抑或是高旷辽远,没法看到它的尽头呢?鹏鸟在高空往下看,不过也就像这个样子罢了。这是因为它飞得太高,无法看清地面颜色的缘故。鹏鸟飞得高有它的原因,可以用水来打比方:如果水汇积不深,它就没有力量浮载大船。倒杯水在庭堂的低洼处,那么小小的芥草也可以用来当作船;如果把杯子放在上面,杯底就会贴在地上不动了,因为水太浅而船太大了。假如风积聚的力量不厚实,就难以托负起巨大的翅膀。所以,鹏鸟高飞九万里,狂风就在它的身下,然后方能凭借风力飞行,以至于背负青天而没有什么能够阻遏它的力量了,才能像现在这样飞到南方。然而这些道理不是大家都明白的。寒蝉与灰雀看到大鹏空中高飞的情景,就讥笑说:"我们在地面上想飞就可以一下子飞起来,够着榆树和檀树的树枝,碰到房梁还可以落下歇息,为什么要费这么大的力气在九万里的高空飞翔呢?"

寒蝉和灰雀真是鼠目寸光,它们与大鹏的不同,就是因为见识小的不如见识大的知道的多,年龄小的不如年龄大的经历得多。要知道,到迷茫的郊野去,带上三餐就可以往返,肚子还是饱饱的;到百里之外去,要用一整夜时间准备干粮;到千里之外去,三个月以前就要准备粮食。寒蝉和灰雀这两个小东西,知道的只是小道理,对大道理一无所知。因为生命短促,清晨的菌类不会知道什么是三十、初一,夏日的知了也不会懂得什么是春天、秋天。而楚国南边有叫冥灵的大龟,它把五百年当作春,把五百年当作秋;上古有叫大椿的古树,它把八千年当作春,把八千年当作秋,这就是长寿。传说中的彭祖到如今还是以年寿长久而闻名于世,人们与他攀比,岂不是很可悲吗?

所以,那些才智足以胜任一个官职,品行合乎一乡人心愿,德行适合做一国之主,能力足以取信全国的人,他们看待自己也像小雀那样自我满足了。所以宋国的贤人宋荣子讥笑他们。还有这样的人,世上的人们都赞誉他,他不会因此越发努力,世上的人们都非难他,他也不会因此而更加沮丧。他清楚地划定自身与外物的区别,辨别荣誉与耻辱的界限,这已经是到头了吧?他在处世方面已经达到了不为小事所累的程度。虽然如此,他还是未能达到最高的境界。

后人常把小鸟与大鹏的故事与人的生活态度联系起来,有"燕雀焉知鸿鹄之志"的说法。事实上由于受各种条件的限制,人对世界的认识能力、人的实践水平是有不同层面的,但人不会永远停留在一个水平上。

这里重要的是，人不要以己度人，以一概全，把自己固守在一个圈子里，以为这是不可逾越的极限，自我陶醉。要知道，人对世界的把握总是不断地由低级向高级发展，总是处在由有限向无限进展的过程中。

THE SMALL SPARROW AND THE GIANT EAGLE

In the northern sea there was a giant fish called Kun. It changed into a giant eagle, called Peng, the back of which might be as wide as several thousand *li*. When it roused itself and flew in the sky, its fully extended wings were like clouds on the horizon. With the turbulent waves on the sea, the giant eagle migrated to the southern sea, which was a huge natural lake. In the book *Qi Xie*, a collection of supernatural things, there are vivid descriptions of the scene of Peng's migration. Its wings beat against the water, causing great waves of three thousand *li*. The fierce wind on the sea spiraled upward to the sky as high as ninety thousand *li*. It took six months for Peng to complete its migration. When it was flying in the sky, the vapor of clouds floating above forests and open fields was like horses galloping and dust blowing, all because of the interaction of the breaths from the various living creatures in the nature. When people standing below looked up, all they saw was white clouds in the blue sky. But was blue the real color of the sky? Or was it because people down there could not reach its end due to the great distance? If Peng looked down from the high sky, the view would have been the same. That was because it flew too high to see clearly the color of the earth. For Peng to fly so high, it had its reasons. Take water for an example: if the accumulated water is not deep enough, it will not have the strength for large boats to float. Pour a cup of water into the pit on the ground of the courtyard, and a mustard leaf can float on the water as if it were a boat; but if a cup is put on the water, the bottom of the cup will be stuck because the water was shallow and the "boat" was too big. If the strength gathered by the wind was not big enough, it would be unable to hold the huge wings of Peng. Therefore the giant eagle Peng flew as high as ninety thousand *li* with strong wind just below it. Relying on the force of the wind, it flew and carried the blue sky on its back with nothing in its way to hinder it. In this manner was it able to reach the south. However, these reasons were not comprehensible to everyone. Seeing Peng flying in the high sky, a cicada and a young sparrow sneered and said to each other, "When I feel like it, I can fly at once from the ground. I can touch the leaves of the elm and the algum, and I can land for a rest if I fly across the roof beams. What is the point of flying in the sky as high as ninety thousand *li*?"

Both the cicada and the young sparrow are as short-sighted as a mouse which can only see an inch ahead, and that's their difference from Peng. Extensive knowledge enables one to learn more than limited knowledge does and the old people experience more than the young. It is known to all that when going to the suburbs, one takes three meals and is able to return with his stomach still full. When going to places one hundred *li* away, one stays awake the whole night to prepare solid food. If one goes to a place one thousand *li* away, one needs to prepare food three months ahead. What the two little things, the cicada and the young sparrow, know is just something insignificant. They know nothing about the bigger truth. Life is short, so the mushrooms of a morning would not know about the beginning and the end of a month, and the cicada of summer would not know about spring or autumn. In the south of the State of Chu, there was a big turtle named Ming Ling. For Ming Ling, 500 years were a spring and another 500 years were an autumn. In the ancient times, there was a great tree named Da Chun which took 8,000 years as a spring and another 8,000 years as an autumn. That was longevity. The legendary Peng Zu has been renowned for his long life even till today. Would it not be pathetic for people to try to compare with him?

Therefore, for those whose wisdom is sufficient to hold an official position, whose conduct meets the expectations of the townspeople, whose virtues are befitting the head of a state, and whose abilities are able to win the trust of the people, they are sure to view themselves in self-satisfaction as the young sparrow. That is why Song Rongzi, the sage in the State of Song, laughed at them. There are also such a kind of people: though the world all praise him, he would not for that reason make more efforts; though the world all criticize him, he would not for that reason feel any depression. He draws a very clear line to separate himself from the external things, and marks out the distinction between honor and shame. Then perhaps it's the time for him to stop, for he has reached the state where he is no longer troubled by trivialities. But even so, he still hasn't arrived at the highest state.

Later generations often compare the story of the small sparrow and the giant eagle to people's attitudes toward life, so today we have such a saying as "How could a sparrow understand the ambitions of an eagle?" Due to the restrictions of various conditions, people may come to different levels of perception of the world and their level of involvement in the worldly affairs varies accordingly. But people never stay on one level permanently. Therefore what is important is that one should never judge others by one's own standards and should never take a part for the whole and confine oneself in a limited space, believing it to be insurmountable and reveling in their self-importance. Constantly evolving from the lower level to the higher one, people's recognition of the world is always in the process of development — from the limited to the infinite.

53. 也说白马非马

有一次,庄子带了些玉米去惠施家做客,进门时看到惠施与另外一个人正在谈论。惠施见到庄子,就起身向庄子介绍说,"这是赵国平原君的门客公孙龙,天下有名的辩才。你知道这样一件事吗?前几年秦国曾与赵国签定条约,双方约定协力共图大业,没有多久,秦国攻打魏国,赵国想发兵救魏,秦国为此很不高兴,说原来定好双方互助,如今怎么能够反过来帮助魏国呢?结果公孙先生反驳说,赵国想救魏国,你秦国不帮助赵国,这才是违约,驳得秦国无话可说。公孙先生常有惊人之论,刚才我们还在辩论几个有趣的话题,你不妨听听,看谁说的有道理。"

于是,惠施与公孙龙又开始辩论了。惠施说:"你说白马非马有什么依据?"公孙龙说:"'马'是用来称呼形体的,'白'是用来称呼颜色的,根据颜色命名与根据形体命名不是一回事,所以白马不是马。"惠施说:"白马黑马不管颜色如何,它总归是马,怎么能说白马不是马呢?"公孙龙回答说:"马圈里有各种颜色的马,人们可以说没有白马,但不能说没有马,这就说明白马与马不是一回事。"惠施说:"认为马有颜色就不是马,但天下没有无颜色的马,难道天下就没有马了?"公孙龙说:"马本来是有颜色的,因此才有白马,如果马没有颜色,那么就只是马。所谓白马就是白与马的结合,白与马结合了,还算是那种没有颜色的马吗?所以白马不是马。我再问你一个问题,你说白马是马,能不能说白马就是黄马?"惠施不假思索地说:"当然不能说白马就是黄马。"这时,公孙龙马上作了类似于三段论的证明:"黄马、黑马是马,黄马、黑马不是白马,所以白马不是马。"公孙龙的这番话把惠施搅糊涂了,一时说不出话来。

在边上坐着的庄子这时说话了,"我见门口拴着一匹白马,是你公孙先生的坐骑吗?"公孙龙点点头。庄子又问,"城门口有告示,说骑马者要交进城费,不知你是否免了?"公孙龙说,"怎么可能呢?"庄子笑了笑说,"既然白马非马,为什么要交进城费呢?其实在我看来,这种争辩没有什么意义,任何东西,不管你想肯定还是否定,都可以找到证明。你可以竖起自己的手指说这是手指,说他人的手指不是手指;别人也可以说他的手指是手指,说你的手指不是手指。你可以用白马来说明白马非马,其他人也可以用白马来说明白马是马。事实上每个人都有自己的标准,这种标准构成了成见,用成见来判断事物的真假和认识事物的是非是没有什么意义的。人总喜欢作出区分,有彼有此,有是有非,想方设法要弄出个谁是谁非,谁输谁赢,这就像竹管观天,实在太可笑了。其实圣人从不去评判是非,而只是客观地反映自然之道,消除彼此的相互对立是获取大道的关键。对迷乱人心的巧说辩言的炫耀,是圣哲之人所鄙视的。"

听了庄子的这番话,公孙龙无言以对,惠施也呆住了。

公孙龙讲白马非马,突出的是"离",看起来违背常识,但"离"对人的认识有合理的一面,能使人们避免犯亚里士多德所指出的那种错误,即把"他是鞋匠,也是个好人"理解成"他是一个好鞋匠"。庄子认为这是小聪明。他有一句名言叫"大知闲闲,小知閒閒",意思是才智超群的人广博豁达，只有点小聪明的人则乐于细察、斤斤计较，谈起事来婆婆妈妈似的唠叨不停，带来的结果就是人们经常说的聪明反被聪明误，甚至是搬起石头砸自己的脚。人要从大处着眼，明白了大道就能处变不惊，四通八达。

A WHITE HORSE IS NOT A HORSE?

Zhuangzi brought some corns and went to pay a visit to his friend Hui Shi. At Hui Shi's house, he saw Hui Shi engaged in conversation with another man. Hui Shi got up at the sight of Zhuangzi and made the introduction, "This is Gongsun Long, an advisor to Prince Pingyuan of the State of Zhao, and a very famous debater in the world. Have you heard about such a story? Several years ago, the State of Qin and the State of Zhao entered into a treaty, under which they were to make concerted efforts in conquering the world. Soon afterwards when the State of Qin attacked the State of Wei, the State of Zhao wanted to send some troops to help Wei. Qin was upset about this and objected, 'Now that an agreement had been reached between Qin and Zhao on offering assistance to each other, how could Zhao go against its word and offer help to the State of Wei, an enemy of Qin?' However, Master Gongsun retorted that it was the State of Qin that violated the treaty when it didn't offer help to the State of Zhao when Zhao wanted to save the State of Wei. At this, the State of Qin had nothing to say. Master Gongsun often has some amazing ideas. Just now we were debating about several interesting topics. Would you please hear us out and decide whose arguments sound more reasonable?"

With that, Hui Shi and Gongsun Long started another round of debate. Hui Shi said, "What do you have to support your idea that a white horse is not a horse?" Gongsun Long said, "'Horse' is used to name the shape, while 'white' is used to name the color. Naming by color is different from naming by shape, which is why white horse is not a horse." Hui Shi said, "A white horse or a black horse is after all a horse regardless of its color. How can one say that a white horse is not a horse?" Gongsun Long replied, "There may be horses of different colors in the stable. One can say that there are no white horses, but one cannot say that there are no horses. So it follows that a white horse is not a horse." Hui Shi said, "According to you, horses that have colors are not horses. Then are there no horses in the world since all the horses are not without colors?" Gongsun Long answered, "Horses do have colors, so there are white horses. If horses are without colors, they are just horses. The so-called white horse is a combination of 'horse' and 'white color'. Can such a combination be called a horse without color? Therefore a white horse is not a horse. I'd like to ask you one more question: if you say that a white horse is a horse, can you say that a white horse is a yellow horse?" Hui Shi gave a reply at once, "Of course we cannot say that a white horse is a yellow horse." At this, Gongsu Long immediately made an argument that sounded like a plausible syllogism, "Yellow horses and black horses are horses, but they are not white horses. Therefore white horses are not horses." Gongsun Long's words completely confused Hui Shi, who remained speechless for some time.

Zhuangzi who was sitting nearby all the time now said, "Is the white horse I see tethered at the door your mount, Master Gongsun?" Gongsun Long nodded his head. Zhuangzi asked again, "There is a notice at the entrance to the city, saying that all horse riders are to pay an entry fee. I wonder if you have been exempted." Gongsun Long answered, "Of course not." Then Zhuangzi smiled and said, "If a white horse is not a horse, why pay the entry fee? In my opinion, it is meaningless to have such debates, because when you want to prove or disprove something, you can always come up with some kind of evidence. You can raise your finger and say that it's a finger while at the same time you deny that other people's fingers are fingers. And others can do the same thing: someone can raise his finger and say that it's a finger while at the same time he denies that your fingers are fingers. You can explain your idea that a white horse is not a horse by using the example of a white horse. But others can use the same example to demonstrate that a white horse is a horse. Everybody has in fact his own standards, which in turn form his prejudices. It is meaningless to rely on one's prejudices to pass judgment on things being true or false and right or wrong. People always like to make distinctions between this and that and between right and wrong. They try their best to work out who is right and who is wrong, or who wins and who loses, but that is as ridiculous as trying to see the sky through a bamboo pipe. Actually sages never pass judgment on things being right or wrong. Instead, they just report in an objective way the Tao of the nature, and the acquisition of the Tao relies on the elimination of mutual antagonism. It is the display of false speeches and misleading eloquence that draws the despise of the sagely and virtuous people."

Having heard Zhuangzi's words, Gongsun Long was speechless and Hui Shi looked stunned too.

When Gongsun Long said that a white horse was not a horse, what he focused on was separateness. His explanations may appear to be a far cry from common sense, yet separateness has its place in the cognitive process of people. It warns people against the mistake cautioned by Aristotle, which is to understand the sentence "He is a shoemaker and a good man" as "He is a good shoemaker". According to Zhuangzi it is just a petty trick. There is a well-known saying of Zhuangzi that "Big knowledge makes people relaxed and limited knowledge makes people idle", which means that people of great wisdom command extensive knowledge and are more generous and broad-minded, while people who know only petty tricks derive fun from showing off their cleverness and haggling over the trivial. When the latter kind of people have to discuss with others about something, they ramble on as if they are talkative old women. In the end they end up being the victims of their own cleverness, or even "dropping the lifted stone on their own feet". People need to proceed with important issues. With the knowledge of the Great Tao, people will be able to remain calm in changing situations and reach their goals in the end.

54. 虎狼也有仁爱

宋国的太宰荡向庄子请教仁爱的问题。庄子说："虎和狼也有仁爱。"太宰荡觉得很奇怪，就问："为什么这么说？"庄子说："虎狼在他们的父子之间也能相互亲爱，这为什么不能叫做仁呢？"太宰荡想了想又问："你说的只是普通的仁，那么什么是最高境界的仁？"庄子说："最高境界的仁就是没有亲。"太宰荡说："我听说，没有亲就不会有爱，没有爱就不会有孝，这就意味着最高境界的仁就是不孝，可以这么说吗？"

庄子说："不能这么说。最高尚的仁是至高无上的，实在值得推崇，孝根本不能与它相提并论。而且，用爱说明道是不恰当的，因为爱不是超过了孝，而是根本没有达到孝的说法。向南方走的人到了楚国都城郢，回头面朝北方也看不见冥山，这是为什么呢？因为距离冥山越发远了。仁义也是一样，它与孝毫不相干，可以说，用外表好像恭敬的态度来行孝容易，以爱的本心来行孝困难；用爱的本心来行孝容易，用'忘掉这是我的双亲'来行孝困难;用'忘掉这是我的双亲'来行孝容易,使双亲忘掉我是他们的亲人困难,使双亲忘掉我是他们的亲人容易,要把天下所有的东西都忘掉困难;要把天下所有的东西都忘掉容易,使天下的人把自己全忘却困难。一个人的德行如果到了能够忘掉尧舜而不为仁义,利益和恩泽施给万世,而不让天下人知道的程度,哪里还会深深感慨去大谈仁孝啊!现在人们说的孝、悌、仁、义、忠、信、贞、廉,这些都是用来劝勉自身而压抑自然本性的,不值得推崇。所以呀,要说最为珍贵的是一国的爵位都可以随同忘却自我而抛弃,最为富有的是一国的资财都可以随同知足的心态而弃置。人的最大的心愿应该是随同自己的本性舍弃名声和荣誉。只有大道是永恒不变的。"

做人是门学问,中国人习惯的是做人与做事并举,做事要做得好,做人也要做得好。有人把这种学问走向极端,那就变得虚伪做作。庄子把矛头对准儒家的忠孝仁义,说这些是违背自然本性的。他举了一个事例:在街上走路不小心踩了别人,对陌生人会连声赔不是,对兄长大不了是怜惜的神态,对父母则无所表示,态度所以会有如此不同,是因为人越亲近就越隐于内心而不拘礼节。庄子的看法是"至礼不人,至义不物,至仁不亲"。

TIGERS AND WOLVES ARE BENEVOLENT TOO

Dang, a high official of the State of Song, went to Zhuangzi for advice on benevolence. Zhuangzi said, "Tigers and wolves are benevolent too." Dang found it strange and said, "Why do you say that?" Zhuangzi answered, "Fathers and sons among tigers and wolves are affectionate to each other. Why can that not be benevolence?" Dang thought it over and asked again, "What you have mentioned is benevolence of an ordinary kind. What is it like at its perfect level?" Zhuangzi answered, "Perfect benevolence is without feelings of affection." Dang said, "I have heard that without affection, there will not be love; without love, there will not be filial piety. Does it mean that perfect benevolence is without filial piety?"

Zhuangzi said, "It can't be put this way. Perfect benevolence is the highly esteemed supreme state, with which filial piety can never be mentioned in the same breath. Moreover, it is improper to explain Tao in terms of love, for love, instead of being something that surpasses filial piety, is just a way of expression for a level below filial piety. One, traveling to the south, comes to Ying, the capital of the State of Chu. When he turns around, facing north, he can't see Mount Ming. Why? Because he is even further away from Mount Ming in the north. It is the same with benevolence, which is far away from filial piety. It is said that it is easy to be filial in reverence, but difficult to be so out of true love; it is easy to be filial out of true love, but difficult to be so when I forget that they are my parents; it is easy to be filial when I forget that they are my parents, but difficult to do so when I have made my parents forget that I am their beloved son; it is easy to make my parents forget that I am their beloved son, but difficult to forget everything on the earth; and it is easy to forget everything on the earth, but difficult to make everyone on the earth forget himself. If one's virtue reaches such a level where he is able to forget about the legendary emperors Yao and Shun as well as their benevolence and righteousness, and bring benefits and blessings to everyone for ten thousand generations without letting them know, will he be talking about benevolence and filial piety with such deep emotion? Filial piety, fraternal respect, benevolence, righteousness, loyalty, sincerity, chastity, and honesty, which are much talked about by people today, are designed to encourage self-development but in fact oppress the very nature of oneself, and therefore should not be advocated. Therefore, nothing can be more precious than being able to give up one's rank of nobility after forgetting one's self-awareness, and nobody is wealthier than the one who is able to abandon the fortune of a state only to enjoy a sense of contentment. The biggest ambition of people is to be able to part with fame and glory in conformity with their nature. Only the Great Tao lasts forever."

It is an art to conduct oneself. Chinese people believe that conducting oneself and handling affairs should be worked at simultaneously. One is required to handle things well but at same time behave well. But if someone goes too far in seeking the perfection in both, then it turns into hypocrisy and artificiality. Zhuangzi directed his criticism against loyalty, filial piety, benevolence and righteousness — the virtues advocated by Confucianism, saying that these are against the real nature of people. He gave an example. One apologizes profusely if he steps onto a stranger on the street; one wears a pitying look if he steps onto his brother; and one does nothing if he steps onto his parents. The difference in attitude is because one tends to be more reserved with feelings and more disregardful of etiquettes when one deals with people who are more intimate to him. In Zhuangzi's opinion, the man with the ultimate etiquettes treats all the people in the same manner, regardless of who they are; the man with the ultimate righteousness treats all the properties in the same manner, regardless of whether they are his own; the man with the ultimate benevolence treats all his relations in the same manner, regardless of how intimate they are to him.

55. 长梧子的教诲

孔子的学生瞿鹊子向长梧子请教:"我从老师那里听到这样的谈论,'圣人不处理具体事务,不追逐私利,不回避灾害,不喜好贪求,不因循成规;没有说也就是说了,说了也等于什么也没有说,因而遨游于世俗之外。'孔子认为这些都是轻率不当的言论,而我却认为是精妙大道的道路。先生你认为应该怎么看呢?"

长梧子说:"这些话就是黄帝听了也会疑惑不解的,而孔丘这样的人怎么能够明白呢!而且你也求之过急,就好像见到鸡蛋便想立即得到鸡,见到弹子便想立即获取烤熟的鹏鸟肉。我姑且给你胡乱说一说,你也就随便听听。人应该与日月并依存,和宇宙同一体,跟万物吻合为一,置各种混乱纷争于不顾,对卑贱与尊贵一视同仁。但人们总是一心忙于去争辩是非,而圣人却好像十分愚昧混沌,与永恒的大道相糅合,处于浑朴而又精纯的状态中。"

"我怎么知道贪恋生存不是一种迷惑呢？我又怎么知道厌恶死亡与年幼流落他乡而老大还不知返家是不同的呢？丽姬是艾地国境守土人的女儿，晋国征伐丽戎得到她时，她哭得泪水浸透了衣襟；等她来到晋国进入王宫，跟晋侯同睡一床而宠为夫人，吃上美味珍馐，也就后悔当初不该那么伤心地哭泣了吧。我又怎么知道那些死去的人不会后悔当初的求生呢？睡梦里饮酒作乐的人，天亮醒来后很可能痛哭饮泣；睡梦中痛哭饮泣的人，天亮醒来后又可能在欢快地逐围打猎。当他在做梦的时候，他并不知道自己是在做梦。睡梦中还会占卜吉凶，醒来以后方知是在做梦。人大彻大悟的时候方才知道自己的一生也是一场大梦，而愚昧的人则自以为清醒，好像什么都知晓，什么都明了，总是说什么君主呀、贱民呀，这种看法实在是浅薄固执。孔丘和你都是在做梦，我说你们在做梦这件事本身也是在做梦。以上这些话听上去有点不可思议，堪称'吊诡'。万世之后假若遇上一位大圣人，解释这个道理就像朝夕相遇一样平常。"

"倘使我和你展开辩论，你胜了我输了，就一定是你对我错吗？我胜了你输了，就一定是我对你错吗？还是有的正确，有的不正确？或者我们两人都是正确的，或者都是不正确？这些我和你都无从知道，而世人原本也都承受着蒙昧与晦暗，我们又能让谁作出正确的裁定？让观点跟你相同的人来判定吗？既然看法跟你相同，怎么能作出公正的评判！让观点跟我相同的人来判定吗？既然看法跟我相同，怎么能作出公正的评判！让观点不同于我和你的人来判定吗？既然看法不同于我和你，怎么能作出公正的评判！让观点跟我和你都相同的人来判定吗？既然看法跟我和你都相同，又怎么能作出公正的评判！如此，那么我和你还有大家都无从知道这一点，还有谁能断定是非呢？"

瞿鹊子问："那该怎么办呢？"

长梧子说："最好的办法是'天倪'，用'天倪'来和是非。天倪就是自然，它认为，对就是不对，正确的也就是不正确的。对的假如真是对的，那么即便对的不同于不对，也无须去争辩；正确的假如真是正确的，那么即便正确的不同于不正确的，也无须去争辩。忘掉死生、忘掉是非，就可以到达并寄托于无穷无尽的境界。"

长梧子对瞿鹊子的教诲，突出表现了庄子"齐是非"的思想。在庄子看来，无穷无尽的是非之争及人所执著的是非观念，产生于人的情感，人的认识象开关一样，可以在是非之间随意转动，所以世界上很难分辨正确与错误。人睡在潮湿的地方会腰痛，但泥鳅却很自在；西施是公认的美人，但鱼看见了就深入水底，鸟见了就飞向高空。这牵涉到一个重要的认识论问题：人能否认识世界，真理是不是含有客观性？20世纪出现的相对主义思潮在学理上与庄子是相通的。

TEACHINGS FROM CHANGWUZI

Qu Quezi, a disciple of Confucius, asked Changwuzi, "I have heard from my Master about such ideas: 'The sages don't get engaged in worldly affairs, neither do they pursue personal gains or avoid disasters. They don't have preferences or desires. They never follow established conventions and rules. They don't speak when speaking, and they speak without saying anything. Thus they roam above the mundane affairs of the world.' Though my Master believes that these ideas are impulsive and improper, I consider them to be the roads to the wonderful Tao. What do you think, Master?"

Changwuzi said, "These words would have perplexed the Yellow Emperor if he had heard them. So how are people like Confucius able to understand? As for you, you have been much too hasty. Seeing the eggs, you immediately expect to get a hen; and seeing the pellets, you immediately expect to get roasted eagle meat. Let me just give you some rough ideas and please don't take them too seriously. People are supposed to exist with the sun and the moon, become one and the same with the universe and blend into the myriads of things, paying no attention to troubles and disputes of all kinds and treating the humble and the honorable alike. But people are always eager to argue about right or wrong, while the sages, seemingly very ignorant and confused, blend into the Great Tao of forever and remain in the state of simplicity and purity."

"How do I know that the love of life is not a delusion? How do I know that the hatred of death is different from not knowing how to return home after being away since very young? The famous beauty Li Ji was the daughter of the Border Warden of Ai. When the State of Jin sent troops to conquer her state and got her, she wept so much that her tears soaked the front of her dress. But when she entered the palace of Jin, shared with the king his bed as the Madam, and had all the rich and delicious food, she regretted having cried so sadly. So how do I know that the dead will not regret their former cravings for life? Those who dream of drinking wine and having fun may wail and weep in the morning; those who dream of wailing and weeping may go hunting happily in the morning. When they are dreaming, they don't know that it is a dream. They may even try to tell their own fortune in their dream and only when they wake up will they know that it is just a dream. So at the time of the Great Awakening people understand that their whole life is also a big dream. Only the foolish believe themselves to be awake with a clear mind, as if they know everything and understand everything. They always talk about monarchs and mobs, which is really shallow and bigoted. Both you and Confucius are dreaming. I who say that you're dreaming am having a dream too. All these words sound very unorthodox indeed. But sages of ten thousand generations later will be able to explain this as easily as if they come across such ideas day and night."

"Even if you and I have a debate, and you beat me, would that necessarily mean that you are right and I am wrong? Or if I beat you, would that mean I am right and you are wrong? Or are we both partly right and partly wrong? Or are we both wholly right and wholly wrong? Neither of us will have answers to these questions. What's more, when people are all in darkness and ignorance, whom can we turn to for correct answers? Shall we ask people who share your ideas or my ideas to make the judgment? Since they hold similar ideas as either you or I, how do we expect them to make sound judgments? Or shall we ask people whose ideas either differ from or are the same with ours to make the judgment? Since their ideas are either different from or similar with yours and mine, how do we expect them to make sound judgments? Therefore you and I and those others are not able to answer these questions. Who else is there to make the judgments?"

Qu Quezi asked, "Then what to do?"

Changwuzi said, "The best way is to use the 'Operation of Heaven' to harmonize right and wrong. The 'Operation of Heaven' is nature. It holds that right is wrong, and correct is incorrect. If what is right is right indeed, then even though right is different from wrong, there is no need to argue; and if what is correct is correct indeed, then even though correct is different from incorrect, there is no need to argue, either. Let's forget about life and death; let's forget about right and wrong. Only then are we able to reach and rest with the infinity."

Changwuzi's teachings to Qu Quezi highlight Zhuangzi's idea on right and wrong. According to Zhuangzi, the endless fight on the topic of right and wrong and people's persistence in distinguishing between right and wrong all derive from the feelings and emotions of people. People's understanding can roam freely between right and wrong as being switched on and off. Therefore it is very difficult to distinguish between right and wrong. People develop backaches when sleeping in humid places, but loaches are quite at home in the same situation; Xi Shi was a renowned beauty, but at the sight of her fish dived into the bottom of the water and birds flew away into the sky. This touches upon an important issue in cognitive science: Are people able to perceive the world reasonably, and are there any objectivity in perceived truths? The Relativism that emerged in the 20th century is an echo of Zhunagzi's ideas in terms of scientific principles.

56. 盗跖怒斥孔丘

孔子跟柳下惠是朋友。柳下惠有个弟弟叫盗跖,盗跖有部下九千人,横行天下,侵扰各国诸侯;穿室破门,掠夺牛马,带走奴婢;一味地抢夺钱财,一点也不顾及父母兄弟,甚至不祭祖先。他所经过的地方,大国赶紧关上城门,派兵把守;小国告急于邻邦,请求保护;人们都很害怕他。于是孔子让颜回驾车,子贡作下手,前去会见盗跖。那天盗跖正好在泰山休整队伍,听说孔子前来求见,勃然大怒,双目睁得圆圆的,头发竖立直冲帽顶,对传禀的人说:"这不就是那鲁国的巧伪之人孔丘吗?替我告诉他:'你编造谎言,假称是文王、武王的主张;你头上戴着树杈般的帽子,腰上围着宽宽的牛皮带,满口胡言乱语;你不种地却吃得不错,不织布却穿得讲究;你整天摇唇鼓舌,专门制造是非,用以迷惑天下的诸侯,使天下的读书人全都不能返归自然的本性,而且狂妄地制订孝悌之道,以求封侯的赏赐而成为富贵的人。你这罪大恶极的东西,快滚！要不然，我将把你的心肝挖出来当菜。'"

孔子不甘心，再次请求通报接见，说："我荣幸地跟柳下惠相识，诚恳希望能够面见将军。"最后盗跖总算答应了。孔子走进盗跖的住所，小心翼翼地叩头拜见。盗跖一见孔子大怒不已，伸开双腿，按着剑柄，怒睁双眼，喊声犹如老虎，对孔子说："到前面来！你所说的话，合我的心意就让你活，不合的话你就去等死。"

孔子说："我听说，天下之人有三德。身材高大，相貌漂亮，无论是谁都喜欢他，这是上等的德行；才智能够包罗天地，能力足以分辨各种事物，这是中等的德行；勇武、慓悍、果断、敢作敢为，能够聚合众人统率士兵，这是下等的德行。人若具备三德之一，就可以南面称王。如今将军同时具备了上述三种美德，你高大魁梧，身长八尺二寸，面容和双眼熠熠有光，嘴唇鲜红犹如朱砂，牙齿整齐犹如齐贝，声音洪亮合于黄钟，然而名字却叫盗跖，我暗暗为将军感到羞耻，并且认为将军不应有此恶名。将军如果有意听从我的劝告，我将出访周边各国，派人为将军建造数百里的大城，建立起数十万户的大国，尊将军为诸侯，跟天下各国和好相处，罢兵休卒，供祭祖先。这才是圣人贤士的作为，也是天下人的心愿。"

盗跖大怒说："凡是可以用利禄来规劝、用言语来谏正的，都只能称作愚昧、浅陋的普通人。如今我身材高大魁梧，面目英俊美好，人人见了都喜欢，这是我的父母给我留下的。你孔丘即使不当面吹捧我，我难道不知道吗？而且我听说，喜好当面夸奖别人的人，也好背地里诋毁别人。如今你一方面用功利来诱惑我，一方面对待我如同对待普通人那样，这怎么可以长久呢！况且我听说，古时候人们自己耕种自己吃，自己织布自己穿，没有伤害别人的心思。然而到了黄帝时代就有了很大的变化，黄帝跟蚩尤在涿鹿的郊野上争战，流血百里。尧舜称帝，设置百官，商汤放逐了他的君主，武王杀死了纣王。从此以后，世上总是依仗强权欺凌弱小，依仗势众侵害寡少。如今你研修文王、武王的治国方略，控制天下的舆论，一心想用你的主张传教后世子孙，穿着宽衣博带的儒式服装，说话与行动矫揉造作，用以迷惑天下的诸侯，而且一心想用这样的办法追求高官厚禄，要说大盗再没有比你大的了。天下为什么不叫你作盗丘，反而竟称我是盗跖呢？你自称是圣哲般的人物，但却不能容身于天下。你尊崇的黄帝、唐尧、虞舜、大禹、武王、文王都是因为追求功利而违反了自然，他们的做法实在是可耻。世人所称道的贤士，就如伯夷、叔齐他们，跟肢解了的狗、沉入河中的猪以及拿着瓢到处乞讨的乞丐相比没有什么不同，都是重视名节轻生赴死，不顾念身体和寿命的人。世人所称道的忠臣，例如比干和伍子胥，最终都被天下人讥笑。老实说，你孔丘所说的，全都是我想要废弃的。你赶快离开这里滚回去，不要再说了！你的那套主张，全都是诈巧、虚伪的东西，有什么好谈论的呢！"

听了这席话，孔子快步走出帐门，眼光失神模糊不清，脸色犹如死灰，低垂着头，靠在车前的横木上，颓丧得几乎不能大口喘气。

盗跖怒斥孔丘这个寓言，是庄子编造出来的，用以批判儒家仁义的虚伪。在庄子看来，儒家的德行本质上就是一种伪行，它当面奉承拍马，背后骂声不绝，当面祝你生日快乐，背后盼你早日归天，内与外、言与行两张皮耍得很开。庄子的这一批判是很深刻的，联想到现实生活，这样的人能说少吗？

ZHI THE ROBBER REBUKES CONFUCIUS IN ANGER

Confucius had a friend, Liuxia Hui, who was famous for his virtues. Liuxia Hui had a brother who was known as Zhi the Robber. Zhi the Robber commanded a mob of nine thousand bandits who pillaged the states and attacked lords, dukes and princes. They broke into people's houses, seized cattle and horses and abducted servants and maids. Their greed for money and property was so intense that they paid no heed to their own parents and brothers, and what's more, offered no sacrifices to their ancestors. Wherever Zhi the Robber passed, big states closed their gates and sent more troops to guard them, while small states turned to their neighboring states for help. Everybody was afraid of him. So with Yan Hui driving his carriage and Zi Gong sitting on his right, Confucius set off to see Zhi the Robber, who was then encamped in Mount Tai and having a rest with his bandits. On hearing that Confucius asked for a meeting, Zhi the Robber flew into a temper. With eyes bulging widely and hair standing up almost beyond the rim of his cap, he said to the messenger, "Isn't this the hypocrite Confucius from the State of Lu? Tell him that this is what I say, 'You make up lies, saying that they are the words of King Wen and King Wu; you have a cap like tree branches on your head, and a wide belt on your waist made from dead cattle; thus attired, you go around uttering nonsense only; you eat well but you don't plow; you dress well but you don't weave; you flap you lips and wag your tongue every day, causing troubles and disputes, misleading lords and dukes in the world, preventing scholars in the world from returning to their nature; you presumptuously decide about filial piety and fraternal respect, seeking to get power and rank and to become rich and influential. Take yourself off quickly with your heinous crimes! Otherwise, I shall have your heart and liver for my meal.'"

Unwilling to give up, Confucius sent in another message asking to see Zhi the Robber, saying, "I have the pleasure of being a friend of Liuxia Hui. And I sincerely wish to be able to meet the General." At last, Zhi the Robber agreed to see him. So Confucius went into the tent of Zhi the Robber. Kneeling down and touching his forehead to the ground carefully, Confucius greeted Zhi the Robber respectfully. On seeing Confucius, Zhi the Robber was fuming with anger. With his legs widely apart and his hand on his sword hilt, he glared at Confucius and roared as loudly as a tiger, "Come forward! If your words agree with my ideas, I shall let you live; if not, I shall kill you."

Confucius said, "I have heard that people in the world may have three virtues. To grow up tall and handsome so that everybody, no matter who he is, likes him—

that is the high level of virtue; to have the wisdom which covers Heaven and Earth and to have the ability to explain various things in the world — that is the middle level of virtue; to be brave, fearless, determined and courageous and to be able to gather a crowd of followers and lead an army — that is the low level of virtue. If one is possessed of either one of these three virtues, one is fit to take a position facing south and the title of a king. Now you, General, are possessed of all the three virtues mentioned above. You have grown to a height of eight *chi* and two *cun*, with bright complexion and shiny eyes. Your lips are red as cinnabar, your teeth are even as a row of shells, and your voice is resonant as bronze bells. Yet you go by the name of Zhi the Robber, for which I feel secretly ashamed. I believe that you, General, should not have had such a bad name. If General will choose to take my advice, I shall visit the neighboring states as your envoy, send people to build a big city which covers hundreds of *li* and contains ten thousand households, and you, General, will be respected as the lord of the state. You will develop friendly relations with other states in the world, lay down your weapons and let your soldiers rest, and offer sacrifices to the ancestors. This is after all the sagely behavior and also the wish of the people in the world."

Zhi the Robber got even angrier and said, "Those who can be persuaded by offers of benefits and ranks and be corrected by words of admonishment are those who are referred as being ordinary, stupid and vulgar. I have grown up to be tall and handsome and everybody likes me when they see me. But that was all bestowed upon me by my parents. Even if you had not praised me to my face, would I not have known it? And I have heard that those who like to praise others to their face also like to speak ill of others behind their back. Now you try to tempt me with offers of benefits and ranks on one hand, and treat me like anyone else on the other hand. How can this last long? What's more, I have heard that in the ancient times people got food from their own plowing and they wore clothes woven by themselves, and they never intended to harm anyone. By the time the Yellow Emperor came along, things have changed greatly. He fought with Chi You in the open wilderness of Zhuolu until blood flowed for hundreds of *li*. When Yao and Shun took the throne, they set up a crowd of ministers. After that King Tang of the Shang Dynasty exiled the previous king and King Wu killed King Zhou, the last king of Shang. Ever since then, the strong relying on their power have oppressed the weak, and the many relying on their big number have overpowered the few. Now with the ruling strategies of King Wen and King Wu that you have studied, you attempt to control the opinion of the world and are bent on preaching your ideas to the later generations. Dressed in your so-called scholar's robe which is loose with a wide belt, talking and moving in a pretentious and artificial way, you aim to confuse the lords and dukes in the world so as to seek high ranks and big wealth. No one is a bigger robber than you are, so why are the world not calling you Confucius the Robber but calling me Zhi the Robber? You call yourself a sagely person, but there is not a place in the world that can tolerate you. The Yellow Emperor, Yao, Shun, Yu, King Wu, and King Wen, all six of them which have been highly esteemed by you, have gone against the nature in their pursuit of power and benefit. What they have done is shameful indeed. The sages highly esteemed by the world, such as Bo Yi, Shu Qi and the like, were no different from a dog that has been dismembered, a pig that has been thrown into the river or a beggar who goes about begging with his empty bowl in hand. They took their death lightly in their pursuit of fame, not caring about their body or their life. The loyal ministers praised by the world, such as Bi Gan and Wu Zixu, all ended up being laughed at by the world. To tell you the truth, what you, Confucius, have said is exactly what I want to throw away as garbage. Begone! Don't say another word! Those ideas of yours are just something deceitful and hypocritical. What else is there to talk about?"

Having heard these, Confucius hurried out of the tent. His eyes were dazed and blurred and his complexion was as pale as dead embers. He leaned against the bar in the front of his carriage with his head bowed down, unable to draw a breath smoothly in his distress.

Zhuangzi made up this story about Zhi the Robber angrily rebuking Confucius in order to criticize the hypocrisy of the benevolence and righteousness advocated by Confucianism. According to Zhuangzi, the virtuous behavior of Confucianism is actually a form of hypocrisy which flatters to the face but abuses behind the back. They may wish you happy birthday to your face, but once you turn your back, they grind their teeth in anger and pray for your early demise. The inside and the outside, the words and the behavior — both are maneuvered expertly. The criticism made by Zhuangzi has been pertinent on this matter. In view of the everyday life, can we say that such hypocritical people are few?